RIVER MONSTERS

RIVER MONSTERS

TRUE STORIES OF THE ONES THAT DIDN'T GET AWAY

JEREMY WADE

HOST OF **RIVER MONSTERS** ON

DA CAPO PRESS
A Member of the Perseus Books Group

First Da Capo Press edition 2011

Editorial production by *Marra*thon Production Services. www.marrathon.net

DESIGN BY JANE RAESE
Set in 12-point Granjon

Cataloging-in-Publication Data for this book is available from the Library of Congress.
ISBN 978-0-306-81954-4
ISBN 978-0-306-81980-3 (e-Book)

Published by Da Capo Press
A Member of the Perseus Books Group
www.dacapopress.com

Da Capo Press books are available at special discounts for bulk purchases in the U.S. by corporations, institutions, and other organizations. For more information, please contact the Special Markets Department at the Perseus Books Group, 2300 Chestnut Street, Suite 200, Philadelphia, PA 19103, or call (800) 810-4145, ext. 5000, or e-mail special.markets@perseusbooks.com.

10 9 8 7 6 5 4 3 2 1

To Matthew, Dominic, Joshua, Tamsin, Ivo, and Luca

CONTENTS

CONTENTS

INTRODUCTION

WHY SOME FISHERMEN'S TALES ARE TRUE

But I will lay aside my Discourse of Rivers, and tell you some things
of the Monsters, or Fish, call them what you will,
that they breed and feed in them. . . .

Izaak Walton, *The Compleat Angler,* 1653

IT'S A DISTURBING EXPERIENCE—seeing something that doesn't exist.

In July 1993 I was floating in a leaky wooden canoe on a muddy Amazon lake, known simply as Lago Grande (big lake), looking for arapaima. Unusually for fish, *Arapaima gigas* are air-breathers. Despite having gills, they have to surface at half-hour intervals to burp stale air from their swim bladder and gulp a fresh mouthful down. It's a quirk that allows these super-predators to stay active in stagnant water, when other fish are going belly-up. And without doubt it's one of the reasons they grow so huge. Just how huge is not known for sure, but they are commonly said to be the biggest freshwater fish in the world, with some supposedly reliable sources quoting a maximum length of fifteen feet. So they shouldn't be too hard to spot, particularly as they're also not exactly camouflaged, being decorated all over with vivid red markings. So why hadn't I seen a single one?

Perhaps they had all been harpooned or netted—the one drawback to being so large and visible. But local fishermen assured me there were still arapaima in the lake, mainly because there's a very deep hole, over seventy-five feet deep, off the southern end of the central island where

1

their encircling nets can't reach the bottom. A few days before, José had even pointed some out to me:

"There! The size of this canoe! . . ."

But the distant ripples looked no different from any of the others that he had pointed out earlier, made by river turtles, caimans at periscope depth, and other fish. Or so he said. As far as I was concerned, he was seeing things that were invisible. I recalled how other fishermen had told me that the lake was *encantado*—enchanted—how an invisible force sometimes held canoes out in the middle, and how the fishermen had strange dreams when they camped here, dreams about ghost ships from an underwater kingdom whose occupants silently beckoned. No wonder fishermen have such a reputation for invention and exaggeration and for being all-around unreliable witnesses. Perhaps the arapaima wasn't a real fish at all but rather a spirit living in another dimension, a spirit you can only see once you've lost your grip on reality after too much time staring at the water.

Or maybe I needed to look harder. Back home, beside an English pond I could locate a feeding carp from the tiniest whorl on the surface, spun by its tail as it rooted head-down in the silt. But this water spoke a different language that I couldn't yet decipher. Where José saw a clear signature I saw a meaningless scribble.

But foreign languages can be learned. In time I started to recognize the subtly different ripple patterns. My eyes began to enhance detail and eliminate noise, to sharpen edges and slow down time, so that I too could tell not just the species but also the size and direction of travel—even, sometimes, whether or not the ripple-maker knew it was being watched. But back then, my first time in the Amazon, it felt as if the lake's inhabitants were mocking me. Dejected, I stared at the water and pondered the strange mechanics of perception—the perplexing fact that you can only see something properly if you already know what you're looking for.

Such was my state of mind when, thirty yards from the boat, the surface opened and something huge heaved into the air. The size was right for a very big arapaima, but the shape was all wrong. What I'd seen—if the blurred afterimage wasn't deceiving me—was an arched back, bright pink in color and bearing a row of large triangular points. It was like some huge gear wheel in the lake's workings, briefly cutting into the air before spinning back into the depths.

What it was not like was any living creature in the real world.

Back at the hut that night I described it to José, who knew the lake better than anyone. He regarded me over his ragged moustache and then asked where I was keeping my secret bottle of *cachaça*—and why I wasn't sharing it with him.

"Nothing like that lives here," he said.

All the other fishermen I told about it said the same thing.

So what do you do with an experience like that? Do you keep talking about it in the face of disbelief or even ridicule? Or, like a puzzled spectator at a magic show, do you admit that your eyes must have been tricked—or, rather, your brain has misinterpreted the signals from your eyes? For the sake of my sanity, I allowed the outlandish vision—which had once screamed for attention—to fade from my memory.

And that's how things would have stayed if I hadn't gone back the next year. I was still looking for arapaima, but I also cast lures into the lake margins for smaller species—*tucunaré* (more widely known as peacock bass), *surubim*, and *aruanã*—usually to return to the water but sometimes for the pot. On one particular day, when these fish were proving more elusive than usual, there were several pink river dolphins breaching in the area of the deep hole. These (the scientific name is *Inia geoffrensis*, but they are known locally as *botos*) are among the Amazon's strangest looking animals—hump-backed with a bulging head that contains an echo-location organ and sports a narrow, toothy beak. I decided to pack up fishing for the day and try to photograph dolphins instead.

With my 135mm medium-telephoto lens, I had to be pointing right at them to get them in the frame. But they appeared through the surface without warning, in random positions, for just a fraction of a second . . . and by the time I'd reacted they were gone. However, with the bright sunlight and fast film, I could set both a fast shutter speed, to freeze the action, and a small enough aperture to give a good depth of field so I didn't have to fiddle with fine focus. I then waited with the camera raised, ready to react to the loud exhaling puff that signaled a breach.

The next couple of hours saw me almost dislocate my neck several times, as I snapped round and pushed the shutter, as well as nearly tipping myself out of the boat, which was wobbly enough even when I was keeping still. I had an idea that I'd clicked on a dolphin or two, but there was no way to know until I had the slides processed.

Several weeks later, when I got back to the UK, most of the frames were much as I expected—shots of the sky and skewed horizons, some with anonymous splashes or spreading rings—but I did have a couple showing a dolphin's humped back.

Then I held another slide up to the light—and there it was: the shape that had been transient and blurred on my retina, now clear and sharp on film. But what on earth was it? The picture was published in *BBC Wildlife* magazine, sparking speculation that it might even be an unknown new species. I returned to the lake the next year with a video camera provided by the BBC Natural History Unit, and after a six-week stakeout I captured it on videotape in just three grainy frames—but unmistakable.

I also looked into the mystery of its identity, and three years later, after talking to countless people, pieced together the shocking story. It's one that, in some ways, I would rather not know. But even so, there is a happy ending, for both the creature and me. The creature is exuberantly alive, almost flaunting its strangeness, and I am not losing my marbles. My fisherman's tale was true.

And in a strange way this discovery gave me a broader validation. Although a few friends saw my shoestring travels as unusual and interesting, in the eyes of most I had lost my way. After attending primary school in southeast England, I had won a full-fees scholarship to an exclusive "public" (meaning private) school, where, at age sixteen, I scored the best exam results in the school's history. But then my trajectory flattened and nose-dived. I emerged from university with a degree in zoology, vaguely prompted by my interest in fish, but no idea of anything

I wanted to do. So instead of crushing knuckles underfoot on the career ladder, here I was, in my late thirties with a trail of abandoned jobs behind me, making less than minimum wage from selling occasional magazine articles.

Part of the problem was my father, who in his youth had been a farmer but who'd been disinherited after he'd abandoned the family trade to become a priest. As a teenager, predictably, I'd rejected organized religion, but I seemed to have absorbed other, more profound things from him that I couldn't shake. One of these was an indifference to the trappings of worldly success. Or perhaps I was just saying this because, with my threadbare employment record, and something else that nobody knew about, those things were never going to be mine anyway. And this wasn't quite true either. On very special occasions, Dad would wear a gold watch on a chain. It had belonged to his father before him, one of the last farmers in England to work the land with heavy horses, and one day, Dad always reminded me, it would be mine, in the unimaginable future when he would no longer be here. Meanwhile, as I squandered time, he did a good job of concealing his disappointment, even when it was compounded by my youngest brother Martin following my erratic footsteps, dropping out of college to become a wandering English teacher in Spain, France, and Italy. Occasionally a letter from a girl in Brazil would turn up at my parents' house and I'd see the looks next time I talked about my "research trips." I felt that if I could only magically transport my father to an Amazon lakeside then he would understand. Because this was where, for whatever reason, despite all the blood-sucking insects and mud like a First World War battlefield, I became properly alive. It was hardly the garden of Eden, but it was the gateway to a state of mind that he would recognize. Because, despite our differences, we shared one fundamental belief: that there is more to this world than what's visible on the surface.

My sighting of the Lago Grande monster and subsequent proving of its existence is also why I have more time than most for other unlikely tales. Now if somebody tells me they have seen a giant animal lurking in the water, I don't automatically dismiss it because there is no photograph. Native fishermen don't carry cameras. Nor do I swallow it without question, however. Such stories need to be subjected to scientific scrutiny. And for all the exaggeration and mutation that can arise in the retelling, some fishermen's tales do contain nuggets of shocking truth.

There's also some hard science on this side of the argument. Unlike land animals, aquatic creatures have their bodies supported by water so they are not subject to gravity as a factor that limits growth. This means that if conditions are right, they can keep on growing throughout their lives—so-called "indeterminate growth." A land animal, however, that kept growing after reaching maturity would start to have trouble moving from place to place and, hence, finding food. This is gravity putting the brakes on growth. Every terrestrial or airborne body design has its optimum maximum size. But it's a very different picture for "weightless" fish, which occasionally throw up giant freaks.

With fish, it's all about food. If there's a lot available and it doesn't cost too much energy to get it—disputing with competitors and watching one's back against predators—a mature fish will have a big energy surplus. Some of this energy will go toward breeding, the seasonal production of large quantities (normally) of eggs and sperm, but some will go toward further growth, which brings the advantages of fewer predators and a bigger mouth, for feeding on even more food. . . .

A dramatic example of this principle at work is what has happened to the size of carp in English lakes over the last forty years. In most waters where they were found, the biggest individuals used to grow to about twenty pounds; now they commonly reach thirty pounds or even much more. The rod-caught record has leapt from a longstanding forty-four pounds to nearly seventy pounds, an impossible monster for any level-headed angler of the 1970s. This can largely be attributed to the vast quantities of high-protein bait, similar to bodybuilders' food supplement, that carp anglers have been shoveling into the water. Compared to tiny grubs and larvae hiding in the gravel or silt, these highly visible balls of food represent a huge energy intake for very little effort, and the carp duly keep growing and growing, with some individuals reaching sizes previously unheard of. So when a freak fish, much larger than those seen normally, is reported from the wild, what appears not to make sense logically might be perfectly possible *bio*logically.

But then we're back to the question of proof, which is another matter. Fish can be very hard to find and even harder to examine closely. And what is surprising until you think about it is that this is truer in fresh water than it is in the sea. Rivers and lakes make up a tiny fraction (0.01 percent) of the world's water, yet we know less about what lives here than in the distant oceans. The reason for this is simple. Seawater is clear: we can see into it. But drop a cameraman into most rivers or lakes, and he won't see or film a thing. Fresh water is a better place to hide. And in the absence of pictures, our preferred form of hard evidence, we're back where we started: with fishermen's tales—which leads to one other way of discovering what's down there.

Casting a line into the water is like asking a question. Something could be right underneath you, but you can't see it—it's there but not there. And sometimes only a line will make it real, despite the odds against this happening being very long. After hanging limp and lifeless—maybe for hours or days or weeks or years—it will twitch and run, and the cane or carbon-fiber in your hands will bend like a divining rod. Then, if your gear and nerves are sound, you will bring something out into the light, seemingly from nowhere, from another dimension. When this happens, it has an element of magic to it, like pulling a rabbit from a hat.

This book is a series of such investigations into the murky world of fishermen's tales. The tales are of river monsters that are frighteningly large or dangerous—or both. Fish that swallow men whole, others that eat them from within, and others that pack a killer punch. And the truth, though elusive and sometimes complex, is often every bit as unbelievable as the myth.

CHAPTER 1

GOONCH

When Atropos who snips the threads of life misses one thread
she cuts another, and we who do not know why
one thread is missed and another cut,
call it Fate, Kismet, or what we will.

Jim Corbett, *Man-Eaters of Kumaon,* **1944**

THE RIVER IS A ROAR IN MY EARS as the unseen creature starts to drag me, step by stumbling step, toward the murderous water at the tail of the pool, and the moment when I can go no further on land. This is the fish I have been hunting for three years—and the archetypal monster I have been after all my life. But such is its power, and the weight of monsoon water on top of it, that my desire to capture it with a line now seems like madness.

I want to stop time, to put off the moment, but the whirlpool in front of me continues to turn relentlessly clockwise between the left-to-right surge along the far bank and the countercurrent at my feet. This wheeling back eddy, spun from the main flow by a bulge in the black rock opposite, was my secret weapon, my means of evening the odds in what would otherwise be an impossible situation. And until a few moments ago, my plan was working. I'd managed to confuse the fish enough to bring it into the narrow strip where the river runs backward, where the weight of the water was working with me, not against me. But now the fish seems to have worked out where I am and what I'm trying to do, and it has turned back into the main flow and is heading exactly where I don't want it to go. If it reaches the outlet, there will be no holding it. And with this side of the riverbank transforming from a boulder beach into sheer cliff and mountainside rearing hundreds of feet high, there will be no following it either.

I picture the fish in the boiling depths, shouldering its way through the lightless water—the great broad head filled with teeth and the thick muscular body trailing tentacles from every fin. Such is its appalling momentum through water that would grind a person to pieces that I can already taste the sickness and despair that will flood through me when the line cracks like a rifle shot and the rod springs back lifeless in my hands.

Then where will my investigation be? This story of a man-eating fish in *fresh* water, hundreds of miles up a rocky river, will remain just a fishermen's tale. Although the biology adds up, I need hard proof, otherwise the outside world will continue to dismiss this tale as the colorful fantasy of illiterate peasants. And I'll be just another poor, credulous soul who swallows anything he's told. A broken line will convince nobody.

The fish skirts a small slack at the tail of the pool, just before the exit funnel. This is my last chance. I clamp down on the reel as hard as I dare, trying to heave it in here. The rod creaks in pain, its Kevlar and carbon-fiber sinews surely about to transform into splinters. But I've edged the fish off its course. The line sings a high, tinny note as a tail like a black flag breaks the surface: it's huge with two pointed lobes— definitely a monstrous goonch. And then it's gone, and the line is being torn away, faster and faster. The moment has come.

As I rip off my radio-microphone, a voice behind the camera yells at me not to do it, but James keeps filming. My privileged role as world-traveling TV presenter is a Faustian pact. In moments like these, my soul is not my own but instead laid bare for millions to see. I can't just shrug and later mourn in private the one that got away. I've got to do whatever it takes.

Even in the knee-high margins, the water almost knocks me over. With the rod held high, I launch myself, pulling with my other arm and kicking with both legs. Immediately I regret my decision. The river seems to have accelerated, turning the far bank into a blur. But I can't turn back because there's now sheer rock behind me. With a start of horror I realize I'm now in the strip of water that falling boulders, dislodged from the cliff above, regularly bomb. Even the small buzzing fragments hit with the impact of high-velocity shrapnel. An irrational voice tells me that my struggles might call down a fatal rain on top of me.

Then I remember the fish. From this perspective, the accounts of people dragged under take on a reality more vivid than ever. I mustn't be swept down over its position—wherever that now is. But I'm tiring with every breath. The water clutches at me, like a malevolent living thing, and a black fear supplants my original motivation for this act of folly, driving my leaden limbs toward the distant shore.

PINPOINTING EXACTLY WHERE THIS STORY STARTS is difficult, but with hindsight I see a slow inevitability reaching right back to the moment I caught my first fish, aged eight or nine, from the River Stour in southeast England. The river ran through the village where I grew up, and beyond its mirrored surface was a secret world, populated with mysterious inhabitants that few people saw. Over the years its winding course led me ever further over the fields, always wanting to see what was around the next bend.

In my above-surface life I was drawn to study zoology, and later to teach it, but I found the emphasis on theory suffocating and, as a result, wandered lost for several years, supporting myself with a variety of odd jobs, from building-site laborer to farmhand to motorbike dispatch rider in London. Meanwhile my interest in fishing was waning. Britain has lots of people and not much water, and by my mid-twenties that water had become crowded with other enthusiasts. Fishing no longer satisfied my craving for mystery and the unknown, so I hung up my rods.

But the chance discovery of a magazine article about a fish in India (the mahseer, a giant golden-scaled carp that lives in thunderous rocky rivers) changed all that. With my dusted-down rods packed inside a length of drainpipe, I boarded an Ariana Afghan DC10 to Delhi. I had only £200 concealed under my clothes and scarcely a clue how I was going to survive the next three months. But I learned quickly—and caught some fish. On my return, having studied some instructional books about journalistic writing, I wrote a couple of articles about my experiences and sold them to a fishing magazine. That was a revelation. Despite later rejections, I realized that here was a possible way to make some kind of living from my interest in fish.

So I started digging for information about other exotic river fish. Over the next ten years I made five more expeditions, each between two and five months: to Thailand, where my hunt for the Mekong giant catfish (*Pangasianodon gigas*) got me arrested for spying; to India again, where I caught a monstrous southern mahseer (*Hypselobarbus mussullah*) of ninety-two pounds; and three times to the Congo rainforest in search of the goliath tigerfish.

Then, after cowriting and self-publishing *Somewhere Down the Crazy River* about travels in India and Central Africa, I made my first expedition to the Amazon on the trail of the arapaima, the mythic fifteen-foot air-breather. After my experiences in the Congo, which included partial blinding from malaria, I thought this would be a breeze, but the difficulty of this new mission exceeded all expectations. For six years the course of my investigation twisted and turned through the many layers, both real and mythological, of this bewildering region before delivering me at the center of the maze, where the armor-plated giant revealed itself.

My picture of that fish made the British national newspapers, where a television producer in London saw it, and for over two years he touted the idea of a documentary about the fish before finally getting it commissioned. *Jungle Hooks*, filmed and screened in 2002, has since gone down in history for showing the first capture on TV of a giant (two hundred–pound) arapaima—and the unscripted crashing of a single-engine plane into the Amazon forest.

But television is a fickle business. Our proposals for a follow-up series (one of them about alligator gar in the US Deep South) were rejected. I tried to be philosophical about this, knowing that the decision often comes down to budget and is not necessarily a judgment on the merit of the idea. In fact, without my own self-funded research and helpful friends in the Amazon, *Jungle Hooks* would never have been made.

Then in 2005 I received a phone call. My friend Gavin Searle, who had filmed and directed me in the Amazon, was having another existential crisis. As usual he was questioning why somebody with a master's degree in anthropology had just crawled out of yet another reality TV show. "I need a break, Jezzer," he said. "Why don't we go to India? You take your rods and I'll take a camera. Maybe we can cut something together when we get back and sell it to cover our costs."

I was at a loose end myself, scratching around for odd bits of proofreading and copy editing, but this was something we could do on a shoestring. Even so, the idea of selling a program made on spec relied heavily on wishful thinking. So we phoned the commissioning editor of *Jungle Hooks* at Discovery Europe for some guidance. The response was not what we expected: an immediate summons to London and a commission to make a five-part series—not because they particularly wanted a series about India but because it was time for another *Jungle Hooks*.

But this stroke of good fortune also made life more complicated. We had to form our own production company and get an official filming permit. This was straightforward in theory, but six weeks later we had no reply to our application. Fishing in India is very seasonal, and the Himalayan snow melt was fast approaching, followed by the monsoon, which would wash away all our plans. But our paperwork had vanished into a bureaucratic black hole. Finally, in desperation, we handed a large sum to a "fixer" based in Delhi, and submitted a new application. Our permission returned after a week. At the time of writing, our original submission remains buried in somebody's in-tray. It has been there for more than five years and counting. . . .

We arrived at the Kali River, a gray snow-fed tributary of the Ganges, where it briefly forms the border between India and Nepal, two months later than we'd intended. Our target was the golden Himalayan mahseer (*Tor putitora*), a fish said to grow to two hundred pounds, although these days a fifty-pounder is a rarity. Traditionally they are targeted during their annual breeding run on their way up to the headwaters as the monsoon waters rise, and then on their hungry return, with river junctions being the most productive spots. But intercepting the migration is a hit-and-miss affair and can cause offense to some local people, who consider river confluences to be sacred.

From Delhi we took the overnight train north to where the flat Gangetic plain abruptly ends and the mountains begin. Then we spent a day in a jeep on twisting roads cut into rock, contemplating the sickening drops just feet from our wheels and the crumpled skeletons of buses far below. When the road ended, we hefted our bags and set off downriver on foot along a path scratched into the mountainside. Soon I was in a lather of sweat, cursing the straps that cut into my shoulders and the long unwieldy rod container that is my constant burden. But the views of the river were breathtaking. I lost myself in the slow rhythm of my footsteps until eventually the path dropped down and approached a pool. The next thing I knew, after emerging breathless from some shrubs, I was looking up at a Mayan pyramid—huge stone steps climbing high into the air. It took a moment to work out what this was: a low-angle view of terraced fields, with only their stone-built retaining walls visible.

After dumping our kit in a stone hut, I clambered over a field of boulders to the river, anxious to fish before dark. At the tail of the pool the water funneled into a fast chute alongside the far bank, which drove a large, slow back eddy on the near side. Approaching low and quiet, so as not to disturb anything lying close in, I selected a six-inch wooden plug, painted in a lifelike fish-scale pattern, and cast upriver (but down the countercurrent) to the wedge of slack at the edge of the pool's outflow. Engaging the reel, I started to retrieve, with the lure's vibrations making the rod-tip bounce as its diving vane took it under. The next casts were progressively closer to the far bank, falling just short of the ridge of spiky waves where fast and slow water met, which in some indefinable way was beckoning me. Drawing a deep breath, I loaded up the back-cast, flinging the lure with all my might, and landed it in the target area. After just a couple of turns, the line caught on something solid, which then moved: a gleaming eight-pound mahseer—long, rubbery-mouthed, with scales like golden pennies. Maybe we weren't too late after all.

But nothing else followed. It was as if the river had been emptied of fish. As fishless day followed fishless day, we started to despair of getting enough material to make even one half-hour program, never mind five. If this had been merely the personal jaunt we had originally planned, we could have just shrugged our shoulders. But the stakes were now much higher. The total absence of anything on my line forced us to dig ever deeper for other, peripheral material. We filmed inch-long snow trout fry in a rock pool. I discoursed on the gentleman anglers from the days when India was part of the British Empire. Gavin made me grab a snake that was lying on riverside boulders on the pretext that it could have been a fish-eating species. So when our guide Vinay said something about the "Dharma Ghat man-eater," our ears pricked up.

Somebody had been pulled under the water, he told us, a couple of miles downstream from our camp. People said it was the work of the *soos*. Downstream, in the Indian plains, a soos is a Ganges river dolphin (*Platanista gangetica*), a creature very similar to the Amazon pink dolphin, apart from its color, which is gray-brown. From my travels I knew that river dolphins aren't always the cuddly creatures of popular imagination. In the Amazon they bite paddles smacked against the surface to shoo them away from nets and grab the keels of canoes, which they then rock furiously in a gesture of defiance. Carnivorous hunters, they locate prey by sonar and then clamp it in a multitoothed beak. Larger prey is given a fatal ramming first. But their normal diet is fish, either swallowed whole or torn apart. A human would not normally be on the menu, although at eight feet long and three hundred pounds, a Gangetic dolphin would be more than capable of grabbing a swimmer's leg and pulling him under if it wanted to. But dolphins aren't found this far upriver. Because they are air breathers, you would see them if they were here. So this soos is not a dolphin.

But they said it makes a sound like a dolphin. When it opens its mouth, the inrush of water sucks its victim down. This, though, could just be a description of the river. Moving water can exert its own fatal suction. Rocks create back eddies, which accelerate into whirlpools. Current lines move in unpredictable directions and at variable speeds. Halfway down our camp pool was a large rock, and sometimes the water flowed past it smoothly and quietly; but then, seemingly at random, it would start to rip and spin. This rock has a ledge just under the surface, where it's possible to stand with the water halfway to your knees. It looks an obvious place to wash dishes or bathe. But take one step further, and you're in thirty feet of water. A little further out the river looks as if it's boiling, with huge up-wellings rolling the surface layers—a reminder that water spins in three dimensions: not just round and round, but up and down too. In this depth of water, a person caught in one of the down-currents would stay on the bottom, with eardrums ruptured and lungs full of water. Perhaps it's no accident that the Kali River is named after the Hindu goddess of death and destruction. Perhaps the perpetrator was the water itself, with no intermediary in the form of an underwater creature.

The only problem with this reasoning is that the Dharma Ghat victim was taken in shallow, slack water at the edge of the pool. The same went for a young man who disappeared at the Roll Ghat ferry crossing a couple of miles upriver. If this was elsewhere in India, a likely culprit would be a mugger crocodile (*Crocodylus palustris*). But the river here is at an elevation of nearly 1,400 feet and the water is too cold for them. And again, if they were here you'd see them hauled up on land warming their cold blood. India's other crocodile, the narrow-jawed, fish-eating gharial (*Gavialis gangeticus*), is likewise not found at this elevation. And the same goes for pythons.

Casting the net wider, could the killer be a bull shark? Unknown to most people, this species, which normally lurks in warm and temperate coastal seas, has the disturbing habit of entering rivers and sometimes wandering a long way up them, something most sea fish are unable to do. Dharma Ghat is a thousand miles from the sea, but bull sharks have been reported in the Mississippi above St. Louis and more than two thousand miles up the Amazon. And the species is known to swim the Ganges. If it were simply a matter of distance, we would have to consider a bull shark a possible suspect. But this is another animal that doesn't venture into the mountains, being restricted to warm water. And although bull sharks are known to navigate small rapids in the Rio San Juan in Nicaragua, the rapids it would have to scale to get here are far bigger, not to mention the man-made barrier at Tanakpur, a hydro-electric and irrigation dam, which effectively puts an end to this line of speculation.

Faced with events that seem to have no natural cause, it would perhaps be understandable if some people invoked the supernatural. Maybe the forces at work are not simply the product of gravity acting on water but also the earthly manifestations of a divine will. In the Ganges, known to Hindus as "mother Ganga," there is a custom of ritual bathing, to wash away sins and hasten the end of the mortal cycle of death and earthly rebirth. But on this stretch of the Kali, it is noticeable that nobody bathes in the river. This fact might just be due to the cold water, which comes from glaciers in the high Himalayas, but it might be something else. Even the buffaloes, which people keep to plough their terraced fields and that normally need no persuasion to wallow in water, have to be driven into the pools' shallower margins with blows to their thick hides.

Then we met Man Singh. One day, two years before, he had heard his young granddaughter screaming from the head of the pool. When he got there, he saw a huge underwater creature dragging his prize buffalo into the water. But he'd seen this animal before and knew what it was. He said it was a goonch.

When I heard this word, a twenty-year-old memory surfaced. It was my first visit to India, and I was on the West Ramganga River in the Himalayan foothills. I was fishing with a bright silver spoon in a rapid, and my lure had just splashed down near the far bank when something took it with a sickening lunge and carried it away downstream. Then, just as suddenly, the line was dead. Either it had swum round a sunken snag or it wasn't playing by the rules and had just decided to sink to the bottom where my eleven-pound line would make no impression on it. So, abandoning the rules myself, I heaved a rock a little upstream of the point where the line entered the water. On the fourth or fifth throw, it was on the move again, and I stumbled downstream after it, trying to draw level and apply pressure from the side. Then it went to ground again, and this time it felt different. Here there were large branches washed up on the banks, and I visualized others on the riverbed, with my line wrapped around one of them. This time the boulders didn't work, so in desperation I laid the rod down and kicked off my shoes in preparation for following the line down, although there was no way I'd keep my footing once the water was past my knees. It was more of a gesture than a realistic plan.

A scraping sound caught my attention, and I saw my rod moving toward the water. Thinking it was only the current, I picked it up and immediately felt the fish, which was coming toward me now. The memory is then a bit blurred. I know for sure that I didn't land it by grabbing the jaw, as the teeth were unlike anything I'd ever seen. Then there were the tentacles festooning its scaleless body, and its tiny eyes. At four feet, eight inches long (including tail tentacles) and weighing about thirty pounds, it was the largest fish I'd ever caught. But there was something repellent about it, even though it would be another twenty-three years before I'd hear this species (*Bagarius yarellii*) stand accused of being a man-eater.

Since then I'd seen pictures of goonch in the water that could have weighed two hundred pounds. But do they grow big enough to take a person? This seemed to be the ultimate tall tale—until I thought about it. When somebody is in the water, with nothing to hold on to, it's possible to pull them under using very little force. As for a fish eating someone, it's not as far-fetched as it first sounds because some fish can swallow whole prey almost the same size as themselves. Going by the relative size of its mouth, I reckoned a goonch would need to be nine or ten feet long to swallow a small adult human. But some freshwater fish *can* grow this big. Earlier that same year, an eight foot, ten inch

Mekong giant catfish, weighing 646 pounds, had been netted in Thailand—the largest freshwater fish to be fully authenticated.

To reach such a size, a goonch would need an abundant food supply. But mahseer populations have plummeted in the last half-century. Then Vinay speculated what the food supply might be. It was something we'd seen ourselves at the pool where we were camping. One morning a procession of people wound down to the river, carrying a bundle wrapped in cloth. At the riverbank they made a platform from the logs they'd also been carrying, set the bundle on top of it, then set the logs alight. After the flames had been going for a while, there was a dull liquid pop, the sound of a skull cracking, believed to be the moment when the soul leaves the body. The mourners then scooped water onto the flames, sending steam billowing into the air, and pushed the fire's remnants into the river with poles. Downstream we saw spreading rings from a rolling fish.

Vinay suggested I put out a super-strength handline, baited with singed goat meat. But there was no time to mount a proper campaign, beyond trying to catch a smaller goonch from elsewhere, to show what the alleged culprit looks like. This turned out to be a mission in itself, but the sixty-pounder I caught was the first specimen of this species ever to be seen on TV. The main story, however, was filed under "unfinished business."

And that's where it might have stayed if another friend of mine hadn't watched the series a couple of years later. Wildlife filmmaker Lucy d'Auvergne had just finished a two-year stint filming chimpanzees in Tanzania, and she saw the story as being of interest to a much wider audience. She put together a detailed proposal and cut a five-minute taster DVD and took this to Harry Marshall, boss of Icon Films in Bristol, the UK's main center of wildlife filmmaking. Harry carefully placed this bait and then waited, a process that took several months, while interested parties circled, until Animal Planet decided to give us the go-ahead.

One of our goals was to get the first underwater footage of goonch. But going underwater into the goonch's environment was a daunting prospect. Because nobody had done it before, there was no telling how one of these supersize predators might react to a person up close. To give ourselves the best chance of the footage we needed, we enlisted veteran underwater cameraman Rick Rosenthal, whose interest we managed to pique. Rick is a passionate fish conservationist, whose work is all about getting close to the ocean's largest and rarest creatures and showing their intimate lives to those of us who cannot go where he goes. Waiting on the edge of a bait ball, while marlin spear and slash just feet away, is all in a day's work for Rick, and having such experience in our team was an enormous boon. Part of the key to Rick's success over the years is that, where possible, he doesn't use air tanks and all the other scuba paraphernalia. His normal dive kit is a mask and snorkel—and one breath of air. And this was all we were going to use in India. Scuba diving, in contrast, would have been a logistical nightmare, requiring us to drag a compressor, tanks, and other bulky gear into the mountains. The size of the team and cost would have multiplied too. All that to turn ourselves into large underwater objects blowing off clouds of noisy bubbles, which would very likely send all other underwater life heading for the horizon.

Although nervous about this mission, I was not a complete novice underwater, having learned to scuba dive in British coastal waters in the early 1990s. I took it up out of a desire to see my imagined land-scapes for real. But diving in rivers and lakes held no attraction for other divers, who saw this as looking for "brown fish in brown water." So I did what they did, and I clocked up the hours sucking bottled air on reefs and wrecks. But free-diving, or breath-hold diving, beyond wandering around on the surface with a snorkel and the odd short duck-dive, was totally new for me. So before going to India I took a course at the British navy's Submarine Escape Training Tower (SETT) at Gosport near Southampton.

Free-diving is as much a mental discipline as it is a physical one. Borrowing much from yoga, it is anything but a macho activity. A re-laxed body and mind means slower oxygen consumption and more time until you need to breathe. In the weeks before the course I'd done exercises to stretch and loosen my ribcage and abdominal muscles along with breathing routines to increase my tolerance to carbon dioxide build-up in the lungs, the trigger that makes you involuntarily inhale well before you've exhausted available oxygen. Lying on my back, I could empty my mind and let time slowly pass, not wanting to hurry it along, familiar now with the spasms that start to ripple through the diaphragm, which I gently ride, aware but detached as I slowly check my watch, now nearing the end of its second, third, or even fourth revolution. But in water the body is more active, as is the mind, which cuts the breath-hold time. In the tank I managed to pull myself feet-first down a rope to thirty feet, pushing tiny squirts of precious air through my Eustachian tubes to relieve the pressure on my eardrums, and puffing through my nose to ease the squeeze on my low-volume mask. But for some reason I couldn't descend head-first. My ears, always a bit "slow," refused to equalize in this position, probably a result of nervous tension constricting the tubes. At ten feet, the pain would stop me going any further, which was immensely frustrating, as I had plenty of air left. My pulse was insistent and loud, and the more I tried to shut it out, the more it hammered for attention. Maybe part of my mind was thinking ahead to cold gloomy water and hidden monsters in caves.

Then we were in India, where news came from our intended location, Corbett National Park (named after the celebrated hunter, conservationist and author, Jim Corbett), that suddenly made our task seem near-impossible. We would not, after all, be allowed to get in any of the pools along the park's stretch of the West Ramganga River because of the risk from mugger crocodiles. We would have to find somewhere else—where the goonch were unprotected and, therefore, much more scarce and wary. The Kali was a nonstarter because it was too dangerous—not only because of the possible presence of a man-eating specimen but also the strong currents and poor visibility, which, according to latest intelligence, was down to zero now following rain.

So we settled on a pool further up the Ramganga, some distance from Corbett Park, where the fish have a degree of protection because of a temple beside the water. But even this doesn't deter the really determined poachers. A couple of years before, Vinay had found a huge goonch here that had been killed by electro-fishing, Indian style. This involves hooking cables up to the power lines that stretch between wooden poles along the valley and then carefully dipping the other ends in the water, thereby also causing the lights to dim in nearby Bhikya Sein. Having removed the wires, the poacher then scoops the dead and dying fish from the surface. At seven feet, six inches to the fork of the tail, and possibly weighing over three hundred pounds, the monster goonch would have been impossible to carry; and even cutting it into pieces might not have been worth the effort, as goonch aren't considered good to eat. (A poacher who sold pieces of goonch saying it was mahseer was later beaten up for his trouble.) More likely, though, the poachers didn't see it. Unlike other fish, catfish aren't weightless in water but rather slightly more dense, thanks to heavy bones in the head and a small swim bladder. So the corpse would have slowly trundled along the bottom, between the cliff that forms the pool's left bank and the boulder beach opposite, to the shallows at the bottom end, where Vinay's friends found it.

But I knew monstrous fish were still there. I had hooked one when filming with Gavin but lost it when it sliced my ninety-pound nylon on a rock. In a state of deepening despair, I then fished on for days and nights without a touch—the pool had gone dead. This often happens with fish, but in this case an overzealous assistant didn't help the situation. One evening he spotted two young lads who had come down to the river from somewhere high above in the valley. They were deploying a loop line, a length of cord with monofilament nooses every few inches, along the base of the cliff. Loop lines are usually strung across flowing shallows, where they can be surprisingly effective. A fish, moving upstream, finds its head inside a noose and panics, tightening the nylon between its gills and pectoral fins. And the more it struggles the tighter the line holds it. Strung along the cliff base, a few feet under water, the loop line would intercept the small species that suck algae from the rock, but it is a low-impact method that just provides occasional fish for the fishermen themselves. Granted, the boys' line could have been a hazard if I hooked a fish, but goonch tend to fight on the bottom and their line was at mid-water, so I was prepared to live and let live. But before I knew it, the lads had been sent packing by a fellow who is normally charming but who, so the story goes, took an iron bar to the last person who crossed him, breaking both his legs.

The incident left me with a nasty taste in my mouth, but soon after dark, when I heard the explosion of a large predatory fish breaking the surface, my thoughts turned to other things. The sound of the fish, in the nighttime stillness, was immense, like a huge boulder falling in the water. Then it happened again, much closer, and then again. Then we were yelling at one another to get the hell away from the water and hurling impotent obscenities at the unseen figures high above. This was the low point of the entire trip. I consoled myself with the thought that the lost fish was "one of those things," something I could have done nothing about even though a camera light had been blinding me at the time, obscuring the direction of the line. But later I realized I was kidding myself. If, after hooking the fish, I had moved out of the corner where I was fishing, I would have been in a strategically stronger position. The fish escaped by swimming into a gully in the cliff, but if I had repositioned myself, this wouldn't have taken the line round a corner and I could have pulled it straight out. This was a painful relearning of a basic lesson. Before you fish, you must have a plan that takes account of all eventualities. Not until our postmonsoon return was I able to make some amends. The sixty-pounder I caught was an impressive fish, but nowhere near the size of the lost monster.

Back at the pool now, these memories returned. Two boys fishing with a thick washing line from a big rock upstream looked on as Rick and I peered down into the water, where it pushed into the pool and then kicked ninety degrees on impact with the cliff. I had promised him clear water, but Rick was not impressed. We could see the bottom near the side, where baby mahseer darted into an eddy, but Rick reckoned horizontal visibility would be only six feet. As we pulled on our wetsuits I tried to still my nerves. Rick and I had free-dove a cold, murky English lake before coming here, but I felt unprepared for this.

Without Rick, I wouldn't have dreamed of venturing into that fearful underwater landscape, but his matter-of-fact approach was reassuring.

As he rubbed liquid soap onto the inside of his mask and rinsed it with water, he said, "What I tell everyone to remember is this: when you find yourself wanting to breathe, you've still got plenty of oxygen left." With that, he took hold of his camera housing and pushed out into the current. The sun was high, but soon it would swing behind the cliff and plunge the water at its base into gloom. There was nothing to do but follow.

I tried to relax my body and let the water take me. With four pounds of lead on my quick-release weight belt to counteract the lift of my thin wetsuit, my buoyancy felt about right. I dipped my head under and felt the water on my face, the one part of me that wasn't enclosed in neoprene. Looking down, I could see my gloved hand, but beyond that, a cloudy green atmosphere thickened to obscure everything else. I lifted back up and saw the cliff approaching fast. Okay, what next? Breathing. Slow and unforced, the rubber weight belt yielding as I took air deep into my abdomen. And long, slow exhalations to quiet the pulse. In the training tank I had closed my eyes and shut off my mind, leaving just a slender sensory thread connected to the outside world. But here I needed to stay aware. The current was now bumping me against rock. Further along I saw Rick's fins flip up and sink from sight as he tucked and duck-dived. Now in his sixties, he told me he didn't have the lung capacity that he had as a young man, but he still seemed underwater for an age. I thought about loop lines and anglers' lines snagged on the rocks down there, some with hooks. We both had knives strapped to our ankles, but we didn't have the luxury of air tanks—only our internal supply, which would last one or two minutes at most. So we had to watch out for each other, diving alternately. This was hugely reassuring when it was my turn to descend, but it was a huge responsibility when I was the one on the surface.

An object with a Perspex dome on the front broke the surface, followed by a camo-patterned wetsuit and a jet of water from a snorkel. Rick hadn't seen anything. I squeezed the air from my lungs and pulled in a full fresh charge, my diaphragm working like a piston, then I pinched my nose, popped my ears, pulled my body into a tuck, and followed my outstretched arms downward. Below me was opaque gloom, but the cliff sliding past at my side was a reassuring presence. My mind flashed back to a sea cliff I dove off Oban, western Scotland, when I lost contact with this reference surface and found myself with equal darkness all around. For a few brief moments I had no sense of which way was up and which was down until I checked the direction of my bubbles. But here I was producing no bubbles. My weight belt had slackened around my middle, now compressed by the weight of water, and I had equalized my ears once more as I finned further down the smooth, sculpted rock. And then, sooner than expected, I saw the bottom, a field of sand and scattered boulders that swept in from a dim horizon to meet the base of the cliff. I pulled myself into an upright position and looked around me. The landscape was cleaner than expected, the loose boulders smaller. I couldn't see any fish, but I couldn't explore further because I had to get back up. I kicked and watched the rock flash past, getting brighter as I neared the liquid ceiling above.

Although I was starting to feel more comfortable underwater, managing longer submersions, and starting to spot sucker-mouthed carp swimming close to the rock in places where a strategically placed loop line could have snared them, the low visibility was a problem. Diving here was like blundering around with a small candle in a dark room. We were only likely to see a goonch if we were right on top of it, whereupon mutual shock would cause it to bolt. Nevertheless, after a half-dozen more dives, Rick surfaced with a whoop: "I've just filmed my first goonch!" But it wasn't a close view, just a shape that disappeared in a cloud of sand. A little while later I was sliding head-first down a forty-five-degree slope toward a lip where the rock fell vertically away, and there, in the overhang under the lip, was an open-sided tunnel with a goonch wedged inside: four or five feet long and inches from my face. I slammed on the brakes by grabbing the rock above and reversed away, and then I explained to Rick where it was. But despite descending from the correct spot, he couldn't find its hideout, and nor could I when I went back down. The landscape we were exploring was a complex abstract sculpture whose features seemed to rearrange themselves when we weren't looking. And with such a short horizon, navigating by following one remembered landmark to another was nearly impossible. A few dives later, though, I was drifting along the excavated angle between sand and rock when something made me stop. I slowly floated up and found myself face to face with the same fish—although a moment later, following a dull thump, there was only a blur of water filling the space it had occupied.

We needed to review our tactics. Perhaps it was time to deploy the ROV. The Remote Operated Vehicle was a minisubmarine we'd brought along inside a suitcase-sized flight case with another watertight case housing the control panel and the screen that displayed the view from the remote camera. Pictures were relayed back through a neutrally buoyant quarter-inch cable, by which the craft was also controlled electronically. It reminded me of Thunderbird 2 from the TV show *Thunderbirds*, which I used to watch as a kid. A scale-model toy was something I had desperately coveted, but Santa Claus had only considered me well behaved enough to deserve mints and tangerines. Okay, this was forty years late, but I was going to be flying this ship on a mission every bit as exciting as those piloted by Virgil Tracy.

We fired up the small generator and launched the ROV halfway down the pool, from the boulder beach across from the cliff. Although the current was scarcely visible here, it was still powerful enough to put a bow in the tether. We compensated for this by swimming it across to the cliff then turning its head up-current, exactly like a fish. With the current slower here, I was able to hold position and then maneuver quite precisely, resting the ROV on sloping ledges and lightly bumping it over and around rocks on its stealthy search upstream. Immediately we were seeing a lot more fish, particularly mahseer, swimming up and down underneath the rock overhangs. And we were getting much closer, without seeming to spook them. I dimmed the lights and periodically flicked to the rear black-and-white camera. I still saw nothing large anywhere. The rock was sculpted into organic shapes, like a living thing turned to stone, portions of which would loom enigmatically, fill the screen, then vanish. Then there was something a slightly different color, more gray than brown, outlined against the cloudy water. Yes! It was the flank of a goonch—I could see the mottled bands now. I eased the ROV back a bit, bumped it down to rest on the rock, turned a fraction to the right and there was its head. We got the DV tape in the recording deck spooling as I then edged closer. The fish reacted as if it was quite accustomed to being visited by black-and-yellow minisubmersibles bedecked with lights. Who knows what was going through its mind? Maybe it just saw the ROV as a weird looking fish, but one that was no threat because it was a lot smaller. Or maybe the goonch hadn't registered it at all. Some fish occasionally become torpid, a state akin to sleeping, and this one was resting on its belly, a bit like some sharks do. Or maybe it had been taken by surprise and was puzzled— in a fishy, worried way—and was pretending to be a rock. I managed to look at it for a good five minutes. Only when I eased forward to nudge it gently did it move away and disappear. Again I put this fish at four or five feet long. We had our goonch footage, but nothing yet that had us quaking in our boots.

The next day we went to another pool a few miles upstream. From a suspension bridge above, we looked down on a shoal of big mahseer, effortlessly cruising in midstream. That looked like a good sign. Again, there was an underwater cliff with lots of hiding places—perfect goonch habitat—but we dove the whole length of the pool without seeing a single one. The spookiest sight was a dead carp snared in a torn net fragment underneath a tangle of sunken tree roots. However, the absence of goonch was most odd, particularly given the presence of the mahseer overhead, which seemed to rule out the cause simply being poachers.

Time was short. We had just one more day, and although we already had the first underwater footage of goonch, it wasn't the blow-away stuff we were after. We piled our stuff into the jeep and took it for a long walk to a smaller pool. Here, again, the current pushed against a wall of rock as it turned a corner, thereby excavating a deep hole. I'd

fished this place a couple of years ago, and I knew there were some serious snags down there, with at least a few lines and trailing hooks. The
pool water had a soupy look to it, thanks to the turbulent rapid feeding
it, and the sun had already gone off the surface. Once in the water, the
looming cliff, which curved around us and formed a rocky cove, gave
the place the feel of an amphitheater. I made my way across to the rock,
tried to breathe away my apprehension, and went under. The smooth
water-worn rock plunged vertically downward. I kept expecting to see
the bottom, but instead the pressure kept increasing and darkness
closed in above me. I couldn't understand how this was so much deeper
than Temple Pool, and I thought of trailing lines. Just as I was thinking
of kicking for the surface, I saw something directly underneath me: a
dark shape against a lighter background. As I got closer it flexed into
a curve, swam a slow tight circle, and was gone. I surfaced with my
lungs bursting and told Rick, who hadn't seen anything. Continuing
here was pointless anyway, he said, because the visibility was too bad
for filming. We had it all to do the next day.

Back at Temple Pool, we decided to start at the tail of the pool and
work upstream. To minimize disturbance, Rick went in with the camera while I watched from the other side. Every few minutes he disappeared from sight and then surfaced several feet along, puffing water
from his snorkel and then breathing quietly to get oxygen back into his
bloodstream. At one point a gully cut into the rock, and when he surfaced from here, after a longer than normal delay, it was with an explosion of water and profanity.

"Holy shit!" he gurgled. "There's one down there the size of a
horse!" He kicked across and explained to me that this was our chance
for a two-shot: me and monster goonch in the same picture in an underwater cave where four or five others surrounded it. He would dive
first and take up position on the bottom and I would follow after a few
moments and come in over the top of him. And we needed to go *now*
because the fish had become agitated and might not stay there long—
even though it meant I would be diving cold, having had no warm-up
dives to build up my underwater time and check the lay of the land.

As Rick disappeared straight down I tried to still my hammering heart before taking my one lungful and following. I saw his dim shape on the bottom and arched my back to look where the camera was pointing. Too late I realized that I should have weighted myself a bit heavier for this, as my body, deprived of its downward momentum, started to drift back up. I kicked a couple of times and managed to get a slippery grip on a boulder, holding myself in a head-down slant. Craning my neck backward, I saw the water congeal into gloom underneath an angular arch. Something in there was moving.

Gray against black, I could make out three or four—or maybe five—vertical against the rock wall, with their downward ends swaying like a pod of hideous aliens. I reached forward and saw my fingers barely span the tail root of the biggest fish. They were getting disturbed, possibly feeling cornered, and my air was getting short. But those few moments burned into my memory with an uncommon intensity—not so much a detailed picture but instead the feeling, like a fragment of a dream, whose residue remains after you've burst back into the light.

We had the footage we came for, the first shots of goonch in the wild. But in order to pass judgment on its capability as a man-eater, we really needed a close look at one out of the water. From previous experience, I knew this was not a fish one can catch to order. So when the ROV found a goonch tail poking out of a dark cleft, Rick suggested I go and "noodle" it. But unlike the flathead catfish pulled from their holes in Oklahoma, goonch have serious teeth, so there was no way I was going to grab it by the mouth. Also, on the screen, there was no telling its size.

With Rick watching the screen and the tape deck rolling, I followed the ROV's yellow umbilical until I spotted its headlights eight feet down. A deep breath, a tuck, and a kick, and I was seeing the fish myself. With no time to waste, I reached forward and grabbed the root of its tail.

The next thing I knew, my arm was possessed, shaking my entire body. I hung on and kicked for the surface as the fish's body came clear and the thrashing became wilder. Then there were too many things in my head: the fish, the water, my twisting-back fingers, and the aching air in my lungs. I couldn't hold them all, and the fish was gone. Back on the shore, I cursed. Rick was right: I should have grabbed with two hands. Fear had made me keep one free, for hanging on—to what? With *both* hands immobilizing its tail, I could have finned its thrashing body to the surface then across to the shallows. But a plan is no good after the event, and I wouldn't get a chance like that again.

Later, as I fully expected, I would curse my mistake with even more fury as I watched my motionless lines around the clock, struggling to keep myself awake with just a sleep-deprived cameraman, James Bickersteth, for company, the rest of the crew having gone home to England. I remember the insane joy we felt on the sixth day, when I finally landed a goonch. Then reality returned: the realization that, at ten pounds, this could be bait for the fish I was after. But at least getting one any smaller was impossible. The next day I caught a nine-pounder.

We moved pools, and I caught a twenty-seven-pounder. With some creative camera work it looked quite big, but who were we kidding? The next day, fishing in a thunderstorm, I got my line stuck and deployed an "otter" to free it: a half-full water bottle attached to a snap-swivel, which I clipped round the line and lobbed into the current. Once it had floated downstream of the snag, I yanked hard on the line and felt it come free. But suddenly there was a force, much stronger than the current, ripping the line out. Hanging on for dear life, I stopped the fish's run, and after a period of stalemate, I brought it back toward me, thanks to a countercurrent on the bottom where the rapid at the pool's top end rolls over a lip into deep water. But I couldn't bring it any closer. Before I'd started fishing, I had planned for this eventuality: I would launch myself into the water and pull for the beach on the other side. But a day's rain had made the river wider, faster, and higher. As I kicked off my shoes, James yelled at me not to do it, and, wisely, I listened to him. But in the chaos, the fish slipped off the hook.

Back in England we faced the cold reality of a film about a monster fish but without a monster fish. Harry Marshall, boss of Icon Films, decided, against everyone's advice except mine, to send us out again. But the monsoon had arrived early. From Europe, finding out if the river was even accessible was impossible. Satellite images showed a dark mass spreading over the region. On our arrival, the river was raging and brown, but a carefully placed bait would still hold bottom. Because of the water color, I ripened my fish baits in the sun to create more of a scent trail underwater. And on the third day I hooked something immense, which hung on the line like a great boulder, not running at all but slowly inching through the dark depths until the line went vertically down into the water at my feet, where a great mass of bubbles now erupted followed by a dark back that was a yard wide. For a moment I thought I'd hooked the biggest goonch in the world, but then I realized it was a huge soft-shelled turtle (*Aspideretes gangeticus*). My guide Alam wanted to cut the line, but I heaved it toward some shallows, thrust the rod at James, and grabbed the turtle by the shoulders. The thing was like a tank and almost carried me into the river while shooting its prehensile neck, fully two feet long, and bolt-cutter jaws toward Alam. With great difficulty we blocked its escape with a rock and then turned it onto its back. This two hundred–pound animal hadn't been anywhere near my suspects list, but if, for any reason, it locked onto a swimmer's foot, there would be no resisting it.

Five days later, at the bottom of the pool, with a heavy fish gaining momentum in the current, James yelled at me again. But this time I ignored him. I had a clear plan and knew what I had to do. Half an hour later, having scaled a steep, muddy hillside, crossed a bridge, sprinted down a riverside road, and stumbled exhausted across a field of boulders, James arrived at the precise moment I yelled at Alam, "Now!"

The camera frame wobbles then holds position. In the foreground Alam reaches through the surface and grabs something, and in the frame's opposite corner a great head rears out of the water. This was the image that launched the series—and probably remains *the* iconic moment of all the episodes so far.

To the end of its tail, the fish was six feet long. It weighed 161 pounds. I also measured the width of its mouth (nearly thirteen inches), its maximum girth (forty-one inches) and the "wingspan" of its pectoral fins (forty-four inches). Armed with this data, I was now in a position to make some conclusions about the identity of the Kali "man-eater."

That people have disappeared in the Kali is fact, but there's no direct evidence so far that goonch have taken and eaten them. Certainly this six-foot goonch could pull somebody under if it grabbed a leg. But it would have to be even bigger to be capable of swallowing someone. The question is: how much bigger? If this fish were scaled up one and a half times, to nine feet, it would have a mouth nineteen inches wide and a mouth cavity two feet deep, extending to nearly twice that when the throat is open. That would comfortably take me head-first until just above my knees, and it would leave many of the local men with just their feet protruding. Given the authenticated existence of near-nine-foot Mekong giant catfish, the existence of goonch big enough to swallow a man cannot be ruled out. Going by the proportions of my fish, such an animal would weigh some 550 pounds.

Such a fish deliberately targeting a human is a frightening thought, partly because this would require a degree of intelligence not normally associated with fish. More likely, perhaps, a goonch made a reflex grab at some movement or splash. The victim then took a lungful of water and sank. And the fact that no corpse ever floated back up points to it having been eaten by something. If that something was the goonch and if it wasn't big enough to swallow the corpse whole, it could have ripped off pieces of flesh or possibly removed limbs by crocodile-style spin-feeding. It's then conceivable, however, that the next time a leg was grabbed, it wasn't a simple reflex, particularly because the large tasty biped was so surprisingly easy to overpower. Indeed Man Singh's description of his buffalo's disappearance definitely sounded like deliberate behavior. With no goonch alive being big enough to swallow such a large animal whole, this story points to a strategy of drowning and then dismembering. If that is case, the Kali man-eater could be a goonch even seven or eight feet long, weighing between 250 and 375 pounds, or maybe more than one such animal.

Part of the problem with fish stories, though, is that we fill in the blanks with assumptions, ascribing will or intent where none exists. A couple of years ago I met a Tibetan man who used to train the Indian army in mountain survival and who had long been puzzled by something that once happened to him. He was rafting a Himalayan river with a group of young men when a wave flipped the raft at the head of a pool. As the water pummeled him against a rock cliff, he felt bodies underneath him in the water and called out the men's names. But when he dragged himself ashore, all the men were there, having remained close to the raft. Before I told him my answer, based on my dives with Rick along similar rock walls, he asked, "So who were those people in the water who saved me?"

CHAPTER 2

WELS

Swimming fish leave wakes containing hydrodynamic and chemical traces.
These traces mark their swim paths and could guide predators.
We now show that nocturnal European catfish (*Silurus glanis*)
locate a piscine prey . . . by accurately tracking its three-dimensional
swim path before an attack in the absence of visible light.

Pohlmann, Grasso, and Breithaupt, *Tracking Wakes:*
***The Nocturnal Predatory Strategy of Piscivorous Catfish,* 2001**

IN THE SUMMER OF 2008 newspapers in Germany carried front-page reports of something attacking swimmers in Schlachtensee, a lake on the outskirts of Berlin. Over the course of just a few days several people emerged with bleeding wounds on their legs and a newfound terror of the water. One victim spoke of feeling something "like a snake" touch her before she was bitten.

Typically there was one long wound, broad and slightly curved, on each side of the leg. Close observation revealed multiple tiny punctures. Hospital staff had never seen injuries like this before and had no idea what caused them. From the shape of the wounds, some fisheries scientists identified the perpetrator as the Danubian catfish (*Silurus glanis*), more commonly known as the wels.

Before I stopped fishing in England in my mid-twenties, I was one of very few English anglers who had caught, or even seen, a wels catfish. It was very much a creature of mystery—an alien that the Duke of Bedford had introduced in 1880 when he put about seventy into the Shoulder of Mutton lake at Woburn Abbey, where they successfully bred and started snacking on His Grace's water birds. A century later their offspring had been stocked into a handful of other waters and were rumored to be elsewhere as well. (Like carp, wels sometimes travel by car, wrapped in a damp sack in the trunk, a means of relocation that the Environment Agency is keen to stop.) Very few were caught, and nobody knew exactly where they were or how big they grew. For me, disillusioned by the increasing predictability of carp fishing, this was precisely their appeal. I approached them with all the obsession I had once applied to carp—camping by the water for two or three days at a time and fishing day and night in a mental state in which I was never properly awake or asleep. So the wels is a fish that has always seemed rather unreal to me—and one that has come to signify an altered perception of time.

I think it was the morning after only my second night at a place called Tiddenfoot Pit when, against the odds, I found myself attached to a strong, deep-pulling fish that had picked up a dead perch. But twenty seconds later I was shaking for another reason, contemplating the end of the line where it had been rasped through. I kept coming back until I got one . . . and then a few more: seven fish over the course of the summer, the biggest a yard long.

For a mystery predator that had existed until then only in the imagination, its appearance didn't disappoint. It was hardly like a fish at all, or at least none that I was familiar with. With its scaleless, elongated body, long tentacles, and cavernous mouth, it was more like the work of some mad geneticist, a cross between slug and snake. At eleven pounds, my biggest one was still tiny: they don't grow well in England, with its long cold winters. But a big one, if you encountered it in the water, would be terrifying.

And wels can reach sizes that are truly immense. European folklore is full of tales of huge fish, and when weights and measures are given, these are truly staggering. The most widely quoted capture, from the River Dnieper in Russia (where they are called *ssum*) in the 1800s, weighed 673 pounds and measured over sixteen feet. Another fish, said to be a wels and caught in 1761 from the River Oder, weighed 825 pounds without the viscera. To drag such brutes from the water, fishermen would tie the rope line to a team of horses or oxen. Based on such reports, the maximum size for wels is widely quoted as 1,000 pounds. However, the heaviest wels for which we have reliable weights, recorded in the last half-century, are just a quarter of this. Thanks to intensive catch-and-consume fishing, numbers of wels are now way down on historical levels, so fewer fish reach old age and their full potential size.

Together with those reports of huge sizes in the past were stories of a correspondingly large appetite. In the 1500s the Swiss naturalist Conrad Gesner, in his *Historia animalium*, told of a human head found in the stomach of a wels, along with a hand wearing gold rings. Other reports talk of entire human corpses, mostly small children. Although there is no physical evidence to support any of these stories, the attacks in Germany seemed to lend them credence and revive speculation that there might be a freshwater man-eater in the heart of Europe. I ventured to Schlachtensee to investigate.

Being back in Berlin was strange. I had been here once before in 1989, just before the wall came down. I remembered crossing on the U-Bahn, underground, to East Berlin, when movement in the other direction was still prohibited, and surfacing into a world of cobblestones and two-stroke Trabant fumes. After dark I ducked down an alley behind a gray residential block and pulled myself up to look at the death strip between the two parallel walls. As I fiddled with my camera I heard a voice—very quiet and very near. My blood froze as I realized it came from a tower right in front of me. Very slowly I lowered my head back down behind the concrete (out of the cross-hairs?) and dropped to the ground. What's more, in West Berlin there had also been a unique atmosphere, a relentless pursuit of modernity that seemed like a collective denial of its encirclement. Later, when I went to the Amazon and visited Manaus, the industrial city at its center, I recognized a similar feeling. Now, two decades later, Berlin seemed sanitized, much the same as any other modern city. This time the unreality came from our filming schedule: traveling at dawn from hotel to lake, then back at dusk, so I experienced the city center as a place of perpetual darkness.

Schlachtensee lies hidden behind trees at the edge of the Grunewald forest, approached by shaded paths through still air. It is a narrow, winding ribbon of water over a mile long, but it is mostly less than two hundred yards across. People jog, walk, and cycle around its banks, enjoying the clean air. Others, I was surprised to see, were swimming, just weeks after the attacks and a warning to stay out of the water. Most were bathing near the banks, including a few "naturists," and a few hardy souls were doing lengths. There had been no more attacks since the newspaper story, even though the culprit—or culprits—hadn't been apprehended and removed, but the water was still a lot less busy than usual.

Unlike piranhas and sharks, wels don't have teeth that cut; instead, they swallow prey whole. A hypothetical sixteen-footer would have a mouth two feet in diameter, wider than my shoulders. The depth of the mouth cavity would be about three feet, but it could engulf an animal twice this length because wels, like many fish, can open their throats to take prey right into the stomach, which extends the whole length of the body cavity, almost as far as the vent. Such a fish, then, would be capable of swallowing an adult human. And like any fish that swallows large prey, they would take it down head-first, as most animals slip down more easily in that direction.

But fish well short of man-swallowing size inflicted the bite marks on the Schlachtensee victims. Typically the marks were about seven inches long, indicating a fish measuring about five feet and weighing around fifty pounds. But the historical accounts of human body *parts* being found inside wels stomachs raised the possibility of another feeding strategy. Could they drown and dismember large prey and then swallow the pieces in the same way that a crocodile does?

I am nearly six feet tall and weigh 175 pounds, and normally I can handle a fish out of water that I have brought to land or into a boat, even if it's bigger than me. In its home element, though, it's a very different story. I remember seeing a report about a diver in a Scottish sea loch who got caught in some fishing line that was attached to a conger eel. He was dragged from the shallows down to 150 feet before managing to cut himself free, whereupon he made an emergency ascent and then blacked out. Later it emerged that other divers had previously seen this eel, and the point is that it wasn't enormous: just 40 pounds. So a full-grown man, used to being in the water and equipped with dive fins, had been unable to resist a fish a quarter of his size. Without his air tank and knife, he'd have been a goner. So the story I read about a wels pulling from his boat and drowning a young Polish man—who was fishing with his line tied to his wrist—does have a ring of truth.

So how big—in real numbers, pounds and feet—would a wels need to be to overpower a person in the water? To find out the pull that would be necessary to pull me under, I attached weights to myself until I couldn't keep my head above the surface. It turned out that a downward pull of just thirty pounds will do it. Then I attached a cord to my waistband and swam against a spring balance to see how much horizontal force is needed to pull me backward. The figure was about the same. So what size wels would exert a pull of thirty pounds? The answer is not thirty pounds.

Although anglers set great store by fish weights, fish (with a few exceptions) weigh nothing in the water. You could hang a dead fish, of any size, on your leg without risk. This is why you don't have to use twenty-pound line to catch a twenty-pound fish. In open water you can land a fish this size with a breaking strain of three pounds as long as you have plenty of it. You let the fish swim around against just enough resistance to keep it moving until it tires itself out and floats belly-up. Then you gently pull its weightless, buoyant body over your landing net or within grabbing range. But if you try to stop the fish when it's running, to hold it from a sunken tree or boulder, it will snap the line. This is analogous to the difference between a boat with its motor stopped, which you can move with your little finger, and the same boat with its motor running. What you feel is not the fish's weight but rather its muscular force and momentum. In general, this is proportional to size: a big fish pulls harder than a small fish. But some species pull harder for their weight than others, depending on body shape, fin area, muscle volume, metabolic rate, and so forth.

As far as I'm aware, there is no accurate data on what different fish pull. Scientists have better things to do. So I'm resorting to educated guesswork here that is based on what line strengths are necessary for "hit and hold" fishing in still water. Going on this, I estimate that, from a standing start, most fish can pull between one-third and half of their weight. (The figure will be higher if they already have some momentum.) So to exert a pull of thirty pounds—the force needed to pull me under or overpower me in water—a wels would need to be only sixty to ninety pounds. In other words, it would need to be only half my size or even less.

Based on this, the fish that attacked the swimmers in Schlachtensee was borderline size: maybe capable of pulling a person under, or maybe not. If that was its intention, it would have to "suck it and see." I spoke to two of the victims, Jonas Wegg and Katharina Saxe, and neither of them was pulled under, which suggests they both had a lucky escape from a fish that was not quite big enough to pose a real danger. But bigger fish are in the lake, and neither of the victims goes swimming there anymore.

Something else they both said was very interesting. In the popular imagination, big fish live in the deepest water, but these attacks happened in the shallowest part of the lake, almost shallow enough to stand up in. Also, although wels commonly feed in shallows at night, the attacks happened in broad daylight. At first this would appear to give the wels an alibi, and indeed some biologists have expressed doubt that the attacker was a wels, but there is one reason why wels would be in the shallows at that time of year.

Summer is when wels breed, and unlike many other fish, they don't just shed their eggs and abandon them. They lay them in a nest in the bottom weed and the male then defends against all comers.

"For this particular catfish it was a *huge* stress to guard the nest, when it had all those swimmers around," Dr. Christian Wolter, from the Leibniz Institute of Freshwater Ecology and Inland Fisheries, told me as we rowed a boat in the area where the bathers were bitten. This was the only shallow, weedy water in the lake, apart from the extreme margins. The fish didn't have anywhere else to breed. In his opinion, these incidents weren't attacks but rather acts of self-defense.

I'd come prepared to fish for something with a large, unsatisfied appetite. Even though this assumption now appeared wrong, to come all this way and not cast a line would have been equally wrong. So I teamed up with a local angler called Horst, a retired butcher with a penchant for yodeling while he fished, and we spent an evening offering up half-pound crucian carp on the drop-off into the deep hole at the top end of the lake. We didn't catch anything, but even blank sessions teach you something. In this case it lent support to what local anglers said about the existence of a very small head of wels here. This in turn chimed with what Dr. Wolter said about the difficulty wels have breeding here. All of this seemed to add up. The Schlachtensee wels are not man-eaters, just caring parents.

But what about those old stories of corpses and body parts? They come from a time, long gone, when wels were much more numerous and reported at massive sizes, so we'll never know for sure how big they grew or just how predatory they were. Or maybe we will because, in a few places, the species is making a dramatic comeback. . . .

Nowhere today holds as many big wels as the Rio Ebro in northern Spain, where hundred-pounders are commonplace and an increasing number go over two hundred pounds. Wels are not native to the river but were introduced just thirty-five years ago in the mid-1970s. Their phenomenal success here can be attributed to three main factors. First, the water is much warmer than their native rivers, so they feed and grow year-round with no shut-down period in winter. Second, they are aquatic golden geese. The local economy is now based on fishing tourism, so these fish are worth more alive than dead, and the fishing is, almost exclusively, catch and release. Third, the river is stuffed with food: not just the carp that were here originally but also the tons— literally—of high-protein bait that visiting anglers tip in the water. The Ebro was a place I had to check out.

Most catfish are omnivorous and are caught on baits such as worms, dead fish, or mussels on the bottom. But the big Ebro wels catfish are highly predatory. Until a few years ago, the preferred bait was live carp or eel. The carp were typically around five pounds, but there are stories of people using twenty-pounders. To keep the bait in the desired spot, a few yards of "weak" line, typically twenty pounds breaking strain, were attached to a swivel above the bait and then tied to a tree branch on the far bank or a large buoy anchored in the water. When the angler tightened the line between the vertical rod and the anchor point, this would then suspend the bait just under the surface.

Wels find live prey by homing in on vibrations. Although fish ears have no opening to the outside or sound-gathering funnel like ours, catfish hearing is highly sensitive thanks to a series of small bones linking the ears to the swim bladder. In this way they use this large buoyancy organ as an amplifier. In addition, they use their lateral line, the sunken canal down each side of the body into which protrude jelly-covered hairs, which move and send nerve impulses in response to pressure changes in the water. So a fish tethered near the surface, even on the other side of the river, is an unmissable target. In fact, their remote sensing is so acute that experiments have shown wels to be capable of tracking down small fish by following the wake they leave in the water.

But live-baiting is now banned on the Ebro largely because fishermen were bringing in bait fish from outside, which carried the risk of spreading disease. Some would also argue that, in these enlightened times, this method is questionable from an ethical standpoint. But if the wels's predatory reflexes are all they're cracked up to be, they ought to hit a lure. To test this out, I spent an afternoon trolling in the "upper lake," which is above the hydroelectric dam just upstream from the Ebro's confluence with the Rio Segre. I think it's true to say that hardly anyone fishes moving baits for any kind of catfish, but such a near-total disregard of their predatory side smacks of preconception or even prejudice. Wels are not sleek, streamlined fish like pike or salmon, and their sluglike looks suggest a nature that is equally sluggish. And although angling should be a lifelong lesson in open-mindedness, anglers on the whole judge catfish by their looks. In my case, however, I had open-mindedness forced upon me. In 1982, while fishing a lake in India, I cast a shallow-diving plug at a large swirl in a muddy bay and hooked a fish that, after an arm-wrenching fight, turned out to look disconcertingly like a wels. A closer look revealed a more silvery coloration and proper teeth, identifying it as a mulley (*Wallagu attu*). It weighed around twenty pounds, and to prove it was no fluke, I caught three smaller ones later. Locals told me it grows to over one hundred pounds but then added, to my lack of surprise, that such fish are an extreme rarity nowadays. Then, when I went to the Amazon, I caught surubim catfish (*Pseudoplatystoma fasciatum*) on plugs. These are beautiful, firm-bodied fish with battleship-like gray-and-black Rorschach patterns on their flanks. To begin, this was "lucky dip" fishing, trying all sorts of lures at all depths to find out what species were down there. Over time, however, my approach became more targeted, and what worked best for surubim was a slow troll, with the rod wedged under one knee and over the other leg and then the clutch loosened right off as I slowly paddled.

So trolling for wels didn't seem too incongruous. Using the sonar to read the bottom, we swam the deep-diving Luhr-Jensen Fingerling as close as we could to the rock tumbles and pinnacles on the edge of the deep central valley. The first couple of times the rod kicked, it was zander, one a shiny, green, spiky-finned four-pounder. When the wels took, though, there was no doubting it, and once we'd survived the first heart-stopping moments, when fish and boat were traveling in opposite directions, the light rod struggled to bring it up. In the end I confess I was slightly disappointed that the wels wasn't quite one hundred pounds, but a ninety-pounder is still a lunker on a lure. More important, though, was what it proved to me: that a hungry wels will hit a moving target.

But that fish hit in an artificial lake, in still, clear water. To test their responses in more realistic conditions, I booked a small rowing boat and a local guide, Enrico, and put in a few miles up the Rio Segre. Here the water was brown and bowling along in places at a fast trotting pace—hardly catfish water in most people's minds. Bait was what Enrico called a "yummy fish," six inches of soft, white plastic with a large single hook threaded through it. What followed was some of the most demanding and exhilarating fishing I've ever done. As the tree-hung riverbank blurred by, the aim was to spot slacks and eddies on the edge of the current and land the lure in them, as close to the side as possible. The difference between a perfect cast and a disastrous hang-up that breaks the line—because in this current, there's no going back—is about six inches. It took me a while to get the hang of it, keeping my feet as the boat spun and bumped down shallow rapids, while also scanning both banks—and all the time avoiding the camera boat without looking at it. At first I was cautious as I found my range. Then I started getting in some good shots in some good places, but I had no takes.

Then I hit on the vital detail. On landing the lure in a bank-side pocket, I left the reel open a fraction longer, to let the lure *sink*, then tightened and twitched it alive. Bang! Something plunged on the line as the boat kept barreling downstream and the drag yelped. Instead of the expected loud crack, I heard the painful reedy sound of line scything through water as the fish was dragged from its holt and started to follow us down. Then it was no longer there. It happened so quickly, this double dose of disbelief. I felt a certain sickness come over me—that aching feeling of loss and not knowing. But I couldn't dwell on it because I knew now what to do, and more lies were passing by. Soon I was absorbed in renewed casting, and I hooked another fish. But that one got off too. Then there was the bridge ahead, where we would have to get out. I was bitterly disappointed and tried to give myself some solace by blaming the borrowed gear: a combination of soft rod and thick wire hook. The fish didn't feel huge, maybe fifty pounds, but what memorable catches they would have been from water like this! You can keep your peacock bass, for all their brash Amazonian finery, which you fish in the same general way but at one-tenth the speed for one-tenth the rod-bending poundage. I told myself that one day I'd come back with a beefy bait-casting rod and multiplier reel and with my casting already sharpened so I could simply look at the spot and the cast would go there, like a basketball clearing the ring. But in a way all of this was beside the point. As much as any scientific paper, those hook-ups confirmed that wels are supreme predators, capable of detecting and seizing prey in turbulent zero visibility. What's more, despite their reputation as bottom feeders, they are very switched on to possible food from above, which in fact is totally in keeping with their protruding lower jaw and upward-looking eyes. And to grab potential food this quickly, their reaction has to be an unthinking reflex: grab first, ask questions later.

But if there's easier food around, they'll go for it. Like all animals, constant biological accountancy, where the currency is energy, drives their behavior. Why chase food if it's served up on a plate? Anglers on the Ebro also make a similar decision: why chase the fish if they will come to you? And, in a way, a deal is struck. Now, following the live-bait ban, the most popular method is a half-dozen walnut-sized fish-meal pellets offered on the bottom. Wels find bait on the riverbed by following chemical trails in the water, trails they sniff out using the taste buds that are spread all over their bodies. (Some say that a catfish is like a giant tongue.) These chemical receptors are most concentrated on the whiskers. Together with four short whiskers on the chin, wels have two long ones on the upper jaw that they can extend to either side in front of them. This, we may suppose, makes their remote tasting strongly directional. They likely home in on food by turning in the direction of the stronger reading.

Bottom fishing for wels, Ebro style, bears more relation to marine beach fishing than to most freshwater fishing. Each rod is set in a vertical holder, and, by means of a small rowing boat, the bait is deposited 100 to 150 yards away along with sixteen to twenty ounces of lead to anchor it and a bucketful of loose pellets to lure the "cats" in. The line is zero-stretch braid with a breaking strain of 150 pounds, and the reel is screwed up tight. When the rod folds over or springs back straight as the line falls slack, this signals a take. In either case, there's a tinkling of the bell clipped to the rod-tip. The little sound is insignificant, but after a couple of days it has everyone reflexively scrambling, kicking over cups of tea and falling over film kit.

A flicked flashlight beam shows my rod is straight—a slack-liner. I grab it and wind up the slack. Yes, there's a weight there that isn't the lead, so I heave back as hard as I can. "Try to pull its head off," is the unsubtle advice of the guides here, but with all that line out, anything less will just bounce the hook feebly off its jaw. The next moment, however, I've lost my balance and I'm being dragged on my backside toward the water. The only thing that stops me going in is a slab of rock that I hit with my feet. Some fishermen here end up with their companions hanging round their waists, but at least I'm spared that indignity. To my right is a large weedbed. If the fish kites round this, I'll never get it in, so once I feel it coming my way, I can't let up for a moment. There's the sound of something breaking the surface, and at first all I see is its head—about a foot across. A hand grips its lower jaw, and then another hand, very quickly, as it tries to twist. The movement is exactly like a crocodile's "death roll," and I can easily see now how this could potentially drown a victim or rip a limb from a corpse. With its mouth unclamped from grazed hands, we zip it into a nylon body bag, and it takes three of us to drag it up onto the bank.

The thing weighs a massive 153 pounds, but my guide, Jason Toye, has seen many fish this size. He says the fish just keep getting bigger and bigger, possibly by as much as 5 to 10 pounds a year with no signs yet of any slowing down, although being precise is difficult when you've got fish that can "put on" 20 pounds in a few moments simply by inhaling a carp. (In the two years since I fished there, the record for the river went up by over 30 pounds. At the time of writing, it stands at 246 pounds, 14 ounces—an 8-foot, 2½-inch fish caught in September 2009. Meanwhile the biggest authenticated wels from anywhere was from Italy's River Po in June 2010, weighing 250 pounds and measuring 8 feet, 2 inches.)

And the Ebro has lots of them. This method brings me another five over 100 pounds, with the biggest weighing 163. Bringing them in is hard work. Apparently some visiting anglers stop fishing because they are exhausted. After a while, there's also a kind of mental exhaustion. I find myself wishing for a 200-pounder, but size is largely a lottery.

And success is largely down to the guides, who have the fishing down to a fine art. Although there's no doubt that having a guide gets results, you don't get the same satisfaction as you would if you worked it out for yourself. But we need a big fish for the film, and we can't complain with the size we've got.

We also hear some fascinating stories—not from a dusty historical tome but bang up to date. Jason tells me of a catfish some four and a half feet long that was coming in on an angler's line when a very big fish grabbed it. The would-be cannibal, well over 200 pounds, only let go several minutes later, just as it was about to be gloved. Another time a big wels, later weighed at 155 pounds, regurgitated something just as it was about to be landed. The object turned out to be the skeleton of a 40- to 50-pound wels, but the big one had still been hungry enough to take a bait. And the stories don't stop there. Wels have also bitten anglers, a few on the leg and one on the side of the chest, when they were back in the water after capture. This tends to happen when the fish has been kept out of the water a little too long—for one photograph too many. Although generally attributing human feelings to animals is wrong, large wels do sometimes seem to get pissed off. And in fact one wels I was releasing, after a long piece to camera about its anatomy, did appear to double round and go for my calf. But I'll never know for sure what its intention was because, having heard the guides' stories, I reflexively pulled my leg away.

The same fish, a 140-pounder, had fading bite marks on its back from a fish of similar size. These, according to Jason, would have been inflicted during spawning, which, with wels, is not a delicate affair. Seeing this, I remembered what Katharina Saxe told me at Schlachtensee about something snakelike brushing her legs before she was bitten. Maybe this fish hadn't been defending a nest after all but had instead been looking for a mate and, in its blind lust, had mistaken a human leg for another wels.

At any rate, the picture that emerges from the Ebro is of a fish with serious attitude. And the prospect of these seven- and eight-footers reaching sixteen feet, at which size they could swallow an adult human being, is quite terrifying. However, after looking at these present-day wels, clearly those historical reports of such dimensions are unreliable. Why? Because the numbers don't add up. Based on a known eight-foot wels weighing 250 pounds, a sixteen-footer would weigh in the region of 1,500 to 2,000 pounds. (If a fish keeps the same body shape, a doubling in length comes with an *eight*fold increase in weight.) This is far more than the quoted 673 pounds—a sixteen-footer with this weight would be impossibly thin, more like an eel, so we have to rule it out. Other heavy fish were possibly misidentified sturgeon, also scaleless with tentacles, which *do* grow (or did anyway) to sixteen feet and whose range overlaps that of the wels. Based on present-day wels, a more realistic maximum length would be ten feet with a weight possibly approaching 500 pounds.

But this is still a huge fish, nearly the length of two people. It could easily pull any person under, and given the reports of wels attacks on dogs and swans, including some recently from Poland and Germany, it's not inconceivable that such a fish could attack and swallow a small child. As those old accounts have indicated, the wels is a potential child-eater.

That it is a man-eater, however, is less likely. All verified "attacks" on adults have been reactions to provocation, of one sort or another, including in the case of the Hungarian angler who was nearly pulled under in 2009 by a large fish that grabbed his right leg when he was releasing it. Normally, too, a predator's eyes are looking for something no bigger than its stomach, not to mention that a large prey animal is normally likely to fight back, so is best left alone. But that doesn't mean that Gesner's report of a human head and hand being found inside a wels is untrue: the fish could have easily fed on a drowned corpse, very likely decapitating and dismembering it by spin-feeding. And even a six-foot wels would have the capability of causing the drowning in the first place, if it were ever so inclined. So whether Gesner's wels was a man-eater or just a scavenger remains in doubt, as does the size to which they used to grow back in the sixteenth century.

But that's not quite the end. Although such a distant past is normally unknowable, with a fishing line, anything is possible. Whereas time goes forward above the surface of the water, beneath it, time can spin backward, and one day somebody standing on the banks of the Rio Ebro will bring in a monster from the middle ages, brought back to life in the shadow of the power lines.

It's powerful stuff, this underwater time travel. Sometimes a fishing line can even reveal the future, or at least one possible version of it. And it is a vision more frightening than anything in the medieval manuscripts and bestiaries.

CHAPTER 3

GOLIATH TIGERFISH

Going up that river was like travelling back to the earliest
beginnings of the world, when vegetation rioted on the earth
and the big trees were kings.

Joseph Conrad, *Heart of Darkness,* 1902

TWENTY-FIVE YEARS AGO I READ, open mouthed, about a fish with a difference: a sumo-sized monster with inch-long teeth that was capable of cutting clean, six-pound mouthfuls of meat from its prey, usually with fatal results. This was the mid-1980s, when the tsunami of terror sent around the world by *Jaws* still swirled in the collective psyche. Even after you'd checked under your bed, you couldn't be certain that a great white shark wouldn't surface in your nightmares. The only consolation was that great whites don't swim in rivers. But this other fish is found in rivers, where, according to the pages that trembled in my hand, it bites pieces out of anything that comes its way, including people. One favorite snack, the author said, is the dangling genitals of passing male swimmers.

This wasn't Pliny the Elder writing in the first century nor some monkish medieval tome but rather a Belgian doctor, Dr. Henry Gillet, writing in the 1940s in a book entitled *Game Fish of the World*. The fish he described is the goliath tigerfish (*Hydrocynus goliath*, which translates to "giant water dog"), and it lives in equatorial Africa in the Congo River. In thirty-six years as a traveling medical inspector, Gillet had caught a number of them, weighing up to 87½ pounds, but lost many more—including one, he said, that was at least twice that weight. So why, forty years later, with the world opened up by cheap, easy travel, couldn't I find a single published photograph of this monster or any natural-history programs featuring it?

The book says that reaching the waters where they swim is not hard, recommending a ship to Matadi, a plane to Leopoldville, or a train from Johannesburg or Nairobi. It talks of good hotels and small boats that are easily hired along with a network of roads into the interior. There's even a list of accessible locations (Lake Matshi, Lusambo on the Sankuru River, Makanga on the Kasai, Port Francqui . . .), complete with details of who to contact for assistance once you're there as well as the assurance that "a stay of a few months here will offer no dangers." But a little research revealed a very changed picture.

The first Europeans to see the mouth of the Congo River were Portuguese sailors under the command of Diogo Cão in 1482. Here, at last, they believed, was a back door to the riches of Africa, principally the gold and ivory trade, which, at the time, Arab caravans crossing the Sahara monopolized. But a hundred miles inland a series of rapids blocked the fast-flowing channel that the people on its banks called *nzadi*, "the river that swallows all rivers." A few years later, in 1492, Columbus landed in the Bahamas, leading to the European conquest and colonization of the "New World." Meanwhile, the Congo's natural defenses kept outsiders at bay for another four centuries.

The river was eventually mapped by John Rowlands, the Welsh-born illegitimate workhouse boy who, after migrating to America and changing his name, worked as a journalist for the *New York Herald*, where his big scoop was finding the missing Scottish missionary Dr. David Livingstone on the shores of Lake Tanganyika in 1871. Now known to the world as Henry Morton Stanley, he returned to Africa for another expedition, to a river called the Lualaba, which flows north up the middle of the continent and that Livingstone believed to be the headwaters of the Nile. But when it started to veer counter-clockwise, crossing the equator twice, Stanley knew it could only be the Congo. He described his epic 999-day voyage, which fewer than a third of the 356 people who set out with him survived, in *Through the Dark Conti-*

nent. But his embellished gung-ho accounts of shoot-outs with natives, although very much in the style of the day, have done him no favors. Many in the establishment saw him as a lower-class upstart, and his achievements were singled out for negative spin.

What really tarnished his reputation was what happened next. Stanley had a vision of opening the Congo for trade, based on a road to bypass the rapids and a fleet of boats above. However, unable to find any government to back the idea, he ended up in the pay of King Leopold II of Belgium, who claimed the Congo—an area one-third the size of the United States' forty-eight contiguous states—as his personal colony. Leopold's excesses are now well documented, but for a long time they were hidden from the outside world. After the invention of the pneumatic tire, there was a fortune to be made from rubber, which Leopold's agents collected from wild vines in the Congo rainforests using forced labor. In pursuit of this commerce, and hidden from any scrutiny, the colonists instituted a reign of terror, using massacre and starvation to subdue the population. Workers who failed to reach their quota had their hands cut off. Recent estimates put the death toll during this period between ten and thirteen million, roughly the same number of Jews and others that the Nazi Holocaust killed.

Eventually, the truth started to seep out, thanks to travelers such as the Irishman Roger Casement and the Polish-born writer Joseph Conrad, whose novel *Heart of Darkness*, since retold for a modern audience in the contemporary setting of *Apocalypse Now*, is a chilling vision of the evils that inevitably accompany absolute power. In 1908 the Belgian government took control from their monarch and started to clean up the colonial act—building roads, schools, and hospitals. This was the period when Dr. Gillet, during his time off, cast his line into the Kasai, Sankuru, and Lubi rivers in the southeastern corner of the vast Congo basin and urged readers of *Game Fish of the World* to come and try their luck.

So what happened since then? In June 1960, when I was four years old, the Congo was granted independence. But days later, secretly backed by the Belgians, the mineral-rich Katanga province declared itself a separate state and a military coup deposed the elected prime minister, Patrice Lumumba, who was then murdered. The coup's leader, Joseph Mobutu, went on to declare himself president in 1965, making much of African *authenticité* by eradicating colonial-era names, which included rechristening both country and river Zaire (ironically a Portuguese corruption of the African *nzadi*). Meanwhile, propped up by foreign powers because of his spurious anticommunist credentials, Mobutu set about amassing one of the biggest personal fortunes in the world while the country around him crumbled into ruin.

By the mid-1980s the roads, railways, helpful officials, and guest houses in the interior were no more. Under Mobutu's dictatorship, time had run backward, creating a remoteness that was more than mere geographical distance. Like a medieval despot, he ruled his vast kingdom through fear, chaos, murder, and bribery. Although some ex-pats were in the capital, now called Kinshasa, the country was effectively closed to outsiders. Certainly nobody went there as a tourist.

There are many who say that recreational fishing is a form of escapism, and I would agree with them. I do it to clear my mind of everyday concerns. But now my interest in a fish had taken me to a dark place and alerted me to some realities that might have been best left unknown. All this strife occurred while I climbed trees in a vicarage garden, stared out of classroom windows, and sat by willow-shrouded carp ponds in the timeless tranquility of an English summer night. Lumumba's body hacked to pieces and dissolved in sulphuric acid; a quarter-million dead; an unpaid army ruling by extortion; and dissidence kept in check by rival secret police services—all so copper and uranium would continue to flow out of Africa to the right countries. I surfaced as if from a bad dream. To be concerned about the fate of a mere fish in the face of all this human misery seemed extremely trivial. But then I found myself looking at it a different way. In a world where rivers are increasingly overfished, poisoned, dynamited, and left high and dry by dams and drainage, the Congo could be the one system in the world where fish populations have remained at historical levels thanks to the sheer size of the river, the low human density, and the dictatorial disorder.

This was also, I reminded myself, why no outsiders went there—certainly none with fishing rods. But my thoughts had a certain momentum. I discovered there were flights to Kinshasa, but these catered only to expense-account businessmen and diplomats, costing three or four times the "bucket shop" prices to India or anywhere else. On top of that, I heard I would need pocketfuls of $50 bills to buy back my passport from immigration and bid for my luggage, item by item, from customs. The whole idea was a nonstarter. Then I found a French charter company, now defunct, that flew an aged 707 from Marseilles to Bangui, capital of the Central African Republic (CAR). From here I could cross the Ubangui River to the small town of Zongo in the northwest corner of Zaire. But neither embassy knew if the border was open. If it was, the CAR staff in Paris informed me, I would need to get a visa in Zaire to allow me back into CAR, but they couldn't tell me where I could get this. The only way to find out was to go. After crossing by bus to France, I took off in April 1985.

When I'd come back from India three years before, emaciated and exhausted but with some fish stories under my belt and pocket change from the laughably small amount of cash I had taken with me, I considered, along with the few other backpackers I'd met along the way, that if I could survive that—the squalid doss-houses, seething trains, days of diarrhea—I could survive anywhere. There was also the knowledge that, with a little more money, India could be quite comfortable. But nothing had prepared me for the Congo. From the moment I set foot in Africa and first inhaled the hot, semiliquid, smoke- and wood-flavored air, I felt out of my depth: the stampede at the airport, the long night drive followed by threats from the taxi driver's sidekick when I refused to hand over more than the agreed fare, and the hour-plus search at the border ("Nice bag. . . . Nice shoes. . . ."), after which I was told, "If you go anywhere you are not authorized, *monsieur le professeur,* you are in big trouble."

The next evening I was one of thirty-three people huddled under a plastic sheet on the back of a truck as we came to a boggy halt in a thunderstorm. We lurched into the next town the following night, where I found a hot concrete cubicle of a room that stank of urine and had no water or light. In the corridor a man I couldn't see asked me the purpose of my journey. I couldn't imagine two months like this, so I was tempted to turn back. But the view behind me was equally bleak. From time to time I sold a magazine article, but this was a long way from making a living. And, thanks to record levels of unemployment, there wasn't much else on the horizon. I was back living with my parents, for God's sake, at twenty-nine years old. Should I go back to being a motorcycle messenger in London, which I'd quit while I was still alive? Or leave the country like Martin, bumming around Europe as an itinerant English teacher? Even in my dreams, the future back home was a wilderness. So I decided not to think too far ahead but instead just get through each day.

I reached the river after two weeks—waiting for trucks that never came and sleeping in rat- and bedbug-infested brothels, the only places with spare rooms. I forced myself to eat the acrid manioc paste that's the country's staple source of carbs as well as blackened fish corpses sold from market stalls, fish that reminded me why I was here.

The sight of the river both lifted and overwhelmed me. What appeared to be the far bank was only an island. The true bank was a hazy band of gray-green on the distant horizon. I've always found big waters intimidating: how do you find the fish in all that water? This is one reason I've stuck to rivers. But this was like an inland sea. Three days later I was steaming downstream on a raft of barges pushed by the towering *Colonel Ebeya*, a floating city housing two thousand human passengers and a population of animals that grew by the hour, as dugout canoes intercepted us to sell smoked monkeys and trussed crocodiles.

As a non-African, keeping a low profile was impossible, and men in plain clothes who were clearly not ordinary civilians constantly asked what I was doing there. My reply, that I wanted to catch an *mbenga*, never left them convinced. After two days I joined several other people in a large dugout that peeled off from the moving riverboat and headed for a village on the shore. Here the chief put me up, as is traditional, and his brother took me fishing. One day we crossed to the large central island, where something hit the silver spoon I was casting, breaking the surface in an explosion of spray as it spat out the hook. It was the only take I had in the whole time I was there, partly because the dugout and brother were rarely available and partly because, even though the rains had long stopped, the river was still in flood and the fish were dispersed in the forest. Even the netsmen were catching next to nothing, so there was very little to eat. They told me that if I stayed another couple of months I would catch goliath, but if I was to make it back to Bangui in time for my flight home, I needed to get going.

For days there were no boats, but then I got a lift in a large dugout with a motor that kept breaking down. Finally, back in Bangui, an immigration officer told me, with a meaningful look, that they'd lost my passport. By chance I met somebody with influence who helped me get it back without paying the bribe, which I didn't have the money to pay, just hours before my flight.

Returning to England—and to a girlfriend who was keen to settle down—the time had come to do some serious soul-searching. Although I was just back from an epic, hazardous, solo journey through a place where few outsiders dare to go, she said it was now time for me to "prove myself." Like the immigration officer, she made no direct reference to what I needed to do, but the implication was clear. So when, after a couple of months, I still hadn't secured myself a proper job with a guaranteed, regular paycheck, she informed me that I was a "waster" and left.

As it turned out, a few months after that I did get a job as a copywriter in an advertising agency. I stayed there for three and a half years, at first overwhelmed by my workload and then, as I found my feet, increasingly jaded and unable to take myself seriously. The future looked much more comfortable, but, boy, did it look dull. The excuse to get out came in the form of a phone call. Paul Boote had recently made a TV documentary about Himalayan mahseer and the production company was keen to capitalize on this by doing a follow-up. How about doing some recon in the Congo?

By rights I should have been in no position even to consider this. However, working in the misinformation business had enabled me to decode the messages that others were sending in my direction. So I hadn't "bought a house," despite a relentless campaign, leveraged by tax breaks and huge doses of collective wishful thinking, to rebrand debt as investment. Instead, I lived in an unheated room in a down-market housing estate, with police helicopters providing the sound-track. However, as ample compensation for the stigma, my annual rent was the same as what many of my friends paid in loan interest every month. So instead of putting off the decision for twenty-five years, I could consider Boote's idea for a few moments and then say, "Yes."

On top of that, I simply needed a break. Because of the intensity of my work, for clients that included property firms and oil companies, I'd taken only a fraction of my holiday entitlement. I had been hoping to take maybe one week of the six weeks I was owed, but my employers had recently told me that they had changed their policy on holidays and that I was no longer entitled to any of it. I was outraged. This job was eating my life, sucking my blood. And although it was true, of course, that I was getting paid for doing it, I had believed that there was more to it than that—that stuff about loyalty and being part of a team. I'd been in a similar place before when I briefly worked as a teacher and saw many of my colleagues, hardworking but undervalued people, des-perate to get out of the profession but imprisoned by debt. Along with nearly everybody else, they'd been made dependent on the money-lending industry—all in the name of independence—and I dreaded the same thing happening to me. But because I had no dependents, I had more freedom than most to indulge my youthful hot-headedness. If I threw it all in—again—I would not be inflicting my quaint vision of the world on anybody else. What I was looking for, I suppose, was a way to live on my own terms, to survive without selling my soul. I'd had enough of going with the flow; it's easy to go far if you take this direction. Kicking against the current, however, is asking to be defeated or drowned. But right then, that was what I wanted to do, with both arms out of the water, not drowning but waving—giving the soulless, sleepwalking world the finger. I would probably go under, but at least I would have tried to explore a new direction. As I held my breath and leapt, I thought: maybe there are paradoxical countercurrents, visible only to those who really look for them.

The Congo trip was a disaster. The destination this time was the People's Republic of Congo, the former French colony west of Zaire—and a more user-friendly part of the river. But again the water conditions were wrong: a thick brown soup, from which we failed to catch anything. Then we got stranded hundreds of miles upriver. In the end we floated down on a log raft that was steered by a small tug skippered by an incompetent drunkard. I had persuaded Martin to join us on this adventure of a lifetime, and it did indeed live up to its billing. He remembers to this day the moment a Congolese man stepped over my prone body as I lay passed out with chronic malaria. "I thought I was going to come back home without you," he's told me many times since. "The man just shrugged and said it was possible that you were going to die."

The TV documentary never happened.

I have a theory that fishing activates some of the same neural circuits that get fired up in gamblers. Many fishermen would disagree with this, arguing that their strategies for success, although not foolproof, are scientific. Luck doesn't come into it. Psychologists, however, might nod and talk about "reinforcement": if rewards come along just often enough with timing that is not totally predictable, the human subject will continue to do the human equivalent of the laboratory rat pushing the food lever. But this doesn't explain the excessive level of lever-pushing in some individuals, even when the person should by now realize that the lever isn't connected to anything. But Paul and I both have a stubborn streak. If television was a nonstarter, this ought to make for an interesting book. All we needed for an end to this story was the small matter of a fish. We now knew the right season to go, so we planned to do a return trip the next year. Martin meanwhile remembered something else he needed to be doing.

The rematch got off to a bad start. In fishing-friendly low water the tributaries are hard to navigate because of sandbars, and doing so became even harder when an engine breakdown meant that an underpowered tug had to push our collection of barges against the current.

Most of the time we moved at a slow walking pace, and sometimes we hardly made any headway at all. In some places the slightest swing of the bow would have swept us around and wedged us immovably in the middle of nowhere. We reached our destination after two weeks, cooking on the tarpaulin-sheltered deck and sleeping in confined bunks below. After this, things improved once we had regained some physical and mental energy. We set up base in a riverside village, presided over by a soft-spoken chief, and started to fish. The villagers told us that this was the right time and place for mbenga. But the livebaits that we laboriously caught and fished under floats in pockets of turning water failed to attract any interest, and likewise for the artificials that flashed and vibrated enticingly. How could such a savage predator be so finicky? We'd written off the Belgian doctor, whose notes had formed the basis of the old book chapter, as an old duffer whose patchy results would be knocked into a cocked hat by modern-day equipment and know-how. But it looked like he was right about goliath's elusiveness. We spoke to an old fisherman who used to catch them on a handline, and he told us to fish lumps of dead fish on the bottom—not dead fish, but pieces of fish meat. Doubting this would tempt a mid-water hunter, we nevertheless tried it, as we'd drawn a blank with everything else.

We set up at the downstream end of a sandbar, where the channel swept from one side of the river to the other. Despite heavy weights, the current carried our baits far downstream and deposited them on the shoulder of deep water. Although the spot looked "fishy," I wasn't really expecting anything, so I was taken by surprise when my reel screamed into life. I engaged the drag and, mindful that there was a lot of stretchy line out, sprinted up the scorching sand while sweeping the rod over my head. Moments later a snarling head shattered the surface, cloaked in spray, while I kept running to straighten the belly in the line. Then the fish was dragging me back, pulling in the current like a kite in a gale as I fought to get line back on the reel. By some miracle, despite further jaw-clacking jumps, the enraged animal stayed attached, right up to the point when Paul slipped the gaff into its chin and pulled it onto the sand.

Lying before us, the fish was a bright bar of engraved silver, terminating in a splash of crimson on the lower lobe of its flaglike tail. Its other fins, all standing proud and curved at the leading edge, were like scythes. Everything about it told of slicing through water—and through flesh. After all, there was just no ignoring those teeth, so diabolical and machinelike. It almost didn't seem real—a creature too impossible even to make up. But here it was, the words of Dr. Gillet made flesh. And if I'd ever been in any doubt about the words of Leander J. McCormick, Gillet's awe-struck translator and editor, then I wasn't anymore. McCormick had declared, on the basis of what he'd read, "that a large Goliath is by all odds the most difficult fresh water fish to hook and land." This 38½-pounder had taken three expeditions and six years to catch.

We returned to England and spent the next year writing a book about it, through which this incredible fish captured the imagination of a whole new generation of anglers. But I was left with a niggle of dissatisfaction, a feeling of unfinished business. My goliath, although impressive, was only medium-sized. Part of me never wanted to set foot in the Congo again, but another part knew I had to. Meanwhile, the person in the mirror was getting older, and I knew a time would come when I would be physically and mentally past it. Maybe life was too short for this particular dream.

The opportunity to return to the Congo came with the second series of *River Monsters*. There's only a short list of candidate species out there, so it was inevitable that goliath would come up for consideration. To show a big one on TV would be an incredible coup, but set against that was the high likelihood of failure. Whereas I can survive next to a river at almost zero cost and stay as long as I like, the daily cost of putting a film crew in the field, plus kit, is very high. To make it possible at all, we had to introduce some economies of scale by shooting a second film in the Congo about its catfish. But we'd still at most only have three weeks, including traveling and all background filming, to catch a goliath.

We arrived in Brazzaville in August 2009, planning to get provisions and head straight upriver. I'd done my best to keep up with developments in central Africa in the two decades since I'd last been here, but all of it seemed overwhelming, even by this region's excessive standards. In the mid-1990s the Rwandan conflict spilled over into eastern Zaire, along with the armies of seven African countries, all helping themselves, on the side, to a slice of Zaire's mineral wealth. This ultimately led to the downfall of Mobutu, who was ousted in 1997 and died in exile shortly thereafter. But the country, now rechristened the Democratic Republic of Congo (DRC), remains in conflict, with the death toll from this recent civil war standing at over four million.

Civil war had also flared in Congo-Brazzaville with the appearance of the "ninja" rebels in 1997. Now the city was even more decayed than I remembered it. Returning with a film crew, I wondered if we'd be staying in the Mbamou Palace hotel, where visiting businessmen used to hole up, but this was now a shot-up shell that was in a state of stalled reconstruction. Elsewhere the mood seemed less easygoing and more desperate. On top of that, despite having secured over a period of months the necessary paperwork for an immediate start, we now needed more permits. Day after day our series producer camped in a succession of offices, constantly being told "tomorrow" while the rest of us lost the will to live. Getting a boat was also proving to be nearly impossible. By the time we were on the river we'd lost a whole week, one-fifth of our total time for two films.

We arrived at the sand beach in front of the village after traveling half the night. On the way, we had negotiated treacherous rocky whirlpools in the dark, all the while cursing the final delay that had kept us, plus food and gear, waiting at the riverside for half a day. But to be away from the city was a huge relief, and we now had only the river and fish to contend with. We'd selected the narrow *couloir* (corridor) region of the river to fish, although "narrow" in the context of the Congo means three-quarters of a mile wide. This runs between hilly banks for about 150 miles above Brazzaville, and because the river above, which braids around countless islands, is up to 11 miles across, it acts like a funnel, its flow fast and powerful. At intervals along its banks are rocky bluffs, and as the flow rips past these, it creates diagonal furls of turbulence, enclosing wedges of countercurrent. The name for such a place is a *bweta*, and these are said to be the home of sirens and spirits. Fishermen also say they are where you'll find mbenga on the shifting shear-line between slack and current, ready to hit anything that is struggling in the tumbling water. Few locals fish for goliath, but the preferred technique used to be a short line under a large float, held in place by thin cord running to the bank, which would snap when the bait was hit, after which the fisherman would pursue the float in his canoe. There were three or four such back eddies in striking distance of our camp. But the problem, as usual, was getting bait. The village's few fishermen caught very little in their nets, so we ended up buying fish, in ones and twos, from fishermen from across the river in the DRC.

I'd been told the best bait was a live *kamba* or *machoiron* catfish of about a pound, fished a few feet under the surface. Dead, unmoving fish are much less effective, although I have caught arapaima in the Amazon on dead fish suspended underneath a float when surface waves sometimes give the bait some movement. Back home, where there's a more sentimental attitude toward fish—apart from the bluefin tuna, monkfish, and Chilean sea bass that we happily exterminate to tickle our palates, along with the fish of all species that our waste products poison—the use of live fish as bait can be a contentious subject. The practice is one that I don't feel totally comfortable with, but sometimes it's possible to do it in a way that allows the baitfish to be released if it isn't taken, little the worse for wear—especially if it's a hardy species like a catfish.

On my first fishing day I started in the turning water at the mouth of a sidestream, but the place didn't live up to its promise. We continued down to a bweta, where we maneuvered the boat underneath towering rock. Once we'd settled on our mooring rope, I nicked a treble hook just under a machoiron's dorsal fin and swung it underarm into the water at my feet, into the slow edge of the countercurrent. Scarcely breathing, I watched my orange-tipped float sidle upriver toward the apex of the slack, a textbook holt for an ambush predator. As it approached, the float started to dance and spin in the tongues of current and then it shot off toward mid-river as the main flow caught it. Holding the rod high and alternately checking and loosing the line, I was able to guide it, after a fashion, along the line of the diagonal furl, at times getting it to pause in a temporary slack before it got swept further out. Finally, with perhaps eighty yards of line out, the float, by now a distant dot, swung back toward me, entering the gyre that would bring it back to my feet. Searching such an area of good water in this way was greatly satisfying, but with each revolution—following a subtly different path, a different radius, a different depth—I could feel my belief uncoil. By experimenting with rod position and length of line, I found I could also hold the bait static in a small area, usually one of the chain of whorls along the outer edge of the slack. But there was still no interest. I drew it in once more, into the current-line that would take it again to the apex, and this time the float trotted closer to the bank, curving out of sight behind a large boulder. I let it go for a few feet, but the braided line was now too close to the rock, so I engaged the reel and raised the rod to bring the float back into view. As I did so, I felt a wrench on the line, which slammed the rod down. Five seconds later the line fell slack.

The last two inches of wire, above the dead, tooth-punctured catfish, came back twisted like curly hair, and for a foot above that the line was filmed with thick slime. My last time here, nearly two decades before, I'd fished with forty-pound monofilament, which has a degree of elasticity. Now I was using the latest zero-stretch braid, virtually unbreakable at two hundred–pounds breaking strain (unless it rubs a rock edge) to transmit all the strike force to the bony jaw, but the fish had treated even that with utter contempt. When I showed the evidence of this briefest encounter to the villagers, they shook their heads. "You should put three of those hooks in the fish," they said. "And others below it, and above it. Maybe ten of them." In other words, if the hook wasn't going to hold in the mouth, they were suggesting that I snag it, either in the back with the trebles above the bait, which would trail behind its head as it ran, or in the gill plate with the loose trebles below, which might wrap around it when it jumped. They couldn't understand when I said I didn't want to do this. Catching the fish fairly was important to me, and I wanted to return it unharmed. I was also dubious about festooning the bait with too many hooks. Doing so would affect the liveliness of the bait, and it would also mean that the force of the strike was divided between several hook points—the bed of nails effect. I wondered if there was any rig that would increase my chances or whether results would always be random.

The next day we went to a *tourbillon* upstream. We had to fiddle with the anchor a lot before the boat settled into a good position, from which I managed to float the bait out to a good spot: sixty yards away and just off the diagonal line of turbulence. To think of rivers as unidirectional is common, but in the big picture there are always these pockets where something else is happening. Usually the surface gives a clue to underwater forces combining and canceling. Here a shifting furl of spiky waves was bordered, along its downstream edge, by areas of smooth upwelling. I was fishing a two-pound *machoiron* with one treble hook nicked through the back and another two suspended from cable ties, one under the belly and the other under the tail, like a lure.

At around midday, simultaneously the float vanished and the ratchet screamed. I pushed the drag lever to the strike position and lurched forward as the rod folded over, but there was no reduction in the fish's velocity. I pushed the lever nearly to its limit, and as my back doubled over and my legs tensed against the gunwales, the rod was almost torn from my grip. At least there was no way the hooks could fail to set, given this amount of force. So when the line suddenly went slack, I assumed the fish was running toward me, and wound frantically to regain contact. But after a few seconds I knew. All I brought back was half a bait, torn and punctured. The score was two-nil, to the fish.

Over the following days, as nothing else took, my mood plummeted. How could it be true that this fish attacked people when it wouldn't go for a free offering? At this rate, we wouldn't have a film. What a crazy idea we had had to bring a crew and all their kit here, to a place where my first catch had taken six years.

But fishermen told us that people had been bitten recently. And we heard there had been a fatality near here, upriver at Kwamouth. A young girl had almost been bitten in half. Apparently she'd been wear-ing a cord around her waist, from which dangled a number of shiny bottle tops, and these flashing in the sunlight likely lured the fish in. Ironically, this cord had been given to her as a lucky charm to ward off evil spirits.

For some here, the mbenga *is* a spirit. This is a culture in which nothing is seen as an accident. It's like looking for someone to sue after a twisted ankle on a footpath, except that in this case the culprit is not the city council but a sorcerer. Thus, if a goliath attacks you, it happened because a sorcerer, paid by your enemy, has taken possession of it. But there is also good magic, and the practitioners of this are *féticheurs*. There was one at the next village, and a fisherman took me to see him.

A boy with a soot-blackened face and a man wearing a dress emerged from his hut door. From inside came sounds like cries of sur-prise. A small man came out and spread some skins on the ground. Sit-ting cross-legged, he took pinches of fibrous matter from inside leaf wraps and started kneading them.

"Do you want snake protection too?" whispered Hector our boat mechanic, pointing to a small scar on his upper wrist. He explained that this was a two-for-one offer: I'd have a substance that would protect me from snake bites rubbed into a cut. "Or do you want just the fish?"

I decided on the latter option and, acting on Hector's instruction, put some CFA francs under the skins and then took the ends of two thin leaves that the féticheur was proffering. On a mimed signal I pulled these leaves and dropped the broken ends behind me. The man then gave me a small pouch made from folded, floral-pattern rag, as Hector translated: "You must take this with you when you go fishing, and sleep with it under your pillow. It will protect you from the mbenga, and it will help you to catch him."

I'd not been expecting this. And I didn't know what to do with my gift. Although I'm sure that some superstitions work through the placebo effect, I also know that if you recognize them as such, they lose their power. In the end, I decided it would be impolite not to comply with the prescription. Certainly I needed something to help my focus.

I myself was almost starting to believe that the mbenga is a spirit and not a real fish at all. Maybe my approach was wrong. Or maybe catching it was just a matter of time. Keep at it and another one will come, and sooner or later one will stay on the line. But whether it will or not is in the lap of the gods. The trouble was that I had very limited time: just two weeks to fish, which were nearly over.

By now our *African Queen*–style launch had returned to its owner in Brazzaville, and our transport for everybody plus kit was a large dugout canoe with an unreliable outboard that a young man called Fred (pronounced Frrred-duh) piloted. Getting around in this was a slow business, and after all this time with no fish, morale was getting lower by the day. We'd not been to the original bweta for a few days, so I decided to give it another try. This time we moored the boat a way upstream and I picked my way over the boulders to a precarious fishing position. The bait had a large single hook nicked through its back and another through the skin of its tail, with a treble dangling loose under its belly, held in place with a twist of fuse wire. This was a newly devised rig with a good hooking capability but not too much metalware, and I felt more confident than I had for a while as I swung the bait out fairly close, about ten yards. And I'd scarcely settled into my uncomfortable perch when the float disappeared.

The next thing I knew I was on my feet wrestling a rod that had come alive. Uppermost in my mind was the knowledge that I mustn't let this fish take too much line. On a long line the fish could swing in toward the side, with me powerless to stop it. Because of my position on the point, this would take it around a corner, out of sight, and if the taut, braided line touched a rock, that would be that. But in front of me was deep, open water: each time the fish changed direction, I tried to counteract it in order to keep it in there. At one point the line cut up toward the surface and I thought the fish was going to jump, but instead I just saw its dorsal fin and a flash of silver. I could see it was a big fish, and as I clambered down to the water's edge I yelled at Fred to bring the landing net. There was a good chance this would be chewed to pieces once its head was inside, but by this time, in theory, we would have grabbed its tail. And between us, despite me nearly slipping right into the water, we executed this plan perfectly. The fish, a massively deep-bodied monster, was ours!

What's more, we had landed it alive. As I held it in the flowing shallows, keeping well clear of its business end, its gills were working strongly and rhythmically. But whenever I took my hands away, it couldn't hold itself upright, and over time its breathing slowed. If I had let it go, it would have slipped into the main flow and sunk from sight. But I'm certain it wouldn't have recovered; it would have suffered a fatal battering on the rocks at the bottom of the bweta, possibly being given the coup de grâce by another goliath.

I have a theory that some fish can suffer a form of decompression sickness when they are caught, the same disorder that afflicts divers ("the bends") if they surface too quickly. This is caused by dissolved nitrogen in the blood and tissue fluids forming tiny bubbles when the pressure around the body decreases—exactly what we see when we twist open the cap of a soda water bottle and the dissolved gas (carbon dioxide in this case) forms bubbles. Such bubbles forming in the body's inner workings can cause skeletal, circulatory, and neurological disorders, which, if not treated by recompression, can lead to paralysis or death. One human symptom that's sometimes visible externally is a skin rash, and this is something that also appears on some fish a little while after capture. I've seen it on wels catfish caught from the Rio Ebro, where it is attributed to general "stress" and wisely taken as a sign that the fish has been out of the water long enough. I have likewise seen it on Thai giant whiprays that have been brought up from thirty feet down, although these fish, recognizable because of their tags, are often recaptured, so clearly they recover. But goliath is a sight feeder of the surface layers and wouldn't experience the same pressure drop on capture as a catfish or stingray from the depths. Besides that, it has a closed swim bladder, which would give an obviously "gassed up" appearance if it had been brought from deep water—and the buoyancy of this fish was okay.

I was mystified but, for want of any better idea, eased out into deeper water and held the fish near the bottom, where the water pressure would have been greater. But still its movements became fainter. At this point I noticed some patches of discoloration on its head, like bruising. As a shoal of tiny fry gamboled around the dying beast, I concluded that, on one of its torpedo-like runs, it must have swum into a rock. Until now I'd been having a running argument with Fred, who'd been insisting that I take the fish back to the village. Now I reluctantly conceded that he would have his way.

At the village they were playing football on the sandbar behind our camp. But as I hefted the fish onto my shoulder, the game came to an abrupt end. In moments a cheerful mob, the chief at their fore, surrounded me. Women held out their babies toward it and then withdrew them, giggling, for a reassuring cuddle, just as the open mouth was about to howl. The scene was incredible and couldn't be explained only by the fact that this fish would soon be a meal, a couple of pounds of meat per family. Everybody was reaching out to touch it—at first gentle pats, almost affectionate, but then, after they'd taken it from me, heavy flat-handed blows. The reality about this fish, I now realized, is that despite the stories of mutilation and death, most people here never see one. If they don't regard it as a spirit, it is certainly a myth. They go to the river every day to wash, but their paths never cross; instead, it's all about being in the wrong place at the wrong time—or, in my case, the right time.

At that time, the féticheur's charm had been in my breast pocket. And whatever I think, I have no way of knowing what would or wouldn't have happened if it hadn't been there. All I know is that, now that I felt I had the fish's measure, I wanted to be on the water again, trying for an even bigger one. But for the film we needed just one "big enough" fish. Now we had to catch up with all the other stuff: the crane shots and reconstructions and traveling shots and pieces-to-camera and general landscapes, all of which set the visual scene for the story. So that was the end of my fishing—and probably the end of my Congo story.

But I still can't help wondering just how much bigger these fish might grow. Most river giants, sadly, are much thinner on the ground than they used to be even a few decades ago. And with much-reduced numbers, the chances of those exceptional, wondrous, extra-large individuals of the old fishermen's tales dwindle away to nothing. So the reality, or otherwise, of these beasts remains unknowable.

Sometime after our film was broadcast in the United States, I received an e-mail from a man who grew up in the Congo, the son of a missionary doctor. He told me about the head of a goliath that he once saw in a fisherman's canoe in the Lubi River in East Kasai province, where the fish is known as *nsonga menu* ("pointed teeth"), which was also the nickname of a tribe who at that time were still cannibals and had the custom of filing their front teeth into triangular fangs. The width at the gill plates of the fish he saw was ten inches—one and a half times the measurement I took from my fish—and would give a total body length of six feet. Using the known weight of my fish, I can calculate the weight of this fish (78 pounds × 1.5 cubed) at over 200 pounds. It's an intriguing corroboration of Dr. Gillet's lost six-footer. And the fisherman, of course, said he'd seen bigger.

But what's even more intriguing is that, uniquely in the Congo—where dams and development, pollution and progress are still held at bay by its troubled human history—the giants of yesteryear could still be there. Sitting in my comfortable armchair I consider this. Then I consider the reality of traveling in this region, particularly to its least accessible parts, as well as the fact that I am now a quarter-century older than I was when I first went there. And I conclude that, maybe, some things are destined to remain a secret.

But then again, a two hundred–pound mbenga . . . that would be something to see.

CHAPTER 4

PIRANHA

They are the most ferocious fish in the world.
Even the most formidable fish, the sharks or barracudas, usually attack
things smaller than themselves. But piranhas habitually attack things
much larger than themselves. . . . They will rend and devour alive any
wounded man or beast; for blood in the water excites them to madness. . . .

Theodore Roosevelt, *Through the Brazilian Wilderness,* **1914**

WE ALL KNOW WHAT PIRANHAS ARE CAPABLE OF. We've seen it, or we think we remember seeing it, or maybe somebody just told us about it. I'm referring to the scene in *You Only Live Twice*, when Blofeld's henchwoman Helga Brandt has just informed her boss that she has failed in her mission to kill James Bond. As she turns and steps onto a bridge above an indoor pool, Blofeld, stroking his white cat (so you know that something bad is about to happen), presses a button with his foot, and the walkway opens underneath her like a trapdoor. As soon as she hits the water, it starts to seethe and boil all around her, and in moments her screams are silenced and the surface is still again. Having thus demonstrated his new staff incentive scheme, Blofeld hisses to his remaining sidekicks, "Kill Bond. *Now!*"

Far-fetched? But the nonfiction accounts, such as Teddy Roosevelt's, are scarcely less graphic: "The rabid, furious snaps drive the teeth through flesh and bone. The head with its short muzzle, staring malignant eyes, and gaping, cruelly armed jaws, is the embodiment of evil ferocity."

Strong stuff indeed. And if you can't believe a former president of the United States, who can you believe? His account, more than any other, is the one that established the piranha's bloody reputation in the outside world.

When I first went to the Amazon in 1993, my main objective was to catch an arapaima. But I was also curious to see the Amazon because the things I was hearing about it just didn't add up. One minute I'd be watching a documentary showing the place as an unspoiled Eden, with the cameraman tripping over jaguars and anacondas at every step, and then I'd read a newspaper that said it was all burning down. Interestingly, the tributary that the twenty-sixth president explored, now renamed the Rio Roosevelt in his honor, was previously the "River of Doubt." In my mind, this name could describe the whole Amazon system.

I worked on Martin to come along on the three-month trip. Although I told him I wanted him for his stimulating company, I mainly needed the extra baggage allowance and another body to carry stuff. Three weeks after our arrival in Brazil we dragged ourselves through thigh-deep mud to an open-sided, palm-thatched hut near a lake in the floodplain of the Rio Purus, one of the Amazon's big southern tributaries. The hut's owner, José, was a stocky fifty-something *ribeirinho* (mixed-race river dweller) with a ragged moustache whose semiwild jungle garden provided an erratic harvest of manioc, cashews, pineapples, and *cupuaçu* (similar to sweet furry potatoes hanging from trees), which he sold in the nearby town, a day's travel away in his ancient covered boat. Every day he walked for half an hour along a nearly invisible forest path to the lake, where he netted the day's lunch, with leftovers for supper. His existence was literally hand to mouth, and the deal we struck with him was that we would be tolerated for as long as we earned our keep. So Martin set to hoeing the manioc patch, plagued by clouds of blood-sucking *pium* flies, and hefting sixty-pound loads of pineapples to the boat in hand-woven baskets hanging from a cord round his forehead, while I went fishing.

The lake, known as Lago Camaleão ("Lizard Lake"), was roughly circular, two hundred yards in diameter, and shelved to about eight feet deep in the middle. But before I tried my lures and fancy rods, José showed me how they did it. In an area of semisubmerged bushes at the lake margin, he picked up a thin bamboo pole from the bottom of his tiny dugout, unwound the eight feet of thick nylon line twirled around it, and put a chunk of fish flesh on the large single hook. The hook, I noticed, had an extra long shank, formed by wrapping the final two or three inches of line inside a thin, flattened cylinder of metal—cut from the case of an old battery, he said. Then, as I held my breath, this renowned, fish-whispering survival expert, from whom I'd hoped to learn the secrets of ninjalike jungle stealth, whirled the line out overhand and brought it down on the surface with a resounding *thwack*. Feeling embarrassed for him, I watched the old duffer make repeated recasts, each one louder and more inept than the last. Somehow, on the last cast he ended up with the rod tip in the water, sploshing it around in a way that was sure to send every fish heading for the horizon. Next thing I knew, however, a flash of red and silver was swinging through the air and then flapping in the boat, where José deftly stilled it with the point of a machete blade behind its clicking jaws.

"Piranha caju," he said. "Same color as cashew fruit." I realized I was looking at my first real live (okay, real dead) piranha—and not just any old piranha, but the notorious red-belly (*Pygocentrus nattereri*). Far from being scared off by the splashing, this half-pounder had homed in on it.

Observing this legendary creature for the first time, I could see that the indigenous Amazonians hadn't minced their words when they named it. Combine the Tupi-Guarani words *pira* (fish) and *ranha* (tooth) and you've got "tooth fish"—and this is exactly what it says on the linguistic tin. Also, just saying the word with their pronunciation, *pir-an-yah*, makes you bare your teeth as if you're about to go into a feeding frenzy yourself. That *nyah!* sound. Whereas the Anglicization, *pira-nah* (which is, incidentally, quite acceptable, as we also say Paris instead of Paree), has lost that edge of menace and sounds a little more friendly.

I took the other rod and—after missing a few sharp pulls, each time bringing in a cleaned hook—swung one of these fish in myself. Its broad, protruding lower jaw gave it a pugnacious expression, and the solidity of its head indicated powerful jaw muscles. Bending forward to look at its teeth—sharp, triangular points that meshed together like scissor blades—I asked José if they really were as sharp as people said. He thought for a moment and then produced a surubim catfish from behind him, which he'd netted earlier. Taking my piranha, he touched its snout to the catfish's thick, gristly tail, and immediately the jaws started working, like some diabolical trimming machine, as José moved the fish from side to side, artistically reshaping the tail until it was no more than a stump.

But the novelty of fishing piranha-infested waters quickly wore off. They would devour the deadbaits I put out for arapaima, frustrating my efforts to tempt one of these bigger predators. They would hit the lures I cast for tucunaré (peacock bass), and on occasion, when they didn't hit the lure, they'd eat half the fish that did while it was on its way to the boat. If I caught nothing else, though, we would eat piranha. They are better fried than boiled, and I have been known to reduce one to a pile of bones in seconds. But they are not a species that people relish, even though a soup made from their flesh is said to be an aphrodisiac. I was surprised once, though, by a piranha I was served by a fisherman called Manoel, who had grown up with the Karajá Indians on the Araguaia River. He cut thin fillets from the back of a small white piranha, marinated the pale flesh in a squeeze of lime juice and red *urucú* (annatto) powder, and served it sashimi style. It was delicious, and I asked him if it was something he'd learned from the Indians, a jungle survival tactic for when you can't stop to cook. "No," he said. "It's just something we picked up from the Japanese." But Manoel was unique. Most fishermen who catch piranhas hack their jaws off and throw them onto the bank to die because of the damage they do to their nets.

Then there were the stories of human deaths. A boat captain told me about a man who fell overboard and disappeared in a boil of attacking piranhas. I also heard about a riverboat that capsized while attempting to dock, tipping all its passengers into the water. Their desperate flailing, in an area people constantly chummed with fish guts and leftovers, provoked a fatal piranha frenzy. But these stories never had any names, dates, or precise locations.

And if piranhas really were so dangerous, why did people commonly swim in places where piranhas also swam? (I knew they were there because I'd caught them, often right next to splashing kids.) I partially abandoned my caution and started swimming myself—and it's hard to describe what bliss it is to have cool water support your body after a long hot day of mud, sweat, and biting insects. But I'd only swim where the locals swim, and I avoided the places they avoided. This seemed a sensible enough rule of thumb even though lots of locals had bits of thumb missing or semicircular scars or bifurcated fingertips or, in one case, a nose-tip that had been bitten off and then regrown. These were either from a millisecond's loss of concentration when fishing or inflicted when they were gutting fish off the side of a floating house. And as an angler I was all too aware of the piranha's potential. I caught black piranha (*Serrasalmus rhombeus*) weighing four pounds that had flanks the size of dinner plates and teeth that made me wince just to look at them. Black piranhas have been recorded close to ten pounds, but fortunately they don't hang out in hundred-strong packs like the red-bellies. But red-bellies can grow to a very solid three and a half pounds, and I've caught them one after another at one pound and sometimes two. So although individually they are far smaller than most other river monsters, collectively they're in the same league in that the combined biomass of a shoal of attacking piranhas could exceed that of a human being—which isn't a pleasant thought.

The most voracious piranhas I've encountered have been in two distinct situations. One day, trying to cut through thick forest from José's hut to a big lake beyond Lago Camaleão, I got hopelessly lost. If I headed in the wrong direction, there was uninhabited forest for over a hundred miles, but if I kept going around in circles as I had been for a couple of hours, drinking stagnant water from puddles, I would end up as food for the ants. Starting to panic, I stopped to think. Far under the canopy, I couldn't see the sun, but I discovered that when I held a stick upright on the ground, one of its multiple faint shadows was slightly stronger than the rest, and getting longer. This meant it was past midday, and this direction was east, which was where I didn't want to go. Using this improvised compass, I was able to head toward the river, where at least I would know where I was—if I could get around the swamps that were in the way. But before I hit the river, I arrived at the southern shore of the big lake. Confident now of my makeshift compass but spurred on by failing light, I turned back into the forest, this time heading due south, and reached Lago Camaleão at sunset. I arrived back at the hut just as José was starting to get worried.

"But I'd have found you," he said, with such assurance that I found myself believing him. Whereas other ribeirinhos were totally at home on water, José had a reputation for stalking the forest with his shotgun and dogs, day and night—something almost nobody else did. With a shudder I remembered that he sometimes rigged his shotgun to a trip-wire next to a homemade salt-lick. He'd once shown me a cartridge he'd made for this, repacked with a solid lump of lead, for smashing the skull of a tapir at point-blank range.

Having made it clear that he didn't think much of my jungle navigation, he then mentioned that two people he knew, hunting wild pigs, had gotten lost in the same area the year before. I asked how long they had taken to find their way home. "Twenty-two days," he answered.

Then I told him about the small lake I'd found, boiling with fish life, before I arrived at the big lake. Surely arapaima fishermen didn't know about this place. He snorted. "Those guys get *everywhere*. They carry their canoes on their backs." But I refused to believe him and, a few days later, having dragged the canoe down the twisting tree-choked creek to the big lake, set out on foot to find the place again.

My bait never had a chance to sink more than a few inches; it was set upon and devoured as soon as it hit the water. In the margins at my feet, a black catfish face appeared and looked at me, as if beseeching, "Please get me out of here!" This was one of those shrunken, hungry, dry-season pools where the piranhas had eaten most of the available food and would set upon any edible newcomer. That I'd not been tempted to take a cooling dip on my first visit was a good thing.

The other type of place to avoid is the outflow from a backwater lake when the water is falling during the dry season. At this time, small fish are getting washed out into the river channels, and the piranhas congregate in ambush. You can hear and see them slashing on the surface, and a small shallow-diving plug cast into some lake mouths will take one-pound red-bellies every cast.

One area of backwaters where the piranhas congregate for this small-fish harvest is a place called the Piranha reserve near Manacapuru, fifty miles west of Manaus. Here I finally found a case of a human fatality that was all too true. Because of the big seasonal changes in water level, the people here mostly live in floating houses. One man I spoke to, Julio, told me how, eight years before, he was looking after his two-year-old grandson when the boy ran from one side of his house to the other and fell in the water. When Julio got there, all he saw was the boiling of the piranhas "devouring" the child. Eventually they retrieved the body with a net, but all that was left was a skeleton.

I also found a newspaper report of a bus crashing into the Rio Urubú, east of Manaus, in 1976, and this reported that piranhas ate the occupants. Thirty-nine passengers died, but I spoke to one man who escaped, Dirceu Araújo. He told me how he climbed through a broken window but had to kick his leg free of a hand that had grabbed onto him. He repeated what the newspaper had said about some bodies being partially eaten. Another passenger managed to get out of the bus, but his clothing got caught. I spoke to this man's brother, who was given the body wrapped in a sheet. Just by holding it, he knew that all the sheet contained were bones.

But the bus had been in deep water for several hours before it was retrieved. So it's likely that piranhas did not kill the passengers but rather ate them after they had drowned. What makes this more probable is that the Rio Urubú is a black-water river, poor in nutrients and thin in fish, including piranhas. Red-bellied piranhas, in their dense, potentially homicidal packs, tend to live in muddy, "white water" rivers, such as the main Amazon, the Purus, and the backwaters of the Piranha reserve—not the Urubú.

Recently, however, there have been clear cases of piranhas attacking live humans. In 2007 more than 180 people were bitten when swimming and paddling off a shallow beach at an artificial lake near the city of Palmas. But these were nonfatal single bites. According to Brian Zimmerman, assistant curator of the aquarium at the London Zoo, these piranhas would have been defending their nests, which they construct in exactly the same shallow areas where people like to bathe. This echoes the attacks on swimmers at Schlachtensee near Berlin, except these were not five- or six-foot-long catfish but rather solitary fish measuring just a few inches. Seen in this light, the picture that emerges of these piranhas is of feisty, devoted parents.

Brian also mentioned that some recent research into piranha shoaling behavior indicates that the formation of "packs" is largely a defensive strategy against the animals that eat them. I have seen giant otters and caimans happily chewing on red-bellied piranhas, and pink river dolphins are also a threat to them.

This is not to say that piranhas are harmless and cuddly; their potential is lethal. But if you understand their behavior, you can avoid those situations when they can be a serious risk to human health—unless, of course, your employer is Mr. Blofeld.

CHAPTER 5

ARAPAIMA

After the doctor's departure Koznyshev expressed the wish to go
to the river with his fishing rod. He was fond of angling and was
apparently proud of being fond of such a stupid occupation.

Leo Tolstoy, *Anna Karenina*, 1877

A FEW YEARS AGO I went for a routine dive medical examination. As part of this I was partially stripped and shaved and then wired up for an electrocardiogram. The printout should have shown a nice, regular sequence of blips. However, the doctor, after a pause, told me I had irregular "ectopic" heartbeats and sent me to a specialist for further investigation.

The cardiologist looked at me and said he was 99.9 percent sure I was okay, as I had none of the normal risk factors for heart disease (I don't smoke and I'm not overweight), but nonetheless, he sent me for an MRI scan to make sure. When I came back for the results, I could tell something was wrong. The scan had revealed two patches of scarring, areas of heart muscle that were dead and that would never recover.

In the six weeks before my urgent follow-up test I had plenty of time to ponder my mortality. With time now revealed as something finite, I was struck by how little I'd achieved, in any conventional sense, in my life. The weight of the things I had done was inconsequential when divided into the years. And it struck me now as never before how much this was due to the immense cumulative weight of something else. This was something inside me that was invisible to all instruments and outside observers, something that had eaten away at my minutes and hours and robbed me of irreplaceable years. In a way it was like a heavy unseen fish pulling down, but I couldn't give the line to anybody else or even expect a word of support as it tried to break my back.

I also questioned why this heart defect should happen to me. Although my diet is mostly good and I'm normally active, I'd had lapses over the years. I had also suffered periods of severe stress, most significantly when a publishing partnership swallowed most of my savings, after which I worked single-handedly for three and a half years simply to get back to where I'd started—this was the period when my hair turned white. I knew that stress can kill invisibly by raising blood pressure, thus causing the walls of the coronary arteries to thicken in response, which further raises blood pressure, and so on—a classic example of runaway positive feedback. Maybe I'd had a small heart attack sometime, a few moments of dizziness and clutching at the nearest surface, before coming round to woozy puzzlement. I racked my brains. Then it hit me. A frantic hour of Internet research confirmed my worst fears. Myocardial contusion is normally the result of a severe blow to the chest, most commonly from the steering column in a road traffic accident. Six years before, I'd suffered just such a severe trauma to the chest. But I was nowhere near a car.

I was in Brazil, helping a scientist friend of mine, Alexandre Honczaryk, and a team of fishermen to net one of Alex's ponds. Alex is an aquaculturist, working at the National Institute of Amazonian Research (INPA) in Manaus, the Brazilian city at the heart of the Amazon. His consuming interest is the arapaima. Specifically, he is trying to breed them in captivity in order to take pressure off the wild population, which, in most of the Amazon, has been decimated by overfishing. What we were trying to do was change the combination of fish in his main pond, to get some fishy love-action going. For female arapaima, size matters—they will kill a male that is too small to satisfy them—so we were trying to make sure that the next date didn't end badly.

I was in the water, to one side of the semicircle of cork floats that marked the net perimeter, following it in as the two ends were pulled up on land, thus making the trap smaller and smaller. On our previous attempt, a fish had leapt clear at the last minute, so I reached forward with both hands and lifted the net's top cord in the air so it was slightly higher than my head. Because Alex had warned me about getting too close to the net, I held my body well back from my outstretched arms as I waited to see what we got this time.

I didn't see it coming at all. From inside the belly of the net, I received a sledgehammer blow to my sternum that sent me flying backward in agony. I struggled to my feet and then doubled over as body fluids squeezed out through my clenched eyelids. I remembered something about a martial arts death blow that sends the heart into arrhythmia, quickly followed by it stopping for good, so I fumbled to find my pulse, and was reassured to find it very strong and regular. But for the rest of the afternoon I kept checking, just to make sure. I now know I should have gone to the hospital for observation and oxygen. But at the time I felt okay, not much different from how I used to feel most winter days as a teenager after an afternoon playing rugby as a punch-drunk prop-forward. And besides, we had a television series to make. So I scarcely gave it a second thought despite the fact that, for six weeks, I couldn't raise myself into a sitting position in bed. In order to get up, I first had to roll onto my front and then slide my knees onto the floor.

But now as I looked back, something else struck me. During my time in the Amazon, which started nine years before this incident, I've heard various tales of fishermen disappearing, leaving only a canoe floating empty on a deserted lake like a miniature *Mary Celeste*. Nobody ever found out what happened to them, but generally people said that a *bicho* got them. This is a generic term for "animal" or "beast." But, if pushed, people would say the most likely suspect was a *jacaré-açu,* or, as we know it, the black caiman (*Melanosuchus niger*), a broad-bodied crocodilian that once used to grow to nearly twenty feet. Or they may attribute it to an anaconda (*Eunectes murinus*). Nobody ever mentioned arapaima, a fact that now struck me as odd. Perhaps this is because arapaima don't have big teeth (although if you're a small fish swimming nearby, this is academic, because you'll be sucked in from a distance and then crushed by a bony tongue). They are also very pretty fish.

Their vernacular name, *pirarucu*, comes from *pira* (fish) and *urucú*, the indigenous name of the *Bixa orellana* tree, from whose seeds, extracted from bright red spiky pods, we get the food dye annatto. So the arapaima is "the red fish," from the coloration that edges its sculpted scales, getting more and more vivid toward its broad paddle of a tail. Normally the background color is dark green on the back that shades to silver flanks and a cream belly, but sometimes it is smoky black. And sometimes, most rarely of all, it is the deepest black imaginable, like ink distilled from the midnight sky. Surely, the thinking seems to go, something so pretty can't possibly be a villain.

My involvement with this fish is long and complicated. After I finally caught a goliath tigerfish, I was looking for a new challenge. The arapaima had always occupied a mental backwater where it surfaced infrequently, but after my successful return to the Congo, the arapaima seemed to breach more insistently, sending out ripples that tugged my attention toward the unseen creature at their center.

Something happens when you start going after fish that are potentially bigger than you, and the arapaima, so they say, is the biggest of them all. Anglers traditionally measure themselves by the size of their catches: the bigger the fish, the greater the achievement, or so the thinking goes. As a product of this tradition, I used to weigh carp to the nearest ounce and rank them accordingly. But since then I'd come to realize that it's also about the things you can't measure: an element of hardship, sometimes shading into danger—and, for those truly obsessed, a whiff of unattainability.

In 1949, writing about the arapaima, Leander J. McCormick had declared, "Nowhere else in fresh water is there a fish so large and sporting . . . and yet this giant fish has hardly been tested on a rod." Nearly a half-century later, this still appeared to be the case: I could find no records of any contemporary captures. Maybe the arapaima was extinct. But surely this wasn't possible. I decided to make catching one my new mission. After my nightmare journeys to the Congo, the world's second-largest rainforest, the world's largest rainforest was a daunting prospect. But with the Congo behind me and a track record of traveling alone, I considered myself uniquely qualified. All I had to do was get myself to a remote lake with enough energy left to chuck out a bait, and the fish would be mine.

First I had to decide where in the Amazon to go. Most statistics about the Amazon are meaningless because the figures are too large to comprehend. As I read that the basin covers an area of 2.72 million square miles, my eyes glazed over. I needed that in terms of something that was familiar, and preferably something better than a multiple of Belgium, which for some reason is the normal unit of comparative area. (The Amazon basin is 230 times the size of Belgium.) More meaningfully it covers 40 percent of South America—which means it is twice the area of the Congo and 85 percent of the land area of the United States' forty-eight contiguous states. For most of this huge, semi-aquatic territory, there are no roads.

I tried to narrow my scope down a bit. I wanted to be away from centers of population, with their fish markets and fishing boats, but not too remote; I needed to be in and out within three months. And I wanted "white water," which, in the Amazon, means muddy: nutrient-rich and abundant in life. So my choice of the Rio Purus, one of the southern tributaries, wasn't a completely random stab on the map.

At two thousand miles in length, the Purus is one of the world's great rivers in its own right, being longer than both the Danube and the Zambezi. To get there I planned to take a boat nine hundred miles up the Amazon to Manaus, the main navigation hub (at the confluence with the longest northern tributary, the Rio Negro), and then find a smaller vessel ascending the Purus. It looked simple on paper, but one thing worried me. I needed to be there in the dry season when arapaima are confined to the floodplain lakes rather than spread through flooded forest. But some sources said the Purus, one of the most winding rivers in the world, isn't navigable at low water.

I was glad to have Martin with me on this trip, the veteran of our heroically unsuccessful Congo expedition. Although he's not an angler, I wanted him to be part of something when things went right, and for an enthusiastic naturalist, what could be better than seeing the mythical "red fish"? He was as keen to see the Amazon as I was, giving up his job and room in Paris for this shoestring journey to the rainforest, for which we'd specially acquired a £9.99 nonwaterproof children's toy tent.

The cheapest flights we could find were to the Brazilian coastal city of Recife, where the shoulder of South America pushes out into the Atlantic. Because we arrived on a day when banks were shut, we changed some money in the back room of a bar-cum-brothel in the port area, which held the biggest piles of cash I've ever seen. Brazilian hyperinflation was running at more than 40 percent per month, and we emerged as cruzeiro multimillionaires. Looking for food that evening, Martin and I came across a political rally and a funfair, where the main attraction was a noisy face-off between two men that ended when one man was floored from behind then repeatedly kicked on the ground. We returned to our hotel, with its strange system of paying by the hour, its wipe-down PVC mattresses, and the contraceptives on sale at the reception desk, and suddenly, with mutual horror, realized why the staff were giving us questioning looks.

The next day we took a bus northwest through the drought-stricken *sertão* backlands, and two days later we staggered out into equatorial humidity at Belém, the city at the great river's mouth.

At Belém you can't see the Amazon's far bank. An island the size of Switzerland is in the way. After two days we boarded a boat, slung our hammocks with three hundred other passengers, and set off up the river. The next day the sun rose out of our wake, slowly climbed and passed above us, and then sunk into the watery horizon ahead. Distant gray islands floated between water and sky. Ghastly yodeling *sertanejo* music blared nonstop from speakers on the upper deck. Where possible, the boat hugged the bank, where the current is slower, with the other bank looking like a pencil-thin line. Looking out through the railings, as five days and nights came and went, I reflected how, if things had gone differently on an earlier trip to Southeast Asia, I might now be rotting in jail. It was something I could imagine only too well, having served eight years, from age ten, at boarding school. To get through this I'd developed the ability to dissociate mind and body, entering a state in which I could pass through empty time without feeling boredom. Minutes and hours lost meaning, ceased to exist. This stratagem served me well at the time, but back in the outside world, it became a handicap. Now this sleight of mind was no longer the default setting—something else had claimed the psychic vacuum—but I could still summon it when required, such as at times like this.

Then there were our fellow travelers. Before coming here, I'd studied Portuguese using tapes and written exercises for three months, for three hours every day. But these people on the boat sounded nothing like the cake shop owner in Lisbon, from whom I used to buy imaginary custard tarts. A young man, if I heard him right, told me he was a "professor" of kung fu and that his baby boy was called Van Damme. A girl named Castia helped me with some colloquialisms, despite her disappointment that I knew neither Tom Cruise nor the New Kids on the Block. And her faux-blonde friend, sunbathing on the top deck, filled me in on Manaus: "There's lots of corruption, prostitution, poverty, crime . . . it's great!"

The presence of this city of more than a million inhabitants in the middle of the jungle is both reassuring and baffling. A noisy sprawl of high-rise blocks, stilt-house slums, and roller-shuttered shops, it owes its existence to the rubber boom of the late 1800s and early 1900s, when thousands of migrants poured into the Amazon to collect latex from wild *Hevea brasiliensis* trees. Along with its neoclassical opera house, Manaus had electricity before London, telephones before Rio de Janeiro, and electric trams when New Yorkers were still staring at horses' backsides. But boom turned to bust when the British created rubber plantations in Malaya and Ceylon grown from Brazilian seeds. After that, to stop the region from becoming depopulated, the Brazilian government made Manaus a free-trade zone. This explained the shops selling tax-free TVs and computers from factories in the *distrito industrial*, mostly destined to be airlifted to Brasilia and São Paulo.

But the high-tech communications didn't extend to the Purus. At the floating port, they told us there were no boats this time of year. But we kept asking because we didn't have any other ideas, and after three days we were directed to a disreputable-looking tub called the *Mario Antonio III*. The skipper, who looked like an incarnation of Beelzebub, assured us he was going up the Purus "tomorrow," although the places he mentioned bore no relation to those on our map. The next day the price changed when the government announced a new currency, the cruzeiro real, which was actually the same as the old currency but with the last three zeros ignored. Three days after that, with our hammocks swinging on the upper deck, we rolled onto the water again.

Once in the Purus, even boat time became distorted. As the river twisted this way and that, the confused sun whirled crazily around us. At night, in the close-packed hammocks, I'd wake to find a stranger's toe picking my nose. Shifting position, I'd head-butt the sleeper on the other side. Some bends seemed to go on forever—past the same fallen tree, the same lonely stilt house. And on board the same pans of rice, beans, and fish (lunch? supper? breakfast?) were again plonked on the table. But something was changing. Each day the river sunk a little further below its banks. We finally disembarked down a narrow plank to soft mud and then climbed a steep flight of steps, at the top of which was the town. To get here from Recife had taken three weeks.

Getting to a likely floodplain lake was equally laborious. In the following month, from a base in the forest, I managed just four days on Lago Grande. To get there I had to manhandle a wooden canoe down an overgrown creek, alternately heaving it over fallen trees and dragging it through mud. Baitfish were hard to catch and then lasted no time against the piranhas. So I trolled a lure behind the canoe, but piranhas cut the line, attacking the vee it made in the surface. But most disheartening was my growing awareness of the scale of commercial fishing for arapaima, which was driven by the imported Portuguese taste for salted fish. Traditionally this was cod, but here was an abundant freshwater alternative. Thus, arapaima became the *bacalhau da Amazônia*, or Amazonian cod. For former rubber tappers stranded up in tributaries, here was a new source of income. Having been left alone for thousands of years because of the pointlessness of hunting fish that were far too large to feed a family, whose leftovers would go rotten in hours, arapaima were now under relentless assault. Their habit of gulping air made them vulnerable to harpooning, and they were also taken on set lines attached to flexible tree branches. A fleet of traveling buyers filled their holds with tons of salted meat. I've seen old photographs from the Purus of unimaginable slaughter, the barrel-bodied corpses of giant arapaima alongside those of harpooned manatees, their nostrils plugged with wooden pegs to suffocate them to death.

Now, with numbers much reduced and the easy availability of nylon monofilament, arapaima are most commonly taken in nets. Teams of fishermen wait for the precise day a lake becomes cut off by falling floodwater and then move in, watching and encircling. Sometimes, if there are branches in the water that would snag their nets, they dive down and clear them with saws. Often they will remove all the large fish from a lake in a matter of days. At first I saw the huge fillets, like six-foot kippers, spread out on drying racks by riverside houses, and took this as a good sign. Then I realized I could never beat the locals to the fish, certainly not on the Purus, which, it turns out, is the Amazon's most heavily fished tributary. Fully 40 percent of the fish eaten in Manaus come from here.

Four weeks before our flight home, we returned to the town and started waiting for a boat. If I'd achieved nothing else, I now understood why I'd seen no recent reports of arapaima caught by rod and line, and I tried to accept my failure philosophically.

I was back in England when the Amazon rains came. The footmarks I'd made in the mud now vanished under fifty feet of floodwater: fish swam where I had walked. Amazon folklore is full of stories about the *encante*, an enchanted underwater kingdom whose occupants enter the dreams of fishermen and lure them away from their human lives. Sometimes this is the explanation given for the empty canoe— the equivalent of being with the angels. A year later I was in a canoe again, back at Lago Grande, a water that fascinated and terrified me in equal measure. I had seen things here that I couldn't explain—huge upheavals in the water, distant snakelike shapes—and my curiosity had drawn me back. I was still trying to make a break as a freelance writer, and I was sure there was a story here—something more substantial than a light piece for the travel pages—but I didn't know what it was.

That year and the next three had no direction that I could discern at the time other than a general lowering, further beneath the surface of the Amazon's aquatic and human life. Slowly I gained fluency in the mutated, hybrid Portuguese of the interior, with its subvocabulary of hard-edged indigenous names. Every year I felt that my knowledge had increased to a point just short of some ill-defined critical mass. And while I reached, I had the sense that something was reaching for me: the line of bubbles, speeding toward me like the trail of a torpedo, then passing underneath the boat; the sudden explosion of air and water, right underneath me, nearly tipping me into the water from fright. These were boto dolphins: massive, hunchbacked, and pink-skinned, like giant fetuses—the malformed offspring of those lost fishermen perhaps. And indeed, Amazon folklore says dolphins do hybridize with humans. This happens when male dolphins take the form of young men and visit village festivals, taking care to keep their hats on to conceal their blowholes. In this way they are the cause of many otherwise unexplained pregnancies.

The locals call this troublemaker the red dolphin, or *boto vermelho*, but foreigners call it the pink dolphin following a 1980s documentary series. "We know it's pink, but its *name* is the red dolphin," a man lectured me in the captain's cabin of a riverboat. "Who does Jacques Cousteau think he is, changing the names of our animals?"

He went on, "Did you know that a female dolphin has parts that are *exactly* the same as a woman's? That's why some of these fishermen try to catch them. So they can *passar regra* with them." I nodded, not knowing what to say, as he gestured toward my notebook. "That's *another* thing Jacques Cousteau doesn't know about red dolphins."

Then there was that outlandish saw-backed animal in Lago Grande—the hallucination that turned out to be real. Finding out what it was took three years. One early possibility was a pink dolphin that a boat propeller had injured. But the profile was too clean for that, and in that part of the Amazon, at that time, nobody had outboard motors.

Most likely, in the end, it was something that a fisherman suggested: a dolphin that had once gotten tangled in a net. This happens rarely because of the dolphins' exceptional ability to "see" underwater by using echo-location. But when it does happen, it results in a torn net or a drowned dolphin. Amazon fishermen are not sentimental about dolphins; they see them as a nuisance and will throw a dead one aside with a curse. But maybe this one was still alive when the net was retrieved and the fisherman, angry about his ruined net, cruelly mutilated it. Then, being a resilient animal, it recovered from its wounds and began its new incarnation as a mystery monster, exacting revenge on the human race by frightening the wits out of the few people who glimpsed it.

The dolphins then introduced me to the snakes. When I showed my pictures of the saw-backed dolphin to fishermen, most had never seen anything like it. But some had seen other things. Commonly this looked like a floating tree trunk, complete with root mass, but it would have been moving upstream, creating a wake. This apparition is the *cobra-grande*, literally "giant snake," and I met several sober fishermen who claimed to have seen it. This set me off on a prolonged anaconda hunt after the real-life giant snake of the Amazon. I was told about a distant creek that held veritable monsters that were the width of oil drums and thirty feet long. If I could verify that with a tape measure and camera, not only would it be the largest snake ever accurately recorded, but it would also qualify for the $50,000 prize, on offer since 1912 from the Wildlife Conservation Society of New York, for evidence of a (live) thirty-foot snake. But nobody ever went up that creek—except one team of fishermen: arapaima fishermen.

They agreed to take me on their next foray. But they were on their own mission, and the snake hunt took second place. It was like a military operation, hacking our way through fallen trees with an axe, dragging canoes through swamps, catching and cooking up small *jaraqui* on the run. And this was just the journey to work. The fishing itself was done at a different pace entirely—silently watching then deploying the nets and then waiting for the fish to rise again. Finally, with the trap set, they would beat the surface with sticks and thrash the branches of sunken bushes to flush the fish out and drive them into the net. But the arapaima showed uncanny intelligence. I saw one gray torpedo launch itself four feet into the air and clear the net, to oaths from the fishermen; luckily no one was in the way. Another time, one of the net floats dipped fractionally then popped back up. One of the men then pulled up the net to show me the hole that had just been made. An arapaima had inserted its snout then expanded its head to break the meshes before sliding through to freedom. Then one day while traveling, I found the partial skeleton of an anaconda that I estimated at possibly twenty feet long. But the arapaima had come back to the fore. I had seen how they were killed and butchered and how the fishermen just ate the chopped-up heads with handfuls of gritty farinha, saving the boneless fillets for the merchants. At night, we rested our tired bodies in hammocks slung from trees while the group's leader, who they called "the fat man"—though not to his face—told tales for hours about other fishing trips: the humanlike screams he'd heard not far from here and the patch of jungle floor near the place known as *Meio do Mundo* (Center of the Earth) that was so hot you couldn't stand on it. On our third or fourth trip, with the live anacondas still not showing, he turned to me and asked what I was really looking for. Many people still thought that I was an undercover gold prospector, so this was a familiar question. I said I wanted to catch an arapaima on a line.

He thought for a moment and then said, "I think there's a place where you could do that. We hardly fish there because it's too deep and there are too many trees in the water. But you've got to carry a canoe through the forest. I'll get my son to take you."

A year later, with a piece of rag on my shoulder cushioning one end of a canoe, I sweated three miles along a twisting forest path to the lake. When we got there, his son Josiney and I were too exhausted to fish right away, so we walked a little way along the bank to a place where we could watch the water. The lake was long and narrow, about four hundred yards by seventy, with inlets at each corner reaching into the forest like tentacles. Along our bank, fallen trees with skeletal crowns sloped down into black water. Opposite, the bank appeared steeper, with vegetation reaching over the surface and creating a dark secret space underneath. A strong wind was blowing up the lake, but we spotted a couple of distant ripple-rings and launched the canoe. Then we saw another fish rise closer, but when we paddled near, the next movement was a tail-slap that flung water in a twelve-foot-high arc. This was the sign that they knew we were here. To have a chance of catching one, I needed their surfacing to be *manso* (calm), not *brabo* (wild). We'd be better leaving the boat and returning fresh in the morning.

The next day a silent creature stalked the lake, twitching the single fin at its rear to creep forward stealthily, almost imperceptibly. At its other end a single tentacle extended, motionless for long periods and then flicking in the direction of its prey. Dangling from this rod was a dead six-inch *arari*, suspended six feet beneath a cigar-sized float. But with the wind blowing again, this time down the lake, and the few rises mostly out of casting range, my chances didn't look good. I decided to change tactics and fish blind in an area where there had been some earlier rolls. With the canoe in the middle of the lake, the cast landed just short of the branches on the far side, and immediately the wind pushed a belly into the line, which started dragging the float parallel to the bank while we drifted alongside. I watched, holding my breath, as it passed some likely ambush spots, close to the *galhadas*, sunken tree-crowns, where I'd seen arapaima move before. Then it was in an open gap. Then I couldn't see it anymore, and my line was running out.

The next minutes were a blur of me yelling at Josiney to keep the canoe *"in the middle!"* as the fish made for the sanctuary of the fallen trees. Then the canoe was spinning as water slopped over the sides, and the line was somewhere behind me as I tried to twist to face it. Then it was straight down, and I had the first feeling that I was gaining control. A mass of bubbles erupted underneath us and the rod kicked back—and then a sight I had waited six years to see: a long, shining, smoky-gray body trailing tendrils of water as it hung suspended in the air, level with my face. Then the back of a machete blade being brought down on its sculpted, bony head followed by a sickness in my stomach that this was part of the deal—my payment for being brought here.

As arapaima go, it wasn't a big fish. At fifty inches in length it would have weighed perhaps forty-five pounds. But caught on a rod and line from an area of intensive arapaima hunting, it was a momentous catch. My photograph of that fish, draped over my shoulder with its mouth threatening to engulf the camera, appeared in a British national newspaper, where it was seen by a TV producer in London who then gave me a call. For the next two years he knocked on doors, trying to get a broadcaster to commission a documentary about this iconic fish, during which time I returned to the Amazon at my own expense and shot DIY footage for a demo tape. Finally, after some tantalizing circling back and forth, the bait was taken, and I was heading back to Brazil with a TV crew.

Actually the "crew" at this point was one person, director/cameraman Gavin Searle. Our multitasking sound recordist Fernando Setta would join us on arrival. Just three days later they would be filming my blow from the arapaima and commenting how lucky I was to be hit in an area of protective bone rather than in the face or lower down the body.

The day after that, we boarded a five-seater plane and flew up the Purus. We had been delayed in Manaus, so straight after off-loading our stuff we took the rear door off, strapped in, and took off to shoot our aerials. My job, sitting next to the pilot, was to relay instructions from behind, shouted above the roar of the wind and the engine. Having circled some backwaters, we were following the river back upstream, flying low, when I heard Gavin and Fernando shout, "More lakes!" I had a shouted conversation with our local boatman, Louro, seated behind me, then asked the pilot to climb. As we did so, a ribbon of silver opened up in the green wedge between the Purus and an entering subtributary. I instructed the pilot to line up on it and then come in low.

We were at five hundred feet or less when we heard a loud pop and then the plane started shaking. In front of me I saw the blades of the single prop becoming visible, and in my peripheral vision I was aware of treetops rising to meet us. From inside a vortex of wordless fear, I heard the gentle flicking sound of something brushing our underbelly. Then again, more heavily, and then there was a second pause, doubly filled with both certainty and unknowing. Then everything went dark and a giant hand was shaking us, the g-forces coming from all directions at once, before slamming us sideways and down with the sound of tearing metal. For a millisecond my thought was one thing only: it was over and I was unhurt. Then my lungs filled with an unmistakable sharp taste, as liquid poured onto my shoulders from above: fuel. I clawed at my harness buckle but found it jammed, as the liquid rose up my body to my chest. Not understanding how there could possibly be this much fuel, I reached for my knife, but the pilot had freed me, and I swam out the copilot's door supported by the stinking liquid, which for some reason now extended in all directions under trees.

As I swam underneath the plane's tail, I saw four figures standing on the water's surface. Moments later they had pulled me up onto the port wing. Sunlight poured through the hole we'd torn in the canopy, illuminating the wrecked plane and shredded trees, and five men without a single scratch between them. Two of our cameras were destroyed, but one had kept recording throughout. Back in town that night, having waded and walked to the river, where a flotilla of boats picked us up, we watched the footage back. Before playing it, we all agreed that the time between the explosion and the plane hitting the trees had been three or four minutes. On the tape it was fourteen seconds.

We also remembered no human sounds, but on the tape there was pandemonium: shouts, obscenities, and then breathless prayers.

Over the days and weeks that followed, I tried to scalpel apart the pages of my memory to find what was locked there. The sheer improbability of our escape haunted me. Establishing the precise sequence of events—and contemplating all the what-ifs—became my obsession. Returning to the wreck, I saw that we'd stalled in the crown of a rubber tree, which had bent and then cracked, dumping us side-on into a much larger tree, which would have crumpled us like a tin can if we'd hit it head-on, depositing the engine in my lap. Afterward, everybody asked us the same thing. Did we think we were going to die? It happened too quickly, we said. Now, however, as I belatedly worked through the mental in-tray, I sensed there was something there that I had to deal with.

It was just a flash, but it was there: a moment of certainty that I was going to burn. And for this to happen, after I'd escaped dismemberment, was just so unfair. That was the feeling: primal and childlike. Then to be spared this fate only to be extinguished by water was just too much, a good-news-bad-news joke without a funny side.

About three weeks later a realization hit me with such force that it woke me up. The swamp we'd landed in got steadily deeper as it neared the lake. If we'd come down just one second later, the water that rose while I struggled to free my harness wouldn't have stopped at my chest.

Cynics have since told me that we could have all retired on the insurance payouts if we'd played the permanent mental damage card. But that never crossed our minds, nor has it since. The best payout is being alive. Besides, we had a film to make. An Amazon beauty contest, a tussle with a ten-foot caiman, and campfire songs from our strange friend *Cabra Bom* ("the good goat") awaited us. And, just when we'd given up on the main event, after a day of piranha fishing with Manoel Karajá, he looked at us and said, "I've heard of a place where they've seen a big pirarucu. You can come there with me, but you've got to catch it our way."

After chugging downriver on the last of our fuel, with no rod in the boat, we followed him to a reed-fringed lagoon where patches of the surface intermittently flicked and distorted. After watching the movements of this baby arapaima shoal for nearly an hour, along with the occasional bulging displacements made by its watching parents, we cut a dead three-pound *traíra* in half and whirled the tail end through the air on a 150-pound handline. As soon as the line settled on the water, it started to move, but so slowly that I had to ask Manoel before I heaved back in response. The next thing I knew, a huge eruption shattered the lake's surface and the line was running hot through my hands, cutting my palms. To keep it out of the weeds and away from a stump, I had to stumble first one way along the muddy bank and then the other as the line sliced the surface with a hiss, and the displacements caused by its sudden changes of direction were like detonations of high explosive. The struggle was over in only a few minutes, but the intensity of such direct contact with a fish that was longer and heavier than me was unlike anything felt with a rod and reel. Dragged onto the bank, the fish jackknifed its body, punching its head four feet in the air, into the space where my head had been only a moment before. This was a fitting finale to our *Jungle Hooks* series, a tale of danger and back-to-basics fishing, with the unspoken message that sometimes you can't get where you want to go by means of a straight line. With a nod from Manoel, I slid the fish back into the water, supported it while it took a gulp of air, and let it go.

The sight of this fish, all 200 pounds of it, from this shallow pond left me shaking. But the claims for arapaima growing to fifteen feet are certainly wrong. This figure can be traced back to the German explorer Schomburgk, who visited South America in 1836 and who gave a corresponding weight of 410 pounds. As Leander J. McCormick wrote, "These figures have been adhered to for more than a hundred years without anyone stopping to consider what kind of shape such a fish would have; but any angler with experience of large fish would be sure to notice the disproportion between length and weight." My fish scaled up to that length would weigh in the region of 2,000 pounds, similar to a real-live sturgeon. So fifteen feet can be ruled out as unreliable. The modern consensus is around eleven feet and 500 pounds.

My only regret was that Martin didn't see my fish. Since getting a job as a stonemason (he worked on St Paul's Cathedral and the Albert Memorial) and then a family, he hasn't had time for any more trips with me. Although he has now given up the regular job, he does have two boys to look after, in between collecting dead animals for his uniquely haunting still-life photographs shot on an old-style, blanket-over-the-head five-by-four-inch plate camera in hyper-surreal black and white. But he did put me up in his spare room for a year before I upgraded to two rooms in a friend's house, where I am now, and he always gets a faraway look when I talk about the Amazon. He's the one person I bring back presents for—usually fish scales or animal bones—which he keeps in his garden shed, now well known as the place where we film the introductory segment for each *River Monsters* episode.

When I finally went for my coronary angiogram, the doctor inserted a tube into my right wrist and pushed it up my brachial artery to my heart, where it injected radio-opaque dye. At the edge of my vision I could see a moving X-ray image, a cluster of dark vessels against a light background, near the window behind which the cath lab staff and cardiologist sat. After I'd been wheeled out, the registrar told me I have a very slight thickening of the coronary artery walls, but it's nothing more than anyone else might have at my age. Confused, I asked about the dead muscle. There was no sign of it: an artifact, a trick of the light. But, from time to time, the missed beats are still there. In itself this is nothing to worry about. It's just a dull thump in the chest, like a distant echo of a flying arapaima.

Sometimes, too, the vision of an empty canoe floats into my mind: a body knocked into the water, with the piranhas, candirus and caimans finishing the job. On one of my last visits to Manaus I ran into José's cousin, buying supplies and ammunition prior to heading back upriver. Arnaldo had introduced me to the dubious delights of small-town nightlife, but I had also seen him with his head and upper body down a wild pig's burrow, digging his way to the tusk-rattling beast with his bare hands while José waited behind him with the shotgun. "We had another tourist up the Purus this year," he said. "He had his own big canoe with a motor, and he was staying with people along the river. When he arrived in the town, he started waving money around and somebody robbed him. They took 5,000 reais."

I felt a surge of envy. With that kind of money (nearly £2,000) and kit, I would have surely found the arapaima far more quickly and comfortably without being taken on such a crazy, exhausting, indirect route: the back-breaking weeks weeding José's manioc patch and lugging loads to his boat, to earn my right to stay in the forest; the whole month waiting for a message from the fat man; the tropical ulcers and bone-deep machete wound; all that paddling and dragging of leaking borrowed canoes. . . .

I re-tuned to the story. Apparently, before the man came to the town, he had stayed with some of Arnaldo's friends, an extended family of fishermen scraping a living from the river. "When they heard he had been robbed in the town, they were outraged," he said.

Despite my bitterness, I found I was cheered by this concern.

"If they'd known he was carrying that much money, they would have killed him," he said. "Somebody would have just found his boat."

CHAPTER 6

PIRAIBA

The waters compassed me about, even to the soul:
the depth closed me round about:
all thy billows and thy waves passed over me.

Jonah 2:5

THERE'S A STORY I'VE HEARD SEVERAL TIMES, from different people in different places: a group of Amazon fishermen, operating from wooden canoes, got one of their nets snagged. So one of them dove down to try to free it. But after several minutes, the man hadn't reappeared, and eventually his companions gave him up for dead. Finally, when they retrieved the net, there was a huge catfish inside, and protruding from its mouth were the legs of their former colleague. Fearful that nobody would believe them, they put the fish, still containing the corpse, inside the ice-filled hold of their mother vessel and took it to the nearest police station.

But nobody was clear about exactly where or when this happened until I met Valmi Pereira. He said he witnessed the incident himself at the mouth of Rio Canumã, one of the subtributaries of the Rio Madeira, in June 2000. This time of year, in the southern sector of the Amazon basin, is the beginning of the *vazante*, the "emptying" of the flooded forest, when the floodwaters of the rainy season, which can raise water levels by as much as fifty feet in places, start to recede. At this time multitudes of small fish, which have hatched and feasted in the flooded forest, pour back into the main waterways, and every year predators, including fishermen, intercept them. On this day, there were several fishing teams working the confluence, and all of them joined forces to retrieve the net and the body of the fisherman. But in Valmi's story, the net, a small-mesh seine for encircling shoals of small fish, was empty: no fish and no corpse. Not until four hours later did the fish appear on the surface, in a state of some distress itself, choking on its meal. The men clubbed it to death and carefully slit its stomach to reveal the face of the fisherman, although they knew he was past hope.

The fish was a *piraiba* (*Brachyplatystoma filamentosum*), measuring nearly eight feet, and weighing 286 pounds. Its mouth was 16 inches wide, easily big enough to engulf a human head and the shoulders of a small man, which most Amazon ribeirinhos tend to be, so the facts added up. But I first heard versions of this story well before 2000, and some of these said the fish was a *pacamão,* also known as the *jaú* (*Zungaro zungaro*), which is not quite as big as the piraiba but is said to be more aggressive. So I left this interview not entirely convinced, wanting some supporting evidence. Perhaps there has been more than one such incident.

What's certain is that the piraiba's reputation for size and aggression goes back a long way. Its maximum length is commonly given as ten feet, making it the biggest fish, by far, of running water in the Amazon. The FishBase website quotes eleven feet, nine inches with a weight of 440 pounds. Theodore Roosevelt, during his journey to the Amazon, heard about a ten-footer that two men killed with their machetes "when it lunged over the edge of the canoe at them." He also reported that people feared piraiba even more than caimans. In the lower Madeira they wouldn't swim in open water but instead bathed in stockaded enclosures at the riverside. There's also a clue in the fish's name. According to some linguists piraiba means "'mother of all the fishes"; others say it means "evil fish." In the modern vernacular we could combine the two, and call it an evil mutha'.

Being an inhabitant of moving water, the piraiba is a streamlined fish with a gray back and white belly, which makes it look somewhat sharklike. But unlike a shark, it has a pair of long whiskers, growing from each side of the upper jaw, and smaller ones on its chin. Its way of feeding is also very different from a shark's. Instead of cutting teeth, it has a broad, curving band just inside each jaw that are made up of countless close-packed short points and have the feel of coarse sandpaper. With these, it grips any prey that can't be sucked straight into the mouth cavity, before swallowing it whole. In other words, its table manners are less refined than those of a shark. But is it really capable of swallowing a man whole?

Although fish don't make a habit of swallowing extra-large food items, they do sometimes bite off more than they can chew. A recent story on the Internet referred to a North American flathead catfish (*Pylodictis olivaris*) that was found swimming on the surface with a basketball stuck in its mouth. It was exhausted from being unable to submerge, but its rescuer was unable to pull the ball free—testimony to the grip of those small teeth. Finally he deflated the ball with a knife. There are conflicting reports as to where this happened, but there are convincing photographs, which can be found by anyone who enters "catfish basketball" into a search engine. But do these authenticate the story? Anyone who has ever tried to bite a floating apple will immediately scratch their head and wonder how the ball got there in the first place and possibly suspect a cruel hoax—until someone reminds them that nonbiting predatory fish can exert incredible suction when they open their jaws. I was also told about a similar phenomenon on the top lake above the dam on the Rio Ebro in Spain where wels catfish were found dead with their mouths clamped to water-skiing buoys. Why catfish would go for floating lumps of plastic is something of a mystery, but they are known to be attracted to slapping sounds on the surface, which a wind-chop on the water could have created.

The capacity of fish to swallow edible items can also beggar belief. I remember as a child seeing a series of photographs showing two fingerling pike, no more than four inches long, swim up to each other in a tank. When they were nose-to-nose, the pike on the left opened its mouth and engulfed the head of the other. The next frames show the second pike slowly disappearing until just its tail is sticking out. And I remember looking back to the first frame, and seeing that the pike that opened its mouth first was actually a bit smaller than its victim.

Many years later, fishing the Rio Teles Pires in the south of the Amazon basin, I spotted a large payara (*Hydrolycus scomberoides*) floating on the surface. I agreed with my boatman Flávio that the thing looked dead, but when we went to investigate, we found it still kicking feebly. On half-pulling it from the water, the reason for its stupor was apparent— another payara's tail was poking out of its throat. Flávio grabbed this with some pliers (to avoid getting his hands near the fish's vampire-like fangs) and, with difficulty, managed to pull the partially digested fish out. It was just a few inches shorter than the fish that had eaten it. Put in human terms, that's the equivalent of me swallowing an eight-year-old child. I guessed that a build-up of gases in the stomach, with their way out blocked, had been the cause of the fish's distress on the surface. When we put the undigested fish back, it swam off fairly happily.

But to swallow a person, a piraiba would need to be phenomenally big. And there are other suspects in the frame to account for the many less specific stories of people going to wash in the river at nightfall and never returning. A man once showed me two curved scars on his upper left arm where an anaconda had grabbed him while he was paddling through flooded forest. As the snake then hauled itself into the boat and started to throw coils round the man's body, he had the presence of mind to push the point of his knife against the inside of a coil, which prevented it from tightening around him. Black caimans are also big enough to easily take a human down.

So how big do piraiba *really* grow? I met up with Julio Cavalcante, the former owner of a fishing tackle shop in Manaus, who landed a 211-pounder after a two-hour battle in the Rio Madeira. But he reckons there are bigger ones in the famous "meeting of the waters," where the tea-black Rio Negro meets the brown water of the Amazon and they run alongside each other, scarcely mixing for four miles. He told me he nearly died here once when his line, with a hooked fish on the end, wrapped around him and started to pull him in. He avoided going overboard by cutting the line with his knife. In fact he had vowed never to fish the place again—until we persuaded him to take us there.

He greeted me with a conspiratorial smile and a sealed metal paint tin. His special bait, he said. Julio is a firm believer that catfish find their food by smell, and he works on that principle to make sure they find his bait. What this meant, when I opened the tin and the layers of plastic bags inside, was that, on encountering his special formula, I could hardly breathe. He'd wrapped each hook in the guts of eight chickens and then left this to bake in the equatorial sun for three days. I fished these baits thirty feet down, suspended under a five-gallon drum, in possibly two hundred feet of water, into and through the night, as riverboats criss-crossed the mile-wide river and storm-clouds piled up over the far bank. But nothing took.

From conversations with other fishermen, it emerges that piraiba of any size have become very scarce in recent years. They used to catch them with drifting juglines (baits set under a large float), but that doesn't get results anymore. Now they tend to be caught, infrequently, on multihook longlines, stretched between the bank and a rock on the bottom. I recall something I saw when traveling on a small boat up the Rio Purus at the end of my first Amazon trip. On a beach up ahead, a man looking like an Indian sadhu—straggling hair, sun-blackened skin, something like a loincloth around his middle—was doing a strange dance. Again and again he staggered forward then shuffled unsteadily backward in a rhythm that had a certain familiarity. Then, as we passed—one hundred yards wide of him so as not to ground on the shallows—a gray fish a yard and a half long slid kicking onto the sand. As this tableau shrunk to a speck behind us, I saw a flash as a machete blade reflected the early-morning sun. But since then I've not seen any piraiba caught from the Purus, which tallies with the fact that it's one of the most heavily fished Amazon tributaries. But I have seen a couple jump there, which piraiba are known to do occasionally, although the reason is not known. This is probably what the "lunging" fish that Roosevelt reported was doing. The fishermen who responded to this perceived attack with their machetes just happened to be in the wrong place at the wrong time.

The picture on the Rio Araguaia is slightly better, and this is where I finally achieved my ambition of hooking one of these rare predators. But I made a mistake. As the fish tore off, I skinned my thumb in my efforts to bring it to a halt. When we'd drifted down on top of it, something didn't feel right. The fish would pull out a few yards, and I'd wrestle some back, but the line stayed in the same position, and my connection to the fish didn't feel direct. The line had gone round something, but it didn't feel like a tree branch. *"Espinhel,"* said Wilson, my boatman. The fish had gone under the main rope of a longline, which shouldn't have been there. So I lost the fish, which Wilson, who once caught a seven-foot monster, estimated at over two hundred pounds. I later learned that you don't have to hang on quite so hard on the first run as long as you've got plenty of line and a quick-release knot to your anchor buoy or mooring tree. Piraiba are renowned for their great strength, but they mainly pull *down* and try to keep in the main river channel. They will not make for bank-side snags, even though they could easily reach them if they tried. Some would call this dumb; others say it's fighting clean. Even staying in open water, there are stories of anglers giving up and cutting the line after a fish has exhausted all three or four boat occupants over the course of several hours. With my tactics perfected, I've since caught a couple of piraiba with Wilson, weighing close to a hundred pounds, but I can't say that's compensated for the lost fish. . . .

To try to catch a piraiba for television, I went to the Rio Teles Pires. A decade before, a fish had been caught here that needed four people to lift it. To get to the river, I had the second-scariest light-plane flight of my life with cameraman James Bickersteth as the weather closed in around us and obscured the jungle airstrip. Twice the pilot circled away while frowning at his watch, the fuel gauges, and the fading daylight. I told him that if we had to go back that was okay, although there were storms behind us now too. On our fourth pass, the weather ahead looked unchanged, but I heard a voice mutter, "Right, let's try and get this thing down." As we banked to start our descent toward rocky pinnacles below, the wind landed a punch that almost turned my stomach inside out. A couple of minutes later, as we bumped and yawed, the trees rose up on either side and we slid into contact with a blur of red mud. No sooner had we come to a stop than the pilot jumped out and lit a cigarette. Later I asked James what was going through his head. He looked at me and said quietly, "I had made my peace."

But such isolation has its benefits. Commercial fishermen can't get in by land or water thanks to hostile terrain and unnavigable rapids. At a deep roiling pool below a fall, with the bait on the edge of the main current, something almost tore the rod out of the holder in the boat's gunwale. Once I'd managed to transfer the rod to the padded rest between my thighs and clip the shoulder harness to the reel, I felt more in control. However, even though I was now putting my back into it with over-the-top one hundred–pound monofilament, the fish refused to come off the bottom. From its behavior, I judged it was clearly a big piraiba, so I told myself to stay calm and not rush things but instead maintain a constant pressure without wearing myself out. As the fight wore on, I sensed the fish starting to tire, and, after a while, it was underneath the boat. As it rose a bit more I strained for my first glimpse, and what I saw when it broke the surface was a shock. This was not a piraiba at all. The fish before me was a *pirarara*, which roughly translates as "parrot fish" because it incorporates the word *arara*, the indigenous name for the vividly colored macaw. In English it's the red-tailed catfish (*Phractocephalus hemiliopterus*), and it's every bit as unmistakable as its avian counterpart. Besides its tail, its main feature is its great head, which makes up nearly one-third of its body. Its body markings are also very distinct, with a sharp delineation between its dark back, the color of an old leather jacket, and its bright off-white belly. They are also very vocal, making a rhythmic bellowing sound when lifted from the water, the result of air being expelled through the gill-flaps. But what shocked me about this fish was its size. I'd caught many red-tails before, most of them around twenty pounds, several around thirty, and the biggest between fifty and sixty. But this dwarfed them all, so we put it in the sling and watched the needle on the scales swing round to eighty pounds, ample compensation for catching the "'wrong" species.

I also caught a few jaú, to sixty pounds, similar in shape to pirarara but dark greeny-brown all over, smoother skinned, and with a liking for rocks—so much so that I caught a forty-pounder in some crazy rapids where nothing had any right to survive.

But piraiba are not so straightforward. Typically, you've got to position your bait at long range in strong flow on heavy tackle but in a sensitive manner. This is not always easy. Then it's about being in the right place at the right time. More often than not, nothing comes along. But the fishing gods saw fit to smile on me. In two weeks I intercepted four. The biggest turned out to be the first, hooked in a wide, deep stretch near a small Indian settlement. Immediately it headed for the middle of the river, announcing its identity as clearly as could be. I was fishing a 150-pound braided line with several yards of thick 100-pound monofilament on the business end before the wire leader to give a combination of easy fishability with some abrasion resistance, because there were unseen boulders scattered on the bottom here. Getting the fish off the bottom took a long time, and then it resisted every inch of the way until I finally saw its streamlined body about to break the surface. Then it was alongside the boat, rolling onto its side, and I was able to grab it by its thick pectoral spines and haul it into the boat. As I did so, it appeared to growl at me, but in fact it was belching air from its expanded swim bladder. Weighing in at 72 pounds and measuring five feet long, it was a big, powerful fish, certainly big enough for our film. But as piraiba go, this was a tiny one. And looking at this fish, with that in mind, I found I couldn't write off as fantasy or hallucination those stories of big piraiba taking people down.

What's more, there are still a few big piraiba around. In 2007 a fish measuring seven and a half feet was caught from the Teles Pires and estimated at 375 pounds. The Czech angler Jakub Vagner recently caught one measuring eight feet, eight inches and estimated at 475 pounds. Meanwhile the International Game Fish Association (IGFA) has recognized as its new all-tackle record a fish caught in May 2009 from the Rio Solimões (the middle reach of the Amazon) that weighed 341 pounds, 11 ounces, although from the looks of the photo, this fish likely did not survive. And five years ago I heard about a remote stretch of jungle river where extremely big catfish, almost certainly piraiba, had smashed up insanely strong fishing tackle. Since then I've been desperate to get there, but other commitments have prevented me so far. (There is a very limited window each year when the water conditions are right.) It's very high up on my bucket list, as long as time doesn't run out for the piraiba first.

Giant piraiba are simply astounding—twice my weight or more—and their muscle power is legendary. In terms of a physical endurance test for an angler, surely there can be nothing tougher in a river. They have unceremoniously sunk the canoes of local handliners, and to meet one at close quarters in the water, regardless of its intentions toward you or lack of them, would be terrifying. And anybody who is skeptical of the stories of piraiba swallowing people would likely reconsider if ever in this position. For sheer size, power, demeanor, and rarity, I long thought that a giant piraiba would tick more boxes than any fish I would likely find in a river. Only after a long gray-and-white shape had pulled my boat five miles in three and a half hours on another continent would I revise that opinion.

CHAPTER 7

CANDIRU

Most journeys, I think, begin and all end with a sense of unreality.

Evelyn Waugh, *Ninety-Two Days,* **1934**

MOST FISH THAT ARE POTENTIALLY DANGEROUS to humans are monsters in terms of size, capable of biting, butting or grabbing us, and they are far stronger than us in the water. But a few small fish are every bit as monstrous in their own bloodthirsty way.

One pocket-sized fish that is guaranteed to put the willies up anybody who hears about it is the candiru. In the popular mythology of the Amazon, this fish swims up the urine stream of men who are unwary and uncouth enough to relieve themselves in the river. Like salmon surging up a waterfall, they too are homing in on the smell of chemicals in the water, driven by a basic urge. But unlike the king of fish, they are not driven to breed but to feed, although to the victim this is in effect a bizarre and painful form of sexual assault, as the fish disappears from sight up his urethra.

This fish sounds like a very good reason for not going anywhere near the Amazon.

One day, on my first Amazon trip, Martin asked a passing fisherman if there were candiru here in this stretch of the Rio Purus.

"Sure," he said. "Do you want to see some?"

He picked up his machete and casually hacked off the head of a sixty-pound red-tailed catfish that was in his canoe, hooked it firmly to one of his handlines, and lobbed it into the river. He then sat holding the line, and after five minutes he pulled it in, quickly and smoothly, hand-over-hand. As he swung it onto the riverbank, I saw that parts of the head were moving. Pale, finger-sized shapes fell out of its gills and mouth and flopped on the mud, where he scooped them up into the bowl-shaped gourd that he used for baling his canoe.

I picked one up, gripping hard to stop it from wriggling free, and it responded by vomiting circular gobbets of meat the same diameter as its mouth. With its soft, scaleless skin, it didn't feel like a fish at all but, disconcertingly, like the body part it is alleged to invade. Its short, fine whiskers identified it as a catfish, but its eyes were minute even by catfish standards, like tiny reflective pinheads. We asked if the stories about this fish were true, and the man said he knew of two women who had been penetrated when bathing in the river. But when we asked about men, he said no. That's another type, smaller and thinner. He didn't know how to catch this other type, at least not in a way that didn't involve becoming a victim. But I discovered a technique a few years later.

I was fishing the Rio Araguaia from an alloy skiff that had one of its bench seats modified into a live well, into which we'd put a couple of silvery *papa-terra* fish for catfish bait. On the floor of this tank were two small valves, an inch across, that allowed water to circulate and stay fresh. After an hour's fishing, I opened the lid to check inside and was shocked to find many more fish than we had started with. The swarming newcomers were the length of a toothpick and must have squeezed in through the tiny gaps in the valves, having located the captive papa-terra by smell—a revoltingly impressive feat. I scooped one out with an aquarist's net and put it on my hand, where it shot forward with alarming speed and tried to burrow into the cranny between two of my fingers. Scarcely overcoming my revulsion, I repositioned it and saw how it moved by wriggling its head from side to side, thereby "walking" with the tiny, backward-facing spines on its gill flaps, like a commando crawling on his elbows.

Normally the candiru would swim and wriggle inside the gill flap of a larger fish as the flap briefly opens to expel water that has passed over the gills. This water has lost some of its oxygen to the fish's bloodstream and also picked up small quantities of waste materials, ammonia and urea—the trace chemicals that, biologists think, lead the candiru to its target. Once inside the gill flap, the host's most vulnerable boundary layer is exposed: the complex system of thin membranes across which oxygen and carbon dioxide are exchanged between the fish's blood and the surrounding water. Here the candiru hooks itself into position so that the strong current that pulses through the gills does not blow it out, and it bites into the delicate tissue, rich in blood capillaries. Gorging on its host's blood, it expands to almost twice its body size before detaching and returning to open water.

With the candiru hanging from my hand by one of its spines, I could now see why they say that this fish, *Vandellia cirrhosa*, can only be removed by surgery if it ever finds its way into a narrow human orifice. But has that ever happened? Reliable evidence is hard to come by in the Amazon. However, for the filming of *River Monsters* we tracked down the victim of one attack that was very reliably documented, right down to internal video footage. Silvio Barbosa took me to the very spot where he was bathing with some friends in October 1997 on the banks of the main Amazon River at the town of Itacoatiara. The water is a turbid yellowy-brown, and you reach it by picking your way down a gloopy mud riverbank—hardly Copacabana or Ipanema, but even landlocked Brazilians are drawn to the local beach on weekends. Silvio and his friends had had a few cold beers, so after a while Silvio needed to answer the call of nature. He knew of the candiru's reputation, so he made a point of standing up, he says, in water that came up to the middle of his thighs.

He felt something that at first wasn't painful, and he looked down to see about an inch of the fish still visible outside his urethra. He tried to grab it, but it was too slippery to hold, and after a few moments it had vanished completely inside him.

Whatever he felt then, it got much worse. At the first hospital he went to, they didn't believe his story. Meanwhile, his bladder felt on the point of bursting because he was unable to urinate. He developed a fever and started to pass blood and pus. Three days later, his abdomen horribly swollen, he traveled 150 miles to Manaus, to the clinic of urologist Dr. Anoar Samad. Medical textbooks did not cover this condition, but something had to be done urgently. After putting Silvio under general anesthetic, Dr. Samad inserted an endoscope into the urethra and found the fish, which the sphincter below the bladder had blocked from further progress. By this point the candiru had died from lack of oxygen—not a problem it has inside its normal host—and to Dr. Samad, it looked as if it had tried to gnaw its way out through the side of the urethra. Aware that the fish wouldn't normally come out backward, he was considering making an incision in the patient's groin, through which he could pull it out head-first. However, by this time the fish had started to decompose, so by grasping the fish near its tail with the pincers on the endoscope and irrigating the urethra with distilled water, Dr. Samad was able to ease it out in reverse.

Silvio came round and, after a course of antibiotics, made a full recovery. He was happy enough to talk to us about what had happened eleven years before and even feature in an impressionistic reconstruction that used a squeezy plastic bottle of river water, although some worried that even this might offend the sensibilities of a prime-time audience. But our director Barny Revill still felt that this was all rather abstract for television and thought of the plan to reunite Silvio with his fish. His candiru, it turned out, still existed, although in a dead state in a jar of alcohol at the National Institute of Amazonian Research (INPA) in Manaus.

On the day in question, Silvio seemed to be scanning the shelves rather eagerly. But with thousands of specimens in the temperature-controlled storeroom, we were confident he wouldn't find what he was looking for before we had the camera rolling. When the moment came, he declined the invitation to hold it or even touch it, and instead he just stared at it in my hand.

"I never realized it was so big," he gasped. "I didn't really see it properly before." He explained that at the time, he'd still been groggy from the anesthetic and only saw something vague in a jar. This fish was 5.26 inches long, with a head 0.45 inches wide—a giant compared to those that I'd seen in the live well and, later, falling out of the gills and mouths of catfish I caught, often leaking blood onto my hands if I picked them up. And once I saw several that were somehow attached to the flanks of a red-tailed catfish I'd caught. Presumably, as they were "empty" and translucent, they were waiting to move forward and enter the gills. The catfish waited without struggling for a few extra moments before being returned, grunting quietly, as I flicked the parasites off.

Silvio's story, although gruesome, had a happy ending—for him at least. But if he had lived further from specialist medical attention, there's no doubt that he could have died. This doesn't mean that he feels like a lucky man. When I asked Dr. Samad to quantify the likely levels of pain experienced, he replied, "This is somebody who has already paid for all his sins, in this life and the next."

So there's no recorded case of the *Vandellia* candiru causing a human fatality, although in more remote parts of the Amazon there have likely been unreported cases in which both parties have paid the ultimate price for their respective mistakes. However, tucked away on a nearby shelf in the INPA storeroom, there are some other fish that are on record as being implicated in suspected homicides.

Dr. Elizabeth Bezerra is a forensic pathologist who used to work at the Medical-Legal Institute (IML) in Manaus. At the rear of the building, away from those awaiting news or called in to identify a family member, is an entrance where anonymous box vans unload steel trays containing the corpses of those who have died in suspicious circumstances. Gunshot wounds are commonplace. On the day I was there, a suspected drug dealer in his twenties was wheeled past, his body bouncing slightly as the trolley turned the corner into the examination room, as if he was merely asleep. His was a straightforward case of a gangland turf war settled in the most common way. I found myself thinking of him getting up in the morning, expecting another normal day.

Other cases, however, are less open-and-shut. One corpse that Dr. Bezerra examined some years before had what looked like gunshot entry wounds, half an inch in diameter. What was truly horrifying, though, was that the body had been hollowed out. Nothing remained inside the ribcage and abdominal cavity except a couple of small catfish.

She sent these fish to INPA, who identified them as the other, fatter type of candiru, the one I'd first seen on the Rio Purus. Local people know this fish as the candiru-açu (pronounced "'assu," or "candy-roo AQ" if you're Ice Cube's character in the dreadful film *Anaconda*), which means "big candiru." Its body shape is also very different from the smaller candiru. The local people have grouped them together on account of their similar bad habits, but genetically they are not closely related. It's a good example of how everyday names can be confusing and of the need for scientific names.

Scientists assign the smaller, bloodsucking candiru to the family Trichomycteridae. Within this family, just a handful of species in the genus *Vandellia* are bloodsuckers along with probably some members of the genus *Stegophilus*. The remaining 150-odd species feed on detritus and aquatic insects. The bigger, flesh-eating candiru belongs to the family Cetopsidae, the whale catfishes. Cetopsids feed on dead or dying fish, often entering their thick-skinned prey by way of the anus. Although they don't work quite as quickly or as surgically as piranhas, on many occasions I've had a deadbait reduced to little more than a skeleton by the attentions of these fish.

The most voracious Cetopsid species is *Cetopsis candiru*, the fish from inside the empty corpse that INPA identified for pathologist Dr. Bezerra. Their normal feeding behavior is to bite and simultaneously twist, thereby cutting a circular hole half an inch in diameter. Once one has gained entry, others follow through the same hole. One two-gallon jar at INPA contains over one hundred of these fish, all retrieved from the hollowed-out body of a caiman. I have also tempted some of these flesh-eaters to feed out of my hand off the side of a floating hut one night, despite noise and camera lights. So intent were they that I even lifted some of them out of the water and onto the deck of the house, still with their jaws fastened into their meal, a small dead fish. Knowing this behavior, to find a drowned human corpse that had been fed on by these fish would not be a surprise. But the condition of the skin in the corpse Dr. Bezerra examined suggested that the entry wounds had been made when the victim was alive.

This raised the unthinkable possibility of a fish potentially more deadly than the piranha. But although the victim might have been alive when the candiru attacked, he was likely already in distress or injured. Since that first case that alerted the scientific world to this phenomenon, Dr. Bezerra has seen the same thing several times. "Monday is the worst day," she told me. "People go to the river on the weekend, have a picnic and a drink, get into trouble while swimming, and drown. A day later the body comes up to the surface and they bring it to us."

At present these hollowed-out corpses are found only in the Amazon. However, a *River Monsters* viewer e-mailed me in a state of some consternation with the news that he had once seen the same flesh-eaters at an aquarist's shop in Florida, being sold under the name of "blue whale catfish." What's more, I've since seen posts on aquarists' forums about Cetopsid catfish being kept or for sale. Some of these might be the fish they call the whale candiru in the Amazon, a plump one-pounder that goes by the scientific name of *Cetopsis coecutiens*, which is anything but a cutie except, perhaps, to an ichthyologist.

As for the bloodsucking and occasionally penis-invading candiru, we kept a lonely one in a tank for some days while filming in the Amazon in 2008, but I've not heard of any being kept as pets, even by the keenest aquarists. In fact, certain parts of the United States expressly prohibit people from keeping members of the Trichomycteridae family even though, as the FishBase website notes, "The incorporation of this species in fish-based house security systems has been suggested."

CHAPTER 8

NILE PERCH

In the tomb of Rahotet, a court dignitary, at Medum in Egypt, there is a fresco of two men carrying a large Nile perch hung from a paddle. The tomb probably dates from about 2650 B.C., or more than 4500 years ago. Above the drawing is a hieroglyphic inscription, which translated reads, "Capturing the *Aha* fish." At Medinet Gurob, south of Memphis, there are cemeteries filled with *Lates* dating back to the XVIII Dynasty [about 1580 B.C.]. The fish was unquestionably an object of worship there in those days.

Leander J. McCormick, in *Game Fish of the World,* 1949

EVEN AFTER TWO HOURS, the fish was showing no sign of tiring. For the fisherman in the boat, however, who was burning in the tropical sun, it was another matter.

"Please, please fish, come on," he begged, as his companions poured water over his head and down his back. But every time he gained a few inches of line, his opponent would take it back again. The fish was about twenty feet down in three hundred feet of water, but it absolutely refused to come any closer than that.

"Maybe there's a crocodile hanging on to its tail," joked Shaban, the boatman.

After four hours, nothing had changed, except a few details: the boat had drifted further from land, the fisherman's legs and back were more buckled and his expression more grim, and his companions were now silent. The scene was like a modern-day reenactment of Ernest Hemingway's tale of endurance and defeat, *The Old Man and the Sea,* except this was not the sea. The fish on the end was not a giant marlin but rather a Nile perch (*Lates niloticus*), one of the biggest freshwater species in the world.

After eight hours, the fish is still not in, and the sky is starting to get dark. The fish is now three miles from where it took the lure. Nobody wants to be out on the lake at night, and if this goes on much longer, they'll never find their camp, tucked somewhere down a rocky inlet on the eastern shore. Despite the fisherman's protests, the others give him an ultimatum. The double line above the leader has shown a few times. If he can get the eighty-pound mono leader within reach, they'll grab that and try to haul the fish in. If he can't . . . well, he doesn't have any other choice.

The rod takes on an even more extreme curve, and the swivel at the top of the leader inches clear of the surface. Hands grasp the thick leader and start to heave. There's a collective holding of breath as everyone prays the line won't suddenly fall slack. Is this the moment when The Big Question is finally answered?

The biggest Nile perch to be accurately recorded from this water, Lake Nasser in Egypt, weighed 230 pounds and is the IGFA all-tackle world record. But another fish, caught in the mid-1990s by retired tea planter Gerald Eastmure, was even bigger. It measured six feet, two inches long with a fifty-nine-inch girth, and it was estimated at over 275 pounds. But they are said to grow even bigger, up to 440 or even 500 pounds.

These captures from Lake Nasser are perhaps more remarkable for the fact that it is a new, manmade water. The construction of the Aswan High Dam above the Nile's first cataract created it in the 1960s. As usual with dams, it has been a mixed blessing. The dam itself radiates a dense web of power lines, carrying electricity down the Nile valley, and the regular flooding of the lower river has been brought under control, although the sediments that used to fertilize the Nile delta are starting to fill in the lake. But tens of thousands of Nubians and the temple of Abu Simbel had to be moved to higher ground as more than two thousand square miles of desert were flooded. Meanwhile, as a vast new habitat for Nile perch, the lake has expanded the local fishing industry and lured anglers from around the world. They come because it is exotic yet accessible and because they'll probably catch their lifetime-best fresh-water fish: fifty pounds is a realistic target, and a lucky few catch one over one hundred pounds. And there's the ever-present chance—maybe the next fish that hits the lure?—of something much bigger than that.

Back in the boat, hands grab the leader and pull. The fish kicks, but after all this time, the men aren't going to let it go, and they heave it onto the deck. For a moment, everyone is silent. Heads shake in disbe-lief as the fish is restrained on the unhooking mat. A hand reaches in with a pair of pliers and removes the lure from its mouth. Its deep flanks are almost luminous, its silver scales gathering and intensifying the fading light like a battery of miniature mirrors. On its back, the spiked dorsal fin stands proud. Nobody wants to say anything, but the scales confirm that this is not a collective hallucination. It weighs only seventy-five pounds. Why did it take so long to land?

The only reason I believe this story is because I was in the boat. The date was May 1998, and I had gone to Lake Nasser to write a newspaper article. The fish took a trolled Depth Raider plug in a bay on the west-ern shore at 12:40 p.m. To keep it away from the rocky shore, we started the outboard and held it clear, and from then on it kept deep. As we drifted over the sunken river channel, which runs down the middle of the lake, we could sometimes see it through the clear water. Although broken and distorted by the surface ripples, it looked big but not huge. One possible reason why the angler, Dave Everett, was making no im-pression was that the fish was foul-hooked, maybe in the back or tail. But the line appeared to be coming from its mouth, so the lack of lever-age was a mystery. We could only conclude that the fish was deeper down than we thought and, therefore, a lot bigger.

We got it in the boat at 9:35 p.m., after eight hours and fifty-five minutes. When we put it back in the water, cradled in the weighing sling, it wasted no time recovering; it gave a strong kick and was gone.

Back at the camp, which Shaban miraculously found in the dark, the reaction was predictable. Had we been trying to set some ridicu-lously inappropriate light-tackle record, like the man who went after mako shark with a fly rod and a 12- or 18-pound tippet? (After he was smashed up several times, a hooked mako obligingly jumped into the boat, and the man is now the proud holder of a line-class record.) Dave was using 25-pound line, which should have beaten the fish comfortably in open water in fifteen minutes at most. (The record 230-pound fish was taken on 20-pound line.)

There were also veiled suggestions that Dave must have been pussy-footing around and not using the full strength of his tackle. But Dave, a former weight lifter, was a wreck, his back muscles shot. And although I can't vouch for the crushed gonads, which were cushioning the rod butt, both groins sported colorful bruises the next day. Perhaps to prove a point, he caught a fifty-pounder from the shore three days later, on the same line and with a lighter rod, this time exerting less pressure on the fish so as not to bring it in to the rocky shallows while it was still lively. It was ready to scoop out of the water after only twenty minutes.

In the decade since then, I've tied my brain in knots trying to work out how this fish punched so far above its weight, and I think I might now have an answer. But I've also wondered what story might have been spawned if we'd never got it in.

I also wanted to go back to try for a big one myself. On that trip I was an observer, first as a journalist and then as an emergency stand-in guide. The fishing is not unlike big-game fishing at sea, right down to the waves crashing over the bow, with lures being trolled behind the boats for several hours every day. But because trolling places are limited, usually to two rods per boat in order to avoid tangles, these places were limited to paying clients.

But I did pick up a rod a few times to explore the rocky margins, a style of fishing that is more to my taste. I find big waters intimidating, boring even, but the Lake Nasser shoreline is 4,500 miles of cliffs plunging straight down, precarious points, shallow coves, and views through clear water of an epic underwater geography. Sometimes you can also see fish right in close, although a looming biped will make them vanish. One day I cast to two moving shadows from a narrow ledge at the top of a sheer cliff, but a third fish that came from nowhere seized my lure. After running straight down the underwater cliff face, the fish then started moving along the bank, with the line scraping on unseen rocks as it did so and with me following on the steep, crumbling mountainside above. When I finally brought it to the surface, my guide Mohammed had to clamber twenty feet down and balance on a small rock in order to secure its lower jaw. As he called up, "About fifty pounds," two other Nile perch materialized, just feet away from him, and calmly observed proceedings before melting away. After being held steady for a moment, my fish launched itself away from the mountainside, gliding high above the sunken desert floor.

I finally got my chance for another crack at this species when we filmed the second series of *River Monsters*. But in the ten years I'd been away, catches at Lake Nasser had tailed off. Commercial fishing could be part of the reason, and it's also possible that the water's productivity has declined after the initial input of nutrients from the flooded land. But a major factor seems to be fish intelligence. Catch and release means that fish learn: a straightforward association between a particular thing in the water and a bad experience. Even when I was there, the perch were starting to reject large, gaudy lures in favor of smaller, more lifelike patterns. Now soft artificials and hard-to-catch livebaits are the order of the day, but even these don't fool the bigger fish.

So we started to look for places that are less accessible. All over the world, fish populations are under attack thanks to the human population's increasing need for food. And with fewer fish, there are fewer big fish. Therefore, for most species we'll never know if the old stories about monsters are true. So the fisherman's El Dorado is a place where you step back in time, where people have kept away. Mere remoteness is not enough of a deterrent. In the Amazon, for example, fishermen will drag canoes through miles of forest for the chance to make a lucrative catch. There needs to be something else protecting the fish.

The range of the Nile perch extends to the Senegal and Niger rivers in West Africa and also to the Congo. But its real heartland is the African Rift Valley, where it is known as the *mbuta* or *netch-assa*. The

Rift Valley is a two thousand–mile-long rip in the earth's crust, where a sliver of East Africa is in the process of pulling apart from the rest of the continent. Eventually the sea will flood this sunken trench, but even now the rift can be seen from space because of the water it already contains. The largest Rift Valley lake is the ribbon-shaped Lake Tanganyika. At nine-tenths of a mile deep (4,800 feet), it is the second deepest lake in the world, after the mile-deep Lake Baikal in Siberia (5,387 feet). But I was more interested in two lakes at the southern end of Ethiopia: Chamo and Abaya. These are said to contain the largest Nile crocodiles in Africa, which, in theory, ought to be keeping the fishermen away.

But before unpacking my rods, I called at the National Museum in Addis Ababa to check out some of the earliest known fishing tackle. The Rift Valley is well known as the home of the earliest human ancestors—Lucy, Ardi, and other so-called missing links—so it was also, most probably, home to the world's first fishermen. I tried to imagine exactly what that meant: the realization not only that water was a potential source of food but also that it contained hidden dangers. I also thought about how this tested and fueled early human ingenuity. Did they first collect fish with their hands from drying out ponds and streams, as I have done from the Luangwa River in Zambia? Did they then progress to making traps, or were spears the next step? The items I was looking at—but wasn't allowed to touch—were fragments of dark bone eight thousand years old with pointed ends and notched edges, and they came from the same site where a three-foot-long skull from an early Nile perch was unearthed. There was also a precursor of the fish hook: a double-ended spike measuring three inches long. I've seen exactly the same thing in the Amazon but made of wood. With a cord tied to a notch around its middle, it is threaded inside the body of a small fish. When this is then swallowed by a bigger fish, the spike turns sideways and impales the predator's throat.

At Lake Chamo the crocs turned out to be very real, but there were still fishermen. I should have known. Some of these were "official" fishermen; others were not. When I arrived at the lake, smoke was billow-

116

ing from one of the bays. An unofficial camp had just been torched by its former occupants after they'd gotten wind that they were about to be forcibly moved. When our boat arrived at another camp that was hidden on the bay's opposite side, a group of men with machetes and grim expressions met us. They had heard we were the fisheries people, and they weren't going to give up this place without a fight. But when we told them that we only wanted to film, they relaxed. They let me paddle one of their flimsy balsa rafts, skirting a pod of hippos, to check their gillnets set for tilapia. I asked about Nile perch fishermen, and they pointed to an island that appeared to be uninhabited. But they advised us not to just motor over and look at the nets: "They're watching you."

At the fishing cooperative in Arba Minch I spoke to the man who'd netted the heaviest Nile perch from Chamo. Its flesh weighed 231 pounds, and the head, guts, and bones would have been nearly half that, giving a total of about 340 pounds. But that was fifteen years ago. Nothing that size has been seen since. This man said that nobody catches Nile perch there on hooks, adding, "It's impossible."

I also met men who had paid the price for getting too close to the lake's wildlife. One had had his foot taken off by a croc; a hippo had horrifically gored another. Not for the first time I reflected on the reality of fishing as practiced by men like these, Labena and Altaye, and how different their reality is from mine. I tried fishing with lures, but I kept hooking nets, so I moved to nearby Lake Abaya. Again, the water was cloudy, so I caught some tilapia in the margins and set off in search of a likely spot. With a strong wind blowing down the lake, we hardly made any headway. Our iron boat crashed down on the waves, soaking us and all the kit, and I kept having visions of a weld going and sending us all to the bottom, where we would be at the mercy of crocs even more aggressive and cunning than those in Lake Chamo. On top of that, there were no underwater features. Despite the hilly landscape around the lake, the sonar revealed a bottom as flat as a pool table, a constant twenty-nine to thirty feet deep. Finally, we found a protruding rock and fished around that, but no result. It was time to move on.

Next stop was Uganda and the northern part of Lake Victoria, which has a greater surface area than Lake Tanganyika but less water because it's much shallower. This lake originally had no Nile perch, but they were introduced in the 1950s. Numbers then exploded, at the expense of native cichlids, and several big ones were caught, including a 191½-pound fish in 1991, which held the IGFA world record for a while. But the size of fish has now declined. At the lake shore I watched a commercial fishing boat unloading and then followed the fish, packed in ice in the back of a truck, to a fish processing plant in Entebbe. Here, in conditions of hospital-like hygiene, they were packed for export. Although the tonnages going through were impressive, the size of individual fish was not. Despite a strictly enforced minimum size, most were about three pounds. They once had a fish of 339 pounds from Lake Kyoga, and other factories had seen fish to 440 pounds, but those days were gone. The biggest fish, of the thousands I saw there, was only 75 pounds.

I was running out of places to try when I heard an extraordinary story—an extreme variation on "the one that got away." In October 2009 an art teacher from Northern Ireland, Tim Smith, hooked a large Nile perch below Murchison Falls in Uganda. The fish had been towing Smith's small boat up and down the river for forty-five minutes when the boat suddenly lurched, nearly knocking him into the water. The next thing he knew, Smith was staring into a crocodile's open jaws. Mercifully, because the animal collided with the side of the boat, it missed him by about a foot. By now the fish was on the surface a few yards away, and the croc switched its attention to the easier meal, sinking its teeth into its tail and spinning it around in a death roll. But the fish kicked and the croc lost its grip, so Tim was able to tie the fish to the side of the boat and start the engine. Once well clear, he tried to revive the fish, but it had lost a lot of blood from deep puncture wounds and, eventually, now well into the night, it died. Lucky to be alive himself, Tim weighed the fish at 249 pounds, nearly 20 pounds heavier than the current IGFA record.

Murchison Falls, on the Victoria Nile below Lake Victoria, had been on my radar for several years after some friends went there in 2000. It's a national park, so there's no commercial fishing, but I'd not previously heard of any real heavyweights from here. As a setting, though, it's spectacular: the river plunges 140 feet as it squeezes through a cleft in the rocks barely 20 feet wide. In 1950 Murchison Falls was the location for a scene in *King Solomon's Mines* with Deborah Kerr and Stewart Granger, and in 1954 Ernest Hemingway crashed a light plane nearby. I duly exchanged some e-mails with Tim, who generously gave me some up-to-date tips about the water, and I arrived feeling confident that I was as well prepared as possible.

Other big fish, I learned, were sometimes lost. Below the falls, they would just keep going in the fast water, and in the slower reaches downstream there were beds of sharp shells, which would slice the line. Most people, I concluded, were fishing too light, although for lure fishing, it is always going to be a compromise: use heavy mono and you can hardly cast it, but switch to finer braid and you'll get cut off on the first rock it touches.

Sometimes the best chance that you'll get on a water comes on your very first day. So before my first cast I prepare my tackle obsessively to make sure there are no weak links. Often I will retie a knot many times until I am satisfied that it is as near perfect as possible. I check the sharpness of the hook, touching it up with a file if necessary, and I inspect the line for nicks and other damage that could weaken it. All this is fine if I'm fishing on my own, but doing this can try the patience of a film crew. And I worry that it can reveal too much about me.

Sometime after I left school, I became aware that I was repeating certain actions: checking that doors were locked, cookers were turned off, basins and toilet bowls were clean. Connected with these things were strange, repetitive rituals: clicking my fingers, flicking my eyes around the top corners of a room, talking to myself, counting. And I would repeat the same sequences of actions over and over, unable to finish whatever simple task it was, even though I knew that, in theory, it should have been a simple matter to control myself. In short, I thought I was going mad. But I didn't want to tell anyone, least of all a doctor, because then I'd never get a job. This soon got to the point that these rituals were consuming hours out of each day. But, for the most part, I concealed them from those around me, making a joke if somebody spotted me repeatedly returning to rattle a door handle. Also if I wrote a letter or a card (this being pre-Internet), I would keep rereading it, over and over, to make sure I hadn't written any obscenities or insults. So I stopped writing to people, including, in one instance, a letter I should have written after a family friend's son had died. I felt as if my mind was possessed or, at any rate, shared, and the daily battle for control exhausted me. After fifteen years or so, I learned that my condition had a name: obsessive-compulsive disorder (OCD), maybe with a bit of Tourette's syndrome thrown in. But the information now appearing didn't offer much help other than knowing that I have plenty of company, some of it quite illustrious. (Charles Darwin, Florence Nightingale, Billy Bob Thornton, and David Beckham are among their number, plus the fictional novelist, played by Jack Nicholson, in *As Good as It Gets*.) Nobody, however, really knows where it comes from, and there's no cure for it. My theory, for what it's worth, is that an overactive mind suddenly deprived of things to occupy and inspire it will freewheel and invent things to do. These things then become more and more ingrained the more those neural pathways are used. It's like a stuck record, the needle following the same groove, over and over, wearing the groove deeper and deeper. To fight it, I prescribed myself some real stress. In the same way that a fever is the body's kill-or-cure response to physical infection, to cook invading microbes to death, I decided to turn up the mental heat. This was the other reason I traveled alone to Zaire and the Amazon.

So I don't talk about obsession lightly. It's something deep in my nature, to an extent that is pathological. But it's also something I have harnessed. As I apply superglue to the twenty-turn Bimini twist that gives me three feet of double line above my crimped and flame-sealed fluorocarbon leader, I'm thinking fractions of percentages. And I'm sure this attention to minutiae, which most anglers would pass over, has brought me monster-sized fish that would have otherwise escaped.

On this first day at Murchison, a little way below the falls, I started by casting a lure from the rocky banks. In one spot, very close in, between two fingers of rock, I felt a small tap and saw a boil in the water. But further casts, fanning out from my position, got no reaction. I heard our director Barny Revill saying we should move further upstream for some scenic shots of the "Devil's Cauldron" beneath the falls. But the river was talking to me too, so I told Barny, "I'll just have one last cast."

The river in front of me was a complex mix of current-lines that swung the lure first this way then that. With the rod high, I guided it again toward the two rock fingers, and when it was nearly there I had a gentle take. It felt disappointingly small, my drag registering a slow click-click-click. But then there was a sudden plunge, as if a sandbag had been dropped on the rod, and the sound rose to a whine of alarm. Looking up, I saw the line heading for a rock point downstream. If I didn't turn the fish, it would be gone. Sprinting over the rocks after it, I struggled to exert some lateral force, and just before the point of no return, it veered into the back eddy near the bank. But once in this squashed vortex, it then sped past me going upstream until it stopped in an area of foam just down from a rapid, where I felt a sickening grate on the line. Exerting as much pressure as I dared, I felt it slowly come toward me. But in that crazy, rocky water, it still felt like too much for my thirty-pound line. Then it was on the surface, and I saw a great circular mouth. Straining to keep it clear of tumbled rocks, I guided it into a bay, where my guide Echie and I pulled it up onto land, away from any hungry crocs.

When I first saw this fish on the surface, I thought it was around 60 or 70 pounds. But the scales went round to 112, one of the biggest Nile perch caught anywhere on a shore-fished lure. And in that wild water, with that thunderous backdrop, I couldn't ask for a more dramatic catch.

But I was after something much bigger. Turning to the slower reaches downriver and fishing livebaits, I geared up with 80-pound mono and a leader of tough 125-pound fluorocarbon, and although one take still resulted in a cut line, I converted two other chances to fish of 110 and 130 pounds, making an amazing hat-trick.

Then, in a weedy bay on my last-but-one day, I hooked a fish that was instantly around a snag. As the line grated and I tried to work out what was happening, the fish surfaced at the edge of my vision, some way upstream of where the line entered the water. By now we'd drifted down to the snag, a sunken tree, but by the time I had extricated the line, the hook was no longer attached. I knew I'd lost a heavy fish, but I hadn't seen it clearly enough to know any more than that. One of the people in the boat, however, did get a clear look. Shaking his head, he just said, "You don't want to know."

SO THE QUESTION OF HOW BIG NILE PERCH GROW remains unanswered. But the mystery of "super perch," the seventy-five-pounder that took nearly nine hours to bring to the boat, might be more solvable.

As most anglers know, a seventy-five-pound fish doesn't weigh seventy-five pounds in the water. Thanks to the air in its swim bladder, its weighs next to nothing. But if the swim bladder is deflated, the fish will become negatively buoyant, although it will still weigh nowhere near seventy-five pounds, because of the partial buoyancy of its tissues. The swim bladder of the seventy-five-pound Nile perch that I saw in the fish factory at Entebbe had roughly the volume of a football. This would give somewhere between five and fifteen pounds of buoyancy, which is the dead weight an angler will feel if this buoyancy is absent. And although that doesn't sound like very much, most fishing rods won't lift this amount. After a certain point they just keep on bending, without exerting any more lift.

Significantly this fish was hooked in shallow water but then went deep. From my experience as a diver, I know that if I am neutrally buoyant near the surface but then kick for deeper water, my buoyancy jacket will collapse and I will keep on sinking unless I quickly squirt more air into the jacket. But a Nile perch can't do this. Its buoyancy adjustments are very slow because gas enters and leaves its sealed swim bladder by way of the blood. And in this case it apparently didn't make this adjustment at all. Either it consciously overruled the normal process or the lift provided by the fishing line tricked its body into thinking that neutral buoyancy had already been regained.

Interestingly, despite the difficulty of bringing this apparent monster up, it was quite easy for the boat to tow it when we needed to keep it clear of the rocky shore. So if there had been a gently sloping beach somewhere, free from snags, we could have brought it up by pulling it into the shallows. The other recourse would have been to take hold of the twenty-five-pound main line. This would have exerted more lift than the rod and, done with care, would have brought the fish up much more quickly.

The other monster, meanwhile—going everywhere with me, invisible under the surface—was immune to the laws of physics and logic. That monster would take far longer to beat.

CHAPTER 9

ALLIGATOR GAR

Since the armor of a big gar can flatten a bullet,
the talons of a hawk probably don't feel like much more than a back rub.

Rob Buffler and Tom Dickson, *Fishing for Buffalo*, 1990

ON MAY 7, 1884, the *Arkansas Gazette* carried a story about a boy who went fishing at a place called Shoal Creek and had a bite he would never forget. He was sitting in a boat with friends, dangling his leg over the side, when something in the water grabbed him and pulled him overboard. His companions managed to rescue him, and he lived to tell this unlikely fisherman's tale, though his leg was "terribly lacerated."

In 1932 nine-year-old Elizabeth Grainger was sitting with her feet in the edge of Lake Pontchartrain in Louisiana when a seven-foot-long fish seized her. Her thirteen-year-old brother ran to her rescue and managed to pull her free, but her leg was left raw and bleeding. She was rushed to the local physician, Dr. Paine, for treatment, from whose report this story survives.

The animal that took the rap for these attacks and countless others with vague details recounted orally was the alligator gar, *Atractosteus spatula*, the second-largest fish in North America next to the white sturgeon. But unlike the sturgeon—and as its name implies—it is equipped with a ferocious set of teeth. Behind its head is a massive cylindrical body encased in armored scales heavier and thicker than those of any other fish. (The French explorers in the 1700s called this near-indestructible fish the *poisson armé*, and some say that to open one up you have to use an axe.) And right at the back, there's a huge propulsion unit, made up of three fins grouped together: the tail and the set-back dorsal and anal fins. These give it a profile somewhat like a pike, except a medium-sized one of these could swallow any pike whole. With looks like these, there was no doubt in anyone's mind that the alligator gar was a danger to humans. In 1922 the *Times-Picayune* of New Orleans went so far as to say that alligator gar are more dangerous than man-eating sharks, claiming that gar had killed three students wading in the Mississippi.

I can't remember where or when I first heard about alligator gar, but I dimly remember an old black-and-white picture of two men in a boat, one with a bent rod and the other with a drawn bow, his puny arrow aimed at a massive head rearing out of the water in front of them. The angler wore a pith helmet, which would have made it prewar. But when I started casting my net for large river species overseas, I'd seen nothing more recent. In *Game Fish of the World*, the comprehensive compendium of piscine exotica published in 1949, the alligator gar merited only passing mention. I assumed it must have been a rarity that was now extinct.

Then in 2003 I received an e-mail from a Dutch angler, Jacques Schouten, who had visited Texas the last five summers and caught alligator gar close to two hundred pounds. This now being the age of the Internet, I went online and found some US anglers who had also caught them, and I put together a dossier of contacts and locations. At the time I was looking to do a follow-up to my *Jungle Hooks* series about the Amazon, and this seemed to have all the ingredients: a spectacularly fierce fish that was unknown to most people, some great locations in the backwater bayous, and plenty of biology and local lore. (A gar is clearly behind the legend of "Champ," the Lake Champlain monster.) But this time the pitch, put together with the same producer, wasn't successful. So the strange fish that had been shadily present in my mind, having now revealed itself to be dramatically alive, sank once more into the depths.

The fact that alligator gar weren't extinct, after all, was not for want of trying, on the part of *Homo sapiens*, to extinguish them. The stories about their attacks on humans had created an anti-gar hysteria. Many also believed that this predator was destroying game fish stocks. So in addition to large-scale commercial fishing for gar meat, self-styled vigilantes were catching gar and throwing them on the bank to rot. Then there was Col. Burr's "electrical gar destroyer." The colonel was the research director for the Game, Fish and Oyster Commission of Texas in the 1930s, and this contraption was an eight-by-sixteen-foot barge rigged with a 200-volt generator and trailing power lines that zapped anything it went near. On its maiden voyage, it fried seventy-five gator gar and a thousand turtles. Electrocution as a control measure caught on and probably accounted for the deaths of millions of gar, thereby helping to wipe them out from vast swathes of their original range. Historically they were found in the low-lying reaches of all rivers draining into the Gulf of Mexico, but now they're gone from the Illinois, the Missouri, the Ohio, and the Mississippi above Memphis, and they are barely clinging on in the Arkansas River and the Florida Panhandle.

This extermination mostly went unlamented, even after a Texas Parks and Wildlife Department (TPWD) study in 1987 debunked the belief that this "trash fish" is the nemesis of the nation's "game" species. An analysis of the stomach contents of 209 alligator gar, caught from Sam Rayburn reservoir using gillnets and juglines and weighing between 18 and 156 pounds, revealed that, far from eating their own weight in game fish every forty-eight hours as was commonly believed, most had their stomachs empty. Of those that had fed, largemouth bass made up just 3.4 percent of their diet. Their most popular prey was gizzard shad (26.4 percent), followed by channel catfish (14.9 percent) and freshwater drum (12.6 percent). Miscellaneous dietary items included two coots, eleven fishhooks, an artificial lure, and a plastic bag. This study was also significant for another reason: it demonstrated that the scientific community, if nobody else, had started to take note of this species. Texas was, by now, the main refuge of the once-widespread alligator gar. Would I get to see one before they disappeared for good?

A documentary film on alligator gar finally got the green light when *River Monsters* went from being a one-time program to a seven-part series, five years after I'd originally touted the idea. I then had to dig out the old notes and cross my fingers that the fish were still there. I'd been told that gar fishing is best in the summer months—the hotter the better—so we had to race to get everything set up before we missed the season. The first stop was a couple of days on the Trinity River with Dr. Dave Buckmeier and some TWPD scientists, who had started a gar-tagging program. But their juglines caught nothing, and the nets brought in only a two-foot longnose gar, one of the four smaller gar species (along with spotted, shortnose, and Florida gar). However, some local men fishing for catfish had caught a small alligator gar on a multihook trotline, and they donated this to the team. To attach the acoustic tag, we covered the fish in a damp towel, including its eyes because we had just brought it into the air from dark water, and then drilled a couple of 1/8-inch holes just under the dorsal fin. But I didn't even feel its muscles tense. My observation that it was like a visit to the dentist was unconsciously apt. Gar scales are made of thick bone and are coated with a tough layer of an enamel-like substance called ganoine. Whatever it was that finished off the dinosaurs sixty-five million years ago at the end of the Cretaceous period didn't put an end to these tough customers, although before that time gars also existed in Africa, India, southern Europe, and South America. Now they are only in parts of North and Central America. But from the scientists' fishing results I wasn't optimistic about catching a big gator gar for the cameras.

Cut to another stretch of the Trinity, with the water so low that it was an obstacle course of tree skeletons. To navigate this twisting, outboard-destroying waterway, we'd booked an airboat, owned by bowfishing guide Bubba Bedre. An unsilenced Chevy engine powered the caged aircraft propeller by way of a reducing gearbox so the blade tips wouldn't disintegrate, and I didn't need to be asked twice to put on my ear protection as we blasted downriver. After five minutes, we cut the motor and drifted seventy yards to a steep-banked L-shaped bend, where the flow had scooped out a deep hole on the bottom. As we quietly floated on the edge of the slow current, a fish noisily broke the surface twenty yards away. My mind did an instant bit of fish-behavior cross-referencing, and I guessed this was both a good sign and a bad sign: good because it was a big fish, easily over one hundred pounds, and bad because it knew we were there and was, therefore, unlikely to take a bait.

This is exactly what you'd read from a similar type of breach from an arapaima. Like arapaima, alligator gar are air-breathers, capable of surviving in poorly oxygenated water, like the shrunken Trinity in September. Their swim bladder, in addition to being a buoyancy device, is also a primitive lung. So from time to time they have to rise to change the air inside. And if they feel unsafe at the surface—perhaps because they have been shot at with arrows before in this place—this operation is not calm and relaxed but quick and noisy. We ended the day with no fish caught, despite transferring to the bank, where the movements of my four-person entourage would transmit less into the water.

The next day's fishing was with another bow-hunting guide, Mark Malfa, who also took rod-and-line anglers, if anyone expressed an interest, but these were very much in the minority. We spent the day moving into holes where fish were moving, only for them to move elsewhere, leaving our water empty. In desperation I reached down the years to the time when I was a schoolteacher, and I then delivered a hissed lecture to the crew about the vital importance of keeping quiet. I wasn't so concerned about talking, which was fine within reason, as I was about knocking and banging on the hull. These are wild animals we're trying to get close to, I reminded them. Just a cable-end dropped in the boat could send them all scattering, and then we'll have to wait two or three hours for them to come back. And with only four days allotted for fishing in our eight-day schedule, we could go home empty-handed. The situation was as serious as that. Like naughty schoolchildren, they considered themselves reprimanded, and I've not been allowed to forget it ever since. But these were early days, and since then I've gotten everybody well trained, which is more to their credit than mine: a mobile, stealthy film crew is a thing to behold.

A little later, something took my bottom-fished carp chunk. I let the line run out, ever so slowly, under no tension, and after maybe sixty yards, I tightened and wound down, bringing back an intact bait. Any other fish would have been well and truly hooked, but people have noted that gar feed in a very characteristic way. When they take a live fish, they grab it crosswise in the end of their jaws and then move off with it to a place where they feel undisturbed, like a dog retreating to its den. Then, the prey's struggles having died down, they will turn it, little by little, until it's ready to go headfirst down the gar's throat. At this point the mouth will fully close and the prey will be in a pelican-like pouch that runs along the lower jaw. Even when feeding on a small piece of dead fish, gar will apparently treat it in the same way, as if this behavior is somehow programmed. As one man said to me, a gar's mouth is like its shopping trolley: they will keep food in there for later. So if the angler tries to set the hook before the bait is passed to the back of the mouth, either the hook is not inside the mouth or it fails to make any impression in the bony jaws. Already I could see why some fishermen of old, always inventive, had done away with hooks altogether and had taken to lassoing gars by the snout with wire nooses threaded with fish pieces. Others armed the bait with a nest of thick line, a short length of frayed rope, or a piece of nylon panty hose to tangle the teeth of this uncooperative critter.

Mark said to let the run go even further, but when I did this the fish dropped the bait, probably because of the drag caused by having all that line out. But later that afternoon I brought in a four-footer, which was not the fish I wanted but nonetheless an indication that, possibly, I was one step nearer to that fish.

The next day, I decided on a new tactic: let the fish make its long, slow, twenty-minute run downstream and then, after waiting for it to move off again, drift down after it, steering around fallen trees with the electric trolling motor. Again, the rolling fish mostly moved away whenever we approached and the day was a slow chase, but late in the afternoon I had the chance to put the plan into action. As I slowly wound more and more of the line back on the reel and we drifted closer and closer to the fish, I scarcely dared to breathe. Then, from the angle of the line, I saw that the fish had started to head back upstream, which probably meant that the bait was now properly taken. This time when I tightened, there was a heavy weight on the line and the fish surged away in response. Thinking of all the dead branches in the water, I strained to keep it on a short line, changing the direction of my pull to keep it confused when it was close to the boat. When I finally saw it, for just a fraction of a second, the plume of water it sent up drenched me despite my position on the foredeck four feet above the surface. The rod doubled over in response, but the 150-pound braid held, and after some more plunges beside the boat, Mark was able to loop a strap behind its pectoral fins and heave it aboard.

By now the sky was dark, but under the light of several flashlights I marveled at this beast with its pterodactyl-proof armor. The body behind the head was round like a barrel, drab olive green on top, and shaded to pale cream on the belly. Then there was a hiss as it expelled air, and I saw the plates of its upper jaw come apart, widening the head to maximize the volume of the mouth cavity before it pushed the new charge back into the swim bladder, releasing a small surplus from the gills as its big yellow-reflecting eye, in its recessed socket behind the angle of the jaw, seemed to pop at the effort of it all. But from this I knew it would be okay once it was back in the water. It breathed strongly a couple more times as we weighed it in the sling and ran a tape along its length. Then the two of us cradled it for photos before slipping it back into the dark water, where it swept its tail lazily and sunk from sight.

I wiped my left forearm where I was bleeding, cut by the rearward points of its diamond-shaped scales where its slimy body had slid backward in my arms—a memorable demonstration of why these were once used as arrowheads. Then there was the relief all around that we had a film. At 123 pounds and six feet, eight inches long, it was a serious-sized fish and a tangible sign that the species is not done for yet. The only down side was that it had swallowed the hook, so I'd had to cut the leader. This is common in gar fishing, but at least I'd been using a single hook rather than the trebles that are normally used for gar. Furthermore, it appears that the fish survive with this minor irritant, possibly dissolving it with their gastric juices. But even so, I resolved to try circle hooks, instead of conventional J hooks, if I ever return. These are hooks I've been using for a decade now, originally for arapaima, and I've found they practically eliminate the risk of deep hooking. If the line is tightened steadily rather than sharply struck, the turned-in point will pivot and lodge, almost without fail, in the corner of the mouth. But they require a leap of faith for each new species, particularly those with teeth that might grip a leader and prevent its gradual tightening.

On our last fishing day, back with Bubba, I managed to cut myself on the outside of the mouth of a lively three-footer, and I followed this up with a 111-pounder. Also with me in the boat was Mark Spitzer, assistant professor of writing at the University of Central Arkansas and a walking encyclopedia on all things gar as well as a tireless champion of this "very despised, hated fish." He summed up their treatment at the hands of humans thus: "Basically they look scary, and so that led to people just wanting to run them out of town. And so they *were* run out of town." As for the alleged attacks on humans: "Where's the evidence?" There are certainly large gar still around, but there are no reliable recent accounts of them injuring people.

Perhaps there are just too few of them or the reason for the lack of attacks is because the *really* big ones are no longer around. Many books (such as *A History of Fishes* by J. R. Norman) say they can grow to 20 feet, but there's no evidence for this, even though there are fossilized gars that are nearly 15 feet. The current consensus is closer to 10 feet, and there are photos that show fish around this size. Perhaps the best known is one in the archive of the American Museum of Natural History. This photo shows a fish caught from Moon Lake in Mississippi in 1910 lying on a sagging plank between two trestles with a top-hatted man sitting behind it. But the fish is unusually thin and its fins are unnaturally flared. My guess is that this could have been just a skin, opened down the side, which had stretched when it was hung up. And the fins could have simply dried out when set in the spread position. In other words, this was likely an amateurish attempt at taxidermy. We'll never know, but nonetheless, this was certainly a very big fish. Other old pictures show gar strung up in trees, as if lynched. One old picture I've seen has "10½ foot gar, 465 pounds" written on the back. It was caught by a net maker, Fred Miller, when he was testing a net in winter in an oxbow of the Mississippi near Memphis. The gar's tail hangs just above Fred's knees, and the whole front half of its body is above Fred's head. Somehow it doesn't look quite as big as claimed, but that could be because its belly is turned toward the camera, and as a result, we don't see the body's full depth. (It's not unusual for a photo not to do justice to a fish's size.) And the weight-to-length ratio is absolutely plausible, being about the same proportions as my 111-pounder. The man who showed me this picture, whose family knew Fred, told me the Memphis newspapers in the 1950s carried lots of pictures of 100- to 200-pound fish, usually caught on sawn-off pool cues with rotting chicken carcasses. But the biggest gar he ever heard of was never weighed. It got caught in a gillnet his grandfather set in the St. Francis River in the early 1900s and had to be pulled in with the help of a mule and then finished off with a shotgun. For years its scales were used as ashtrays. (I have some scales from a six-footer, discarded on the bank by a bow hunter, that measure just over 1½ inches, so that gives some idea of the size of this other large gar.)

Another man, Bobby Fly, who caught a seven-footer weighing 162½ pounds from Lake Livingstone, told me he's seen a fish twice this length: "I was tied up in the top of a willow tree in a fourteen-foot flat-bottom, and this bad boy came right up beside, and just surfaced right there. And I seen the front of my boat and the back of my boat, and I've seen fish all the way. So I . . . went home to the house. I didn't hang around."

As for rod-caught specimens, the IGFA record is a fish of 279 pounds that a man named Bill Valverde caught from the Rio Grande in West Texas in 1951. But this was surpassed by a nine-foot, six-inch fish, weighing 365 pounds, that was caught by Trinity fishing guide "Capt Kirk" Kirkland in 1991. Since then, well-documented fish over 200 pounds have been caught most years.

Fish of this size are easily big enough to grab and pull in a person, if they were so inclined. So why aren't they still snaffling the occasional child or toe-dangling fisher-boy? For a start, alligator gar only eat prey that they can swallow whole. Compared to a goonch or piraiba, their jaws are narrow, so a human would be beyond them. And they are not like sharks or goliath tigerfish, which can bite pieces out of large animals. That leaves a territorial response: perhaps they're just aggressive, like wels catfish. But I've heard from people who have happily swum with wild seven-foot gator gar and survived unmolested.

To test this myself, I decided to get personal with a couple of two hundred–pounders that live in a pond at the Texas Freshwater Fisheries Center. Seen through the observation window, they looked like mobile sculptures—huge flexing slabs of carved marble. Diving down, I almost bumped into one of them that was lying loglike between some stumps under a floating weedbed. Seen this close, even allowing for the magnification of my mask, its bulk was astounding. You could have put a saddle on it, as the old boys say. I reached out a hand, but it slid away faster than I could follow. I wanted to lie on the bottom and become part of the underwater landscape, but every time I dove, both fish edged away until I had to return gasping to the surface. Once, for a brief second, I ran my hand down a cobbled flank, but I got the feeling my clumsy advances unnerved them, and they wanted to be left alone. Although the encounter left me awestruck, at no time did I feel threatened.

On reflection, though, I think some of those old tales might have a grain of truth. Back in the early 1900s, before houses had running water, fish were commonly gutted and cleaned at the sides of rivers and lakes. And fish of all species would come to feed in such places, associating splashing with food. This is exactly what still happens with piranhas in the Amazon—except with one difference. If a piranha nips you, you lose a piece of finger. But if you get your splashing foot shut in the jaws of a hungry alligator gar, with its five hundred needle-sharp teeth up to an inch long, it's entirely possible that you'll end up in the water or get your leg shredded. But this wouldn't be an intentional "attack." And because of changed living conditions, there's almost zero risk of anything similar happening today.

So it's high time we reevaluated the gator gar and saw it for what it really is: a unique zoological relic that is worthy of our protection—and not just for its own sake either. Perhaps if this misunderstood predator hadn't been extirpated from the Illinois River, the current plague of Asian carp in that waterway would never have happened. So when, on September 1, 2009, shortly after the *River Monsters* gar episode aired in the United States, the state of Texas limited the number of gar that recreational or commercial fishermen can take from the water to one per day, this was indeed momentous news. Previously there had been no protection whatsoever in this last hiding place. Spitzer cites one commercial fisherman who removed 38,200 pounds of gar in 2008, the equivalent of four hundred 100-pounders. Yet people, even some bow hunters, have gradually welcomed the move.

So when I go back, even if that's not for a while, there is a chance that I might encounter one of the real monsters. One man who has contacted me, who I'm not inclined to doubt, saw a very large fish in rather unusual circumstances in a tucked-away corner where nobody goes. I'm being rather vague because, when I get the time, I want to take him up on his invitation to see the place for myself, where he had a clear look at a fish he put at fourteen to sixteen feet long.

Maybe they'll even wait us out, like they did the dinosaurs.

CHAPTER 10

FRESHWATER SHARK

Unique, then, but not beautiful. Its jaw is wider and squarer than any other,
its incisors proportionately more fearsome, its eyes tiny, since sight,
in turbid waters, need not be perfect. And those purblind eyes stalked
this river: steel ball-bearing eyes, set deep in the side of its skull.

Edward Marriott, *Wild Shore*, 2000

MIAMI LAKE WAS NOTHING LIKE I EXPECTED. I had pictured a wild place, fringed with reeds, the houses far from its shore. But Australia's Gold Coast is not like that; instead, it's a high-density development where trimmed lawns go right down to the water. Originally a swamp, the area was developed in the 1950s and now comprises more than 150 miles of canals that are crowded with condos and boat jetties—a supreme embodiment of the popular idea that water is a place of fun and leisure.

Looking at the lake's bright surface, I had difficulty reconciling what I saw with the newspaper reports. They reported that here, in December 2002, a twenty-three-year-old man had gone for a cooling dip at night with a friend and then had disappeared. His body was found three days later, showing the unmistakable marks of a shark attack. From what a lakeside resident told me, the two men had set out to cross a narrow neck where the water is shallow, but in the dark they got separated and the victim strayed into the main body of the lake, where there is a steep drop-off close to the edge. A few weeks later, while locals were still consoling themselves with the fact that this was a freak event, an eighty-four-year-old early-morning swimmer suffered a fatal shark bite to his leg in nearby Burleigh Lake. The police brought in netsmen from Queensland's offshore shark control program, and they then captured three female bull sharks (*Carcharhinus leucas*) ranging from five feet to seven feet, four inches, but none contained any human remains.

From Miami Lake to the sea, by way of the canals, is about ten miles. Although inland, the waterways are tidal, but sluice gates partially restrain the outgoing tide in order to prevent the picturesque green borders from extending to mud. When the sluices are open, however, any fish with a body up to four feet deep could, in theory, pass through. Authorities reckon there are hundreds of bull sharks in the canals. In fact, one man fishes for them from the balcony of his sixth-floor apartment, overlooking Lake Orr. He says in eighteen months he has caught twelve and lost around eighty. To land them, he sends his friend running downstairs with a gaff.

Normally we don't need a physical barrier to prevent sea fish from moving inland. The transition from salt to fresh water is a barrier in itself, as secure as any metal grill. This is because, in order to take up oxygen, fish have a convoluted expanse of thin membrane, the gills, in intimate contact with the surrounding water. But this semipermeable membrane (whose microscopic pores allow the passage of small molecules but not large ones such as salts) also allows the passage of water. The direction of this movement depends on whether the surrounding water is more or less salty than the fish's tissue fluids. In fresh water, water molecules diffuse inward; in sea water they diffuse outward. For this reason, freshwater and sea fish have fundamentally different strategies for keeping their body fluids at the correct concentration. Freshwater fish must constantly excrete the surplus water they take in; sea fish must constantly replace lost water by drinking. (The salt contained in the seawater that sea fish drink is actively removed from the body by special cells in the gills.)

A freshwater fish dropped in the sea would, therefore, experience runaway water loss, whereas a sea fish placed in fresh water would become waterlogged, its cells exploding from increased osmotic pressure.

Even brackish water, the zone where the water is neither fresh nor salt, is uncomfortable for most fish. Most sea fish can't tolerate the half-and-half mixture of salt and fresh that sluices the inland waterways of the Gold Coast. So the presence of sharks here appears to offend the laws of nature as well as our sensibilities. In fact, sharks are the last sea fish you would expect to find inland because their tissue fluids are even more concentrated than those of other fish. This is because they retain certain waste products in the body, specifically urea and trimethylamine oxide (TMAO), to the point at which their bodies are marginally more "salty" than the surrounding sea water. This allows water to gently diffuse in, with low-level excretion removing any surplus. This increased internal saltiness is a near-perfect adaptation to living in the sea, but a shark transferred to fresh water would experience an even greater shock to the system than its less well-adapted marine brethren: an inrush of water that would demand very high-volume excretion to counteract it—like frantically baling a holed boat to stop it from going under.

So how do bull sharks manage to break the rules? And they're not just in the Gold Coast canals but also in estuaries and rivers worldwide where these are accessible from the warm coastal shallows where bull sharks are normally found. In 1993 I wandered into a gloomy shop in Manaus, where the Rio Negro meets the Amazon, looking for rope and tarpaulins. Hanging from the ceiling were several stuffed fish, dark brown with age and varnish, the biggest of which, thick bodied and seven feet long, I at first took to be a piraiba, the Amazon's giant catfish. The general body shape was about right, but closer inspection revealed an asymmetric tail and five parallel gill slits. The shop's owner told me that one of his employees, now dead, caught it from a spot just downriver. This bull shark had been nine hundred miles from the sea, and there are other reports from near Iquitos, in Peru, more than two thousand miles inland. A fisherman I met later told me he'd caught four or five in the '60s and '70s on long lines set for catfish. Another man told me he'd seen one in the '80s when he was working at the fish-freezing plant in Iranduba near Manaus, where many fishing boats unload their catch. "They called everyone to see it. It had no scales, like a catfish," he said. "When you moved your hand down its body toward the tail, it was smooth. But in the other direction it was rough, like a file."

More recently, in a bar in Zambia, I saw some jaws with broad-based serrated teeth in the upper jaw (for cutting, like steak knives) and narrower, more pointed teeth in the lower jaw (for gripping). People originally thought the "Zambezi shark" was an endemic species, but now we recognize it as the same species as the Ganges shark and the Lake Nicaragua shark, not to mention the bull sharks that have been found in US rivers. These include an eighty-four-pounder that two commercial fishermen, Herbert Cope and Dudge Collins, from Alton, Illinois, caught in 1937 1,750 miles up the Mississippi. Something had been chewing through their wood-and-mesh fish traps, so they set a wire one baited with chicken guts. Although some dismissed this as a hoax, this catch is now widely considered to be authentic, although bull sharks would now find dams blocking their way. In addition, three of the five notorious Jersey Shore attacks of 1916, which inspired Peter Benchley's 1974 novel *Jaws* and the subsequent Spielberg film, were likely the work of bull sharks, not a rogue great white as originally concluded. Even though the attacks stopped after the capture of an eight-foot great white in Raritan Bay, reportedly with human remains in its stomach, the last three attacks were up the narrow Matawan Creek, which would be a very unusual habitat for a great white. And subsequent newspaper stories refer to other sharks seen and captured in the creek after the alleged culprit was killed. More recently, a reported attack in Lake Michigan was almost certainly a hoax, but they have been reliably identified in inland Louisiana.

The fact that the very shark species that swims into rivers just happens to be the one that's the most dangerous to humans, more so than hammerheads, tiger sharks, and even great whites, appears to be a very cruel irony. But this is no coincidence: the reason bull sharks have attacked more people than other sharks is precisely because they live so close to humans in shallow coastal waters, estuaries, and sometimes rivers. Compared with where other sharks live, this water is often murky, so identifying objects or other animals is difficult for their small eyes. Not having hands, fish often feel with their mouths. Rory McGuinness, our cameraman on this shoot, once had his kayak bumped by a bull shark while he was paddling in the Gold Coast canals. So the bull shark's "aggression" is likely sometimes simply curiosity or even self-defense when a swimmer inadvertently gets too close, although this doesn't make them any less dangerous.

The bull shark's ability to penetrate fresh water is thanks to a quirk of physiology that is unique among large sharks. When entering fresh water, bull sharks are able to reduce the saltiness of their tissue fluids by about a third. They do this partly by excreting salt via their rectal gland. Studies have also found that the concentration of urea in their tissues drops by more than 50 percent. Despite this, however, their body fluids are still more than twice as salty as those of typical freshwater fish, so they need to increase their rate of excretion to get rid of surplus water. Experiments suggest that they excrete more than twenty times the volume of water than they do when in the sea. This increased work-load on the kidneys requires the expenditure of more energy, so by the mathematics of biological accounting, which all creatures unconsciously carry out, there must be some benefit to offset this cost in order to make moving into fresh water worthwhile. The question is: what?

One advantage of fresh water is fewer predators, especially other shark species, to prey on bull shark pups. This tallies with the fact that river mouths and estuaries tend to be used as bull shark nurseries. The choice of estuaries, rather than completely fresh water, is interesting and is probably a compromise based on a weighing of pros and cons. Despite the bull shark's tolerance of fresh water, small bull sharks have a harder time in a river, water balance—wise, than large bull sharks. This is thanks to the geometry of growth: small animals have a higher surface area to volume ratio than their larger brethren. And with more surface area per unit of body mass, they take in water more readily and hence need to get rid of it faster. So stick to the estuary, where predators are few and energy costs are not too high—the ideal combination.

But why *adult* bull sharks, apart from gravid females, are in rivers is less certain. Maybe it's simply because they can, and they wander back and forth on a whim. The biggest bull sharks I'd heard of in this part of Australia were in the Brisbane River, further north up the coast. In 2007 Terry Hessey caught a nine-foot, six-inch specimen at the mouth of the river, which pulled 440-pound scales to their limit and was estimated at well over 500 pounds. This was identified as a gravid female by virtue of its distended abdomen (adding to the general stockiness, which gives the bull shark its name) and the absence of penislike claspers on the underside of the body.

The bull shark pups, up to a dozen of them, are born a year after fertilization. Shark scientist Dr. Richard Pillans estimates that there are two to five thousand juvenile sharks in the Brisbane River—so many, in fact, that local anglers hold an annual shark-fishing competition. Terry caught his monster during this event. And although I'd seen a picture of this fish, beached in tidal shallows, I needed to see one in the flesh. Despite knowing about the bull shark's osmoregulatory bag of tricks, the idea of a shark in a river was still something to get used to, as it is for most people.

So I met up with Terry and his fishing buddy Ben Cole at a place called Luggage Point, which even at night has to be one of the least picturesque fishing spots I've ever been to, although this in itself makes it stand out in the memory. The place is known informally as the "poop shoot" because it is the site of a huge sewage treatment plant that perfumes the air and the intertidal mud. But fish have different sensibilities from humans, and the peculiar water quality here likely attracts them, from small bottom feeders right up the food chain. Terry had gotten a hold of a couple of good-sized freshwater eels, about as thick as my wrist and three feet long, which are a favorite meal of bull sharks, along with stingrays. Bull sharks are mainly bottom feeders, and because they often feed in cloudy water, they don't rely much on eyesight to find food—hence their small eyes. But they are far from blind in the water thanks to a sixth sense that humans don't possess. On a bull shark's snout are pores known as the ampullae of Lorenzini, which are sensitive to minute electrical currents, such as those produced within the body of a prey animal. The effectiveness of this sense has been most clearly demonstrated in hammerheads, which sweep their ampullae-rich heads over the bottom like a metal detector, locating buried stingrays that are otherwise invisible.

But this super sense makes things difficult for shark anglers because metal leaders, crimps, and hooks create electrical microcurrents, thus advertising their presence in the water. In an attempt to make his leader invisible to bull sharks, Terry was using PVC-coated wire rope as leader material, the thickness of washing line and with a breaking strain of 1,300 pounds for bite-resistance. He wrapped the hooks with plastic insulating tape, except for the very points, which he gave a final few strokes of the file before rigging the baits—a small touch that marked Terry as somebody who knew what he was doing. Bait rigging was equally meticulous, with cable ties holding the 16/0 hooks firmly in position with their points well exposed. Meanwhile Ben was filling a large cloth bag with several pounds of sand and tying it closed with a length of 40-pound mono, which was then tied to the swivel at the top end of the leader. Casting this assemblage of weighted metalware was of course out of the question, so Terry now hopped into his kayak with the bait and sandbag and set off toward the brightly lit wharves, cranes, and moored ships on the other side. After a few moments we lost sight of him, but the big reel continued to spin out line, about two hundred yards of it, until it went quiet and we saw a light flash out on the water. Then the reel's clicker made a final rasp as the sandbag plummeted to the bottom. As Terry returned, we slowly tightened the line, taking up the slack until the rod, vertical in its metal holder, took on a slight bend at the tip. Then the drag was engaged, just enough to counter the push of water but no more, and the trap was set. After repeating the procedure with a second rod, we settled in to wait.

Above the drone of the mosquitoes, which continued to fly despite the breeze coming off the water, Terry told me how he'd nearly not landed his big shark. The line had gotten snagged on the drop-off that runs parallel to the bank, and he had to wade out in the dark to free it. After hearing this, I was almost relieved when dawn arrived with the reels still silent. Terry and Ben had to go to work, and they weren't sure when they could manage another session. Getting good, fresh bait was also going to be a problem, as was coinciding with an incoming tide. So in the meantime I decided to follow the river upstream, past the high-rises of downtown and the southwestern suburbs to Kookaburra Park, some fifty miles away as the shark swims. Here I trundled into a small car park and walked a short distance over grass to a steep bank. I baited with dead sprat and didn't have long to wait before something snatched at the line. But nothing else happened, and I eventually retrieved to find a bare hook. This happened a few times before I finally connected, only to find that the culprit was a foot-long catfish. My next trip was the same story. Then some local anglers told me the secret: live mullet at night. They also said some people eat the small sharks from here because they're tastier than sharks from the sea. This squares with the lower urea levels of sharks in fresh water (which in a dead shark is broken down by bacteria to form ammonia), so I judged their tip to be reliable.

Getting the mullet was a mission in itself. First, I had to master the art of throw-net fishing, a method I'd steered clear of until now. I'd had a couple of lessons from Amazon fishermen, who hold part of the lead-weighted margin in their teeth and release this by opening their mouth at the correct moment. It's all about timing, said my toothless instructors. But the Australian method, I was pleased to discover, doesn't involve teeth, although otherwise it's very similar, particularly the novice's tendency to land the net in a tightly knotted clump. Eventually I got the hang of it and found a place where I could catch bait, returning, then, with greater anticipation.

The water here is still tidal, rising and falling a good few feet. I arrived at dusk, some hours before high tide, which I'd heard is when there's the greatest chance. But rather than wait, I lip-hooked a small mullet and swung it out on a running lead. Maybe it's because I wasn't expecting anything to happen and wasn't mentally in hunting mode that the spool was suddenly whining. I picked up the rod and tightened the line—not a sweeping strike, as I was using a circle hook—and immediately knew this was a shark. Its reaction on the line was different from any fish I'd caught before: dashing in all directions seemingly at once, including straight toward me, when I struggled to maintain contact. I took some time to get the initiative; then it was a case of judging when to grab it. If I left it too long, it would have a hard time recovering; if I tried too soon, it might still be too much of a handful. I was using a short, one hundred–pound wire leader and eighty-pound braided line, which was amply strong enough to ease the shark onto the shelving mud, where I grabbed it behind the head with one hand and then ran with it up to the grass. I could feel its body tense and flex—a different feel from other fish, possibly because of its different anatomy: the more flexible skeleton made from cartilage not bone and the muscles attaching to the inside of the thick skin, which forms a kind of exoskeleton. It was about ten pounds and thirty inches long. I couldn't look at it for too long, but even though I had it in my hands, it still seemed so incongruous: a shark from a river, about the width of the Thames at Henley, and not that different looking either.

But how much further up did they go? I'd heard a story about a thousand-pound racehorse that had been attacked in the water another thirty miles upstream, and I was curious to know the details. The horse's trainer, Alan Treadwell, witnessed the incident while he was swimming the horse back and forth across the river as part of its training program. Alan had bought the horse, Glen Burns Arm, at a bargain price because of an injury that had supposedly finished the horse's career. But Alan's novel training methods had given it a new lease on life, and it had started winning again. On this day, March 23, 2005, Alan as usual attached a half-inch rope to the horse's halter and then kept abreast of it as it swam by walking along the footway of the road bridge above. The horse was nearly halfway across when, for no apparent reason, it started to flail and sink. "The horse looks like it's going to drown," said Alan. "All of a sudden I saw something hanging off the back of him. As the horse rolled over, the color lightened, and it went to white underneath, whatever it was."

Alan ran to the shore and, together with his stable hand, heaved the horse out of the eleven-foot-deep hole below the bridge. "If we hadn't got him out, I don't think he would have survived," he said.

From the vet's photographs, I saw that Glen Burns Arm had a single crescent-shaped cut on his right flank, with five or six broad tooth marks visible, together with parallel scratches about an inch apart, as if made by teeth that had skidded across the flat hide and failed to penetrate. When I showed the picture to Vic Peddemors, who heads shark research for the New South Wales state government, he declared it was definitely a shark bite. From the orientation of the wound, which ran vertically not horizontally, it appeared that the shark must have turned partially on its side when it attacked, and just the broad-based serrated teeth of the upper jaw, rather than both sets, had penetrated.

From the gentle curvature of the wound, Vic deduced the front teeth of quite a large shark inflicted it, but the shark had been unable to take a bigger mouthful because of the horse's bulk. This tallies perfectly with what we know about bull shark physiology: that larger ones cope more easily in fresh water than small ones. And this was totally fresh water, as I had verified with a salinity meter. But Vic was then visibly shocked when he compared the tooth spacing with a bull shark jaw in his collection and found an almost perfect match. His reference jaws came from a shark nine feet long.

The case seemed open-and-shut, apart from one thing. Five miles down from this bridge is Mount Crosby weir, a twelve-foot step in the river's water level and a barrier that would block the way upstream to any fish. Maybe something else was responsible, something that can circumvent weirs. The only other large aquatic predator in Australian waters is the saltwater crocodile. However, the official limit of the saltie's range is some three hundred miles north, although isolated individuals have been reported well south of this in the past. But then again, crocodiles have to breathe air and haul out of the water to warm their bodies, so you'd expect to hear of other sightings.

Things didn't add up. But then came a piece of information that solved the puzzle. Over the years the Brisbane River has occasionally burst its banks. The biggest recent flood before 2011 was in 1974, when archive photos show the water below Mount Crosby weir at the same level as it is above. Information about shark lifespan is incomplete, but the FishBase website quotes thirty-two years for bull sharks. So it's conceivable that a juvenile swam upstream in the floods and has been there ever since—and very likely not just one.

You can't help wondering what might have happened to a human, a fraction of a horse's size, if they'd gone swimming there that day. This isn't just idle speculation. This place is a popular swimming hole, right next to the road with a convenient parking lot, deep water next to a clean bank, and a bridge from which the more adventurous can jump. And when I was there in early 2009, four years after the attack, there was a total absence of any warning notices.

Sharks are an emotive subject. Unlike most of the other predators in this book, they claim victims from the developed world, people with verifiable names, grieving families, and backgrounds similar to our own. When this program aired, it was one of the few that prompted negative comment. I received a couple of e-mails accusing me of demonizing sharks. Why draw attention to these attacks? Sharks get bad enough press anyway, they said. A couple of others asked why I returned the sharks I caught to the river if they might potentially attack people. Surely this was irresponsible. Both these views miss the point.

Yes, the stereotypical image of sharks is indeed incorrect. They are not the ruthless exterminators of popular imagination—but neither are they benign and cuddly. Some sharks do attack and kill people. Ignoring this fact won't make it go away. In fact, ignoring it will help to ensure that it continues to happen, which will help to keep alive the ignorant antishark mentality that these would-be conservationists claim to be fighting. People are right to be afraid of sharks. What's important is what they do with this fear, which brings us to the second objection.

Killing what you are afraid of is not the answer. In fact, as my next bull shark encounter would make very clear, trying to do so may even make matters worse. No, the answer lies in understanding the predator—not in some wishy-washy, metaphorical head-patting sense, but instead in terms of its biology, *why* it does what it does. Then we can adapt our behavior accordingly. In the case of bull sharks, not everybody knows that they can come into fresh water. For most of us this is academic, but for those living in the risk areas, this could be a matter of life and death. If bull sharks are present in significant numbers, then humans should not get in the water, particularly between dusk and dawn when bull sharks tend to be most active. Another wise precaution, in the bull shark's range, is not to swim in river mouths, especially after rain, which flushes extra food into the water.

It's a question of being informed and taking basic precautions. Shark "attacks" are actually very rare—some seventy to one hundred worldwide each year, of which about ten are fatal. In fact, they mostly make the news because they are unexpected. Just before we returned home from this shoot, a navy diver lost a hand and a leg to a nine-foot bull shark in Sydney harbor.

Meanwhile, back at Luggage Point for a few more night sessions, my baits stayed untouched. Or rather, sharks didn't touch them. I did hook something, though, in a part of the river that had recently been dredged. But the back-breaking weight felt strangely inert. Terry and Ben ran down the mud beach with flashlights to see what was on the line, and their reaction, on the filmed recording of the event, was a series of electronic bleeps. With its cavernous, diver-swallowing mouth (so they say) and crest of nail-like spines down its back, it needed all three of us to lift it—and even more of an effort to take it in mentally. It was a six-foot giant grouper (*Epinephelus lanceolatus*), or as they call it here, a Queensland groper, normally an inhabitant of reefs and the last thing anyone would expect to find here.

In some ways I was disappointed that it wasn't a shark, but then it occurred to me that this fish, with its angry stare and mosaic flanks, was, in its own way, an answer: a graphic embodiment of the unexpected. But nowhere near as unexpected as the behavior of the next bull sharks I encountered.

CHAPTER 11

RIVER STINGRAY

The tail is whipped forwards in a curve with the sting pointing to
the area of body contact. The sting easily penetrates rubber boots
and is powerful enough to be driven into wood.

Michael Goulding, *Amazon: The Flooded Forest,* 1989

THE DATE IS AUGUST 1993, and we are at Lago Grande again, the remote
lake near José's hut in the floodplain of the Rio Purus. I've beached my
wooden canoe on the central island, in one of the few places where getting out on the shore is possible; everywhere else is either knee-deep
mud or jungle right down to the water. But my relief at being able to
get the circulation back into my buttocks is short lived. Although this
is the dry season, with the water level near the bottom of its annual
forty- to fifty-foot flood cycle, a storm has swept in and is blasting the
lake's surface.

I have two lines out, each baited with a dead piranha, half-pound
red-bellies, lying on the bottom. The lines twitch and shudder from the
impact of the raindrops, as distinct from the sharp continuous jumping
followed by stillness that signals the attentions of other piranhas, so I
resist the urge to check the baits. I picture them down there in the
gloom: luminous silvery shapes reflecting the weak light from their
small scales.

I saw an arapaima breach here yesterday, and for once I have half-
decent baits, rather than bare hooks, well placed to intercept it. I try to
ignore my rain-soaked clothes and the chill that is starting to seep into
my body, instead entering that mental state outside normal time in

which everything contracts to one endless still moment. The rain on the water is like the roar of radio static, and plump droplets slide down the line, which, I now notice, is slowly spooling off the reel.

I pick up the rod and tighten into something heavy, which responds by wrenching the rod and ripping line from the reel. At length it slows and stops, becoming immobile. Just as I'm wondering if it's snagged, it runs again, parallel to the bank. The sidestrain I'm applying doesn't seem to affect its course, and its movement is strangely smooth. This doesn't feel like a fish at all: there's no sense of a tail beating—just long glides interspersed by immobility. Gradually I shorten the line, whose angle now tells me the creature is coming up. I feel a repeated jarring, then there's a boil on the surface—not a swirl but a compact eruption. Then a repulsive warty limb emerges into the air, flailing from side to side behind a wall of spray. Halfway along its tapering brown length my eyes fix on the blurred shape of a four-inch blade: stingray.

The stingray is an animal that, until now, I've known only by reputation. But I know enough to be aware that they're potentially lethal. This notoriety goes way back to the story of Odysseus, who was killed by a spear tipped with a stingray spine, thus fulfilling the prophecy that his death would come "from the sea."

I'm momentarily transfixed, torn between curiosity and fear. I can pull it up the gently sloping mud bank, but then what? Already thought is lagging behind events, as the blotchy brown mass slides up wet mud toward me, its amorphous margins flowing into the craters left by retreating feet. In the center of the yard-wide disc is a raised turret where two eyes open and close, flashing black. And it's *bellowing*. A loud rhythmic sound that is at first inexplicable until I realize that those blinking eyes are its spiracles, now sucking in air instead of water, which it is pumping out via the gill slits on its underside. And all the while it brandishes that blade, stabbing the air like a scorpion. I reach behind me for my machete and cut through the tail at its root. Then I hack into the region that I take to be its head. The flesh is jellylike on a frame of gristle. Already I feel sick and ashamed at what I have done: the instinctive, unthinking response to fear—and a frightening reminder of what lurks inside all of us when we feel threatened. Next—so predictable—come the excuses. I remind myself that I'm fishing, some of the time, for food. And that, unavoidably, means killing my catch. But that wasn't why I killed this fish. Then, something fluttering in the water catches my attention. It's a saucer-sized miniature of the beached mother, a translucent baby stingray still with its yolk sac. There are three others the same size, one of which is stranded on the mud. I lift it into the water with the flat of the machete, but doubt any of them will survive, having been expelled before full term.

When I present the fish to José back at his hut, he snorts in disgust. "*Arraia!* I don't even feed those things to the dogs!"

The normal response to a ray on the line, it turns out, is the same as mine. If its sting hits you, locals told me, you won't walk for a month. If you can't get to a hospital, folk wisdom decrees you should get somebody to urinate on your leg. For the remedy to work best, it's apparently best administered by a member of the opposite sex, ideally a virgin, although locals cheerfully admit this is even less likely than finding a fully kitted A&E department around the next river bend. All in all, these alien invaders from the sea are more feared than piranhas, and I didn't see anybody ever go near a live one, apart from one fisherman who gently disentangled a ten-pounder from his net and let it fall, alive and unharmed, back into the water. I took to avoiding them by not fishing bottom baits in areas where I knew they were. Those I did catch I flipped onto their backs and then unhooked with a stick. And I learned that if you do have to wade, you do the stingray shuffle: sliding your feet forward rather than lifting them and planting them down. Rays don't like being stepped on, even if it's accidental, and will respond to this as if under attack.

But what are they doing here so far from any ocean? Like some shark species, especially bull sharks, some rays have the ability to reduce the concentration of solutes in their bodies, which allows them to swim into fresh water—albeit at the cost of having to pee twenty times as much as they do in the ocean. But these Amazon rays didn't swim here from the Atlantic. Their closest marine relatives are in the Pacific. This only makes sense in the context of the continent's geological history. Originally the Amazon flowed west to the Pacific until the rising of the Andes blocked its exit, thus creating a vast area of lake and swamp. A couple of million years later, the water breached the highlands in the east and the basin drained into the Atlantic, thereby creating the river mouth that exists today. By this time the rays, trapped in fresh water, had lost the ability to vary their tissue fluid concentration. So if you put an Amazon stingray in the sea, it would die. They have become true freshwater fish.

And the rivers and lakes are full of them. They are particularly abundant in shallow water—river beaches and the bays and margins of lakes—where they are the largest predatory fish. There's one muddy bay in Lago Grande where I wouldn't wade for any amount of money. But the spine is purely for defense; it is not used to attack prey. One evening, when fishing from a canoe, I spotted something moving in the extreme margin in mere inches of water. For several minutes, in the gloom, I couldn't work out what it was. It was a glistening hump, moving with smooth stealth and occasionally appearing to pounce. Peering more closely, I thought I could see black eyes, and I realized this was a stingray hunting small fish. Another time, I observed one in a small stream, throwing itself like a blanket over something too small for me to see and then wriggling its body forward to manipulate the prey into its mouth to be crushed by its multiple rows of small teeth like flexible, uneven paving. This ability to hunt the extreme shallows, which are off-limits to other predatory fish, is clearly key to their success, along with the fact that they are the only sizeable fish that fishermen leave alone. They commonly hunt at night, and often in very cloudy water, which raises the question of how they detect prey, considering that their small eyes sit in the middle of the body on the opposite surface from the mouth. Like their marine cousins, they have scattered ampullae of Lorenzini to detect the electrical aura of small creatures buried in the bottom mud, but with fresh water being a poor conductor, these have very limited sensitivity. Certainly smell plays a part, as a bait of dead fish will too often attract a ray, and doubtless vibration too. At any rate,

THE AMAZON LAKE MONSTER that nobody believed was real, including me—until I took this picture. This is the reason I don't automatically dismiss other fishermen's tales.

IN MY EARLY TWENTIES I was an obsessive carp angler, escaping whenever possible to camp beside English lakes.

THERE'S MORE TO some fish than meets the eye. Carp have powerful teeth in the back of the throat that would crush a finger just as soon as a snail shell.

A FIFTY-EIGHT-POUND MAHSEER, which dragged me down rapids on the Kaveri River in South India on my thirtieth birthday. Local handline fishermen have been nearly drowned.

IN ZAIRE (now Democratic Republic of Congo) in 1985 I traveled on one of the legendary giant riverboats— with two thousand other passengers, uncounted stowaways and secret policemen, and trussed live crocodiles.

ZAIRE VILLAGE CHILDREN show me a standard-issue, striped (not goliath) tigerfish. Its feared larger cousin, they told me, can almost bite a person in half.

LEFT: **PEOPLE'S REPUBLIC OF CONGO,** 1990. When I took this picture I was incubating a near-fatal dose of malaria.

BATTLING WITH SOMETHING that grabbed a ten-inch piranha. Something about that compact eruption tells me it's not made by a normal fish.

FIRST AMAZON EXPEDITION, 1993. Fishing from the island on Lago Grande. Plank-built canoes are precarious in bad weather.

MY FIRST TEACHER of Amazon jungle-craft. Hard-as-nails José fishing with gillnets on Lago Grande.

BECAUSE OF THEIR GREAT WEIGHT, fishermen butcher arapaima at the lakeside. Mostly you just see their huge, kipperlike fillets.

FISHERMEN SELLING THEIR CATCH on the waterfront at Manaus. The amount of commercial fishing in the Amazon truly shocked me.

IN MOST OF BRAZIL, fishing for arapaima is now banned, but river people have few other sources of cash. The man on the left became a body-guard for the town mayor and was wounded by shrapnel in an assassination attempt.

THE LAST-GASP ARAPAIMA caught on my *Jun Hooks* shoot, using neither rod nor reel. From painful experience I know this fish can be ve dangerous indeed, but in an unexpected way

REVISITING THE SCENE of my Amazon plane crash. Only weeks later did I realize how close I'd come to dying.

THE FISH THAT HIMALAYAN VILLAGERS say is a man-eater. My capture of this 161-pound goonch, after plunging after it into monsoon floodwater, gave weight to their stories.

BREATH-HOLD DIVING IN UNDERWATER CAVES in a cold, cloudy Himalayan river with trailing poachers' lines was not my idea of fun. But we did, eventually, get the first-ever footage of goonch in their natural habitat.

THIS *CUIU-CUIU* **OR "RIPSAW CATFISH"** was a rare catch. But this armor didn't stop a piranha from taking a mouthful out of its back on the way to the boat.

THE BUSINESS END OF A PIRAIBA, one of two catfish species that Amazon fishermen say have swallowed people whole.

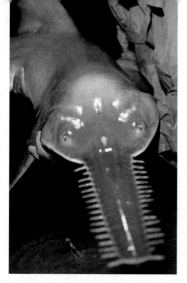

WITH A CHAINSAW-LIKE SNOUT on a shark's body, sawfish require careful handling.

LIKE AN ALLIGATOR WITH FINS. But is the much-maligned alligator gar as dangerous as it looks? And how reliable are the reports of fourteen-footers?

GIANT GROUPERS have been known to attack divers by grabbing arms, legs, and, even once, a man's head. But this 250-pounder from a river surprised even local fishery experts.

BLEARY-EYED DAYBREAK ON THE BRISBANE RIVER.
Not such a good time for darkness-loving
bull sharks, but at least you can tell if
that's an oil tanker you just hooked.

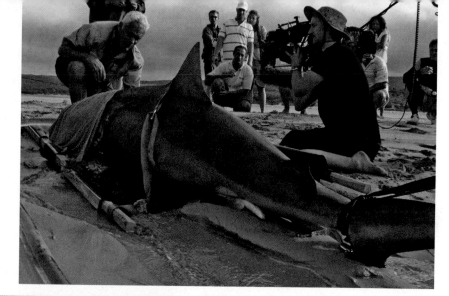

AT NINE FEET, EIGHT INCHES long and weighing five hundred pounds, this is one of the biggest male bull sharks (note the "clasper") ever seen anywhere. What was it doing in a river?

A BULL SHARK made short work of this leg-sized kob in South Africa's Breede River. They also check out people—but why aren't the Breede sharks man-eaters?

THIS FISH HAS SMALL TEETH and very little muscle, but touch it and you could die. Hence the protective clothing.

GET STABBED BY THIS SPINE, with its coating of toxic slime, and the pain is like holding your foot in a fire. Death can follow from gangrene or blood loss.

CAUGHT WITH A LINE BUT NO HOOK, the longfin eel is an unlikely man-eater—until you piece together its grisly modus operandi.

THE TWO THOUSAND–MILE RIO PURUS was my second home for nearly ten years. On its way to join the Amazon, the Purus is a confusion of bends and hidden backwater lakes. Annual floods raise the water level by up to fifty feet.

THE DJOUÉ RAPIDS, where the Congo River squeezes down to just 1,200 yards. Further downstream it's 350 yards. Surely an insane place to cast a line.

"HE CRIED IN A WHISPER at some image, at some vision . . . 'The horror! The horror!'" (Joseph Conrad, *Heart of Darkness,* 1902).

THE FISH THAT TOOK TWENTY-FIVE YEARS to catch.

the desensitizing of their electrical sense hasn't proved to be an undue handicap.

I've also had the opportunity to see rays up close through a dive mask, ten feet down in a crystal-clear lagoon beside the Rio Teles Pires in the south of the Amazon basin. In this aquarium-like setting, fed by springs bubbling up through white sand, I watched the rays glide and scuttle, powered by the graceful undulations of their flexible body margins, where the radiating rods of stiffening cartilage are clearly visible.

In such surroundings, you get a sense of how pretty their blotched body patterns can be and even start to appreciate why some aquarists want to keep them as pets. Even the most common of the twenty-plus species, *Potamotrygon motoro*, the ocellate stingray, resembles a hypnotic galaxy of dancing suns.

Some specimens are also among the biggest fish in the Amazon. In December 2000 US fishing writer Keith "Catfish" Sutton caught a discus stingray (*Paratrygon aiereba*), measuring six feet, two inches across and weighing 116 pounds, 2 ounces, where the Rio Branco flows into the Rio Negro, two hundred miles northwest of Manaus, and he also saw a bigger one the previous January, perhaps seven or eight feet across. In Peru there is talk of rays nearly ten feet across. In 2001 I watched from the comfort of a hammock in a wooden fishing boat as my friend John Petchey was reduced to a physical wreck by something he hooked downstream from Ilha Arraia (Stingray Island) in the Rio Solimões. After breaking John's reel, this stingray finally allowed our skipper Josimar to grab it through the spiracles and haul it aboard our jumbo-sized canoe. This was also a discus ray, sandy-colored and a near-perfect circle, with a tiny afterthought of a stingless tail and a body pattern like cells seen under a microscope. We returned it unweighed, but I guessed 80 pounds. I've also seen a couple of solid-bodied 100-pounders from the Rio Purus that were caught on handlines.

But recently I've learned that these are not the biggest stingrays in fresh water. In 2008 I heard reports of giant whiprays (so called because of their extremely long tails, sometimes more than twice the body length) being caught in Thailand, from the Maeklong (not to be confused with Mekong), and Ban Pakong rivers. These fish were so massive that some people are now claiming this species, *Himantura chaophraya*, is the biggest freshwater fish in the world. Although Thai fishermen have doubtless known about this fish for generations, scientists only formally described it and gave it a scientific name (the Chao Phraya is the river running through Bangkok) in 1989. This was on the basis of just three specimens, which is either an indication of their rarity or the difficulty of catching them, or both. Now a group of scientists from Chulalongkorn University, working with British ex-pat angler Rick Humphreys and a team of Thai fishermen, is trying to fill in all the gaps in our knowledge. By means of tags and a growing database, they hope to find out its growth rate, maximum dimensions, population size, and distribution—as well as the chemical make-up and mode of action of the black viscous venom coating its barb.

Thailand is a well-trodden holiday destination, popular with backpackers, scuba divers, sex tourists, and affluent sun-seekers. But I was nervous about going there. After my first foreign fishing trip, to India in 1982, I had managed to get a couple of articles published in fishing magazines, and I was digging around for another destination and another fish story. The articles paid £40 and £25, which admittedly didn't go far toward repaying my £285 air ticket and £160 travel costs (especially as I've yet to receive the latter fee). But suddenly, at age twenty-six, I had a glimmer of a possible direction in life. I had visions of my writing making other trips possible and, maybe—who knows?—even turning a profit. What I really needed to get things moving was a *big* story. I recalled an old picture I had seen in a textbook in the zoology department library at Bristol University. It showed an Asian man in a coolie hat peeping over the top of a huge smooth-skinned fish: deep-bodied, blunt-headed, and with a tail that looked a yard wide. At first I thought the creature was blind, a monstrous cave-dweller perhaps, until I noticed its eye low down near the corner of its mouth. The accompanying text said it was a Mekong giant catfish (although I could see no barbels). When I first saw that picture, the fish's home was a war zone. But when I called it to mind again, the Vietnam conflict had been over for nearly a decade. I started scouring the London "bucket shops" for a discounted flight and found what I wanted with Tarom, the Romanian airline. A couple of months later, in March 1984, I arrived in Bangkok.

In the meantime I'd found out a little more about my quarry. Unlike most catfish, the Mekong giant catfish, known as *pla buk* in Thailand, is a vegetarian that feeds on algae. No one has ever caught a noncaptive specimen on a line. Rather than being discouraged by this, I saw this as my story. I would be the first, possibly using some kind of stinky mashed paste bait of the kind I'd used to tempt carp, which is also normally a feeder on tiny food items but catchable if you know how.

I headed for the northeast of the country, where the Mekong forms the border between Thailand and Laos. Because many countries are sensitive about their borders, I did the rounds of fisheries stations and obtained a letter of introduction explaining what I was doing. On top of that, a helpful English speaker checked me in with the border patrol police who, as if this were the custom at police stations throughout the world, invited me to stay. Their sleepy outpost was right next to the river, and they seemed to enjoy the novelty of a foreigner in their midst, patiently setting about trying to teach me Thai. But my inability to repeat even simple words with the right tones (low, mid, rising, high, falling) in the right places had them puzzled. If even infants and halfwits could cope with this exercise, why did this foreigner insist on coming back with made-up nonsense words or completely different words entirely?

"*Ngaw.*" This was my allotted minder-cum-guide, an athletic cheerful man in his mid-twenties.

Me: "*Ngaw.*"

There were concerned shaking heads all round, but also encouragement to have another go. But still I kept getting it wrong. Then, on maybe the twentieth attempt, people were clutching their stomachs, slapping each other's backs and wiping away tears. When they finally calmed down, they tried to explain to me, in nasal sing-songy Thai, that I'd just said (starting to giggle again) something that sounded like *ngaw.*

My fishing, meanwhile, was meeting the same level of success. At the nearby gorge, fishing a slow, deep, silver spoon, I quickly found myself with a bent rod as I hooked one of the countless nets and long-lines that were strung across the water. Even a hook dropped at my feet got snagged. So, instead, I went with a local fisherman in his leaky canoe, retrieving a longline that had been out overnight. He'd put out a hundred hooks, baited with grasshopper, but not a single one had a fish. I met a pla buk fisherman who showed me his nets, with meshes so wide that I could have squeezed through them. But he rarely put them out now because hardly any fish were left. I started to realize that my quest was turning into a failure.

So when my hosts invited me to an evening of Thai boxing at the nearby town, I happily went along. I was given a front-row seat next to a bespectacled man who spoke some English and kept ordering me bottles of beer. He turned out to be the District Officer paying a visit, and I was told I'd be spending the night at the town's police HQ. I was shown to an upstairs office, where I slept with an armed policeman beside me, and in the morning the man continued to ply me with beer and questions. Most of these seemed designed to uncover my political views, but I kept my replies noncommittal. He also said, many times, "You could disappear here—nobody would know." I took this to be concern for my well-being, so I told him I'd be careful, but this didn't seem to be the response he wanted. After a few hours of this, my host, by now quite drunk, suddenly snapped, "Give me your passport!" Looking at the photo page, which in those days listed one's occupation, he declared, "This is not a teacher! This is a spy from the Middle East!"

That my passport photograph looked rather villainous was true. And that embarrassing youthful attempt at a moustache, a bit like Prince, probably did merit some kind of punishment. But escorting me off to the cells, as they were doing now, seemed to be taking things a bit far. The next thing I knew, I was being repeatedly measured, with the results compared with the height in my passport, as if they now thought I was some kind of impostor. A few hours later, despite the quiet politeness of the lower ranks holding me, I was seriously worried.

I wasn't keen to end up with those other Westerners, shackled and forgotten in the "Bangkok Hilton." I considered making a run for it, but that would be seen as confirming my guilt. Instead, using gestures, I asked that somebody go and fetch my bags from the border post, and a couple of hours later, to my surprise, they turned up. I rummaged inside and found my envelope of spare passport photos: one with Jimi Hendrix hair, one showing a scowling biker, and so on—but all *me*. "Look!" I indicated, to puzzled frowns, appealing to some logic in a situation that didn't seem to have any. This is just what we're like in England, always changing our hair and look. It's just a fashion thing, not a disguise.

Shortly after that, they let me go. I got straight on a bus going south and headed for Bangkok, anxious to get as far away as possible. During my questioning, the officer had confiscated all my film. This included shots of an eighty-six pound *Probarbus*, a relative of the Indian mahseer, that I'd seen doubled into a freezer at a fisheries station, and a stuffed pla buk that I'd seen in an old shed. This fish was as long as my outstretched arms and immensely deep-bodied. It was the biggest fish I had ever seen in my life, and I hazarded a weight of two hundred pounds. There were also several shots of the river, and this was what concerned me. They had all been taken with the permission of my police minder, but the District Officer wouldn't know that. When he saw all those pictures of the border, he might conclude I had been a spy after all. (However, he might not see anything at all, as I had loaded bulk 35mm film into an assortment of used canisters, whose markings bore no relation to the contents. I did this to save money on film rather than it being an espionage thing, and I had given him written details of the correct development process needed. But his expression told me that he would be going by the canister labels, which might make him think, when everything came back blank, that he'd been double-bluffed.) So I headed to the British embassy to see if there was any way I could repair the situation and establish myself as a bona fide tourist. After telling me twice to come back the next day, they had an answer: "Our advice is to leave the country as soon as possible."

A few days later, traveling by bus and boat, I crossed overland into Malaysia. My savings from a year of teaching in London had financed a spectacular "blank."

Five years later I came across a newspaper article that made me break out in a sweat. It stated that around the time I was there, the British government had secretly sent members of the Special Air Service (SAS) to northeast Thailand to train Pol Pot's Khmer Rouge. At first the British government denied this. Why would we upstanding Brits aid a genocidal dictator-turned-terrorist? The answer lay in the algebra of realpolitik. Because the Khmer Rouge had been overturned by the Vietnamese, some in the West now saw the people who had killed two million Cambodians as the good guys. This was a case of our enemy's enemy being our friend or, rather (one more sideways step, because this was about the UK's "special relationship" with the United States), our friend's enemy's enemy. My Kafkaesque nightmare suddenly made sense. There were things going on in this remote, tourist-free area that the world was never supposed to know about, and along comes this person with a notebook and camera, spinning some cock-and-bull story about fish. . . .

But in 2009 the world had moved on. All this was now old news that nobody, it turned out, cared much about—except those people who'd had their legs blown off courtesy of our taxes. I walked through arrivals at the spanking new Suvarnabhumi airport without feeling a hand on my shoulder and continued by van into Bangkok.

The stingrays, known as *pla kaben* in Thai, are also little known about, and their enormity shocks those who encounter them. I'd been hearing about battles lasting up to six hours, with rods sometimes broken. The biggest recent catch was nearly eight feet across and estimated at around 600 pounds. (Some put it even heavier—at over 750 pounds—but it was not weighed because it was a pregnant female, and lifting such a heavy fish out of the water could have damaged it internally.)

I was also surprised to find out how close the captures were to Bangkok. The tidal reach of the Maeklong, just forty miles from the capital, flows right through a built-up area, past houses, temples, and markets, all of which inevitably raised questions about the potential danger of these fish.

One member of the fishing team had had a scary encounter. While handling a "small" (100-pound) stingray in a net, its spine scratched him at the base of his left index finger. "After five minutes, it feels like I'm holding a heavy stone," he said. Then his whole arm and the left side of his trunk went numb as his heart raced and sweat poured from his face. At present there is no antidote to the venom, which appears to be similar to that of a pit viper. So he was more than relieved when he recovered after three hours.

Another fisherman I spoke to, hauling a small one in by the spiracles, had its spine pierce his thigh to a depth of three inches. He crawled back to his house and was rushed to the hospital. Luckily, the spine went in at an oblique angle—any steeper and it could have opened his femoral artery, which, if not immediately shut off by applying pressure to the groin, could have caused fatal blood loss.

So catch-and-release fishing for them is a serious business. For a start, stingrays can attach themselves, like a giant suction cup, to the river bottom, sometimes covering themselves with an equal mass of mud. This dictates the use of extremely heavy-duty tackle and a complete lack of subtlety in playing them. Light gear simply will not shift them. Period. On the first day I motored onto the river with the fishing team in a canopied long-tail boat, a narrow wooden vessel with a rear-mounted automobile engine driving its ten-foot propeller shaft. The place we were heading for is nicknamed Area 51 because people say, "It's full of aliens," which do indeed look like underwater flying saucers. Once in position we put out multiple lines baited with live ten-inch snakeheads that were lip-hooked on size 10/0 circle hooks. Line was 160-pound monofilament, ridiculous in fresh water (and in the sea for that matter), that was backed with 100-pound braid. There's a tide of a few feet at Area 51, and at low-water slack something took one of the baits. After letting it run, we tightened to set the hook and then I slackened the drag momentarily while I clipped into two harnesses, one round my lower back and another round my shoulders, and inserted the rod butt into a gimbal in front of me. Meanwhile, a second boat rafted up to our narrow vessel to create a broader platform. Otherwise, we risked rolling over and capsizing with a powerful fish under the boat. The other danger was that I'd go over the side if the line coming off the reel, under extreme tension, cut into the coils behind it and jammed. So one of the team was hanging onto the back of my harness. In my pocket, as a last resort, was a knife to cut the line.

After only a couple of minutes, I know I have a very big fish here. My broomstick-stiff rod is bent into a semicircle, its tip just inches from the surface and occasionally disappearing under it. For extra leverage, my feet are up on the gunwales, and after ten minutes my bent legs feel like those of a weight lifter holding a squat halfway up. Even with the harnesses, my back is starting to complain—this is precisely what backs aren't designed to do, and exactly the position in which the bent and compressed spinal column can pop a disc or two. I listen to the pain, but I can't do anything to lessen it. In fact, I increase the drag a notch and strain harder because I want this to end. As I double and groan in response to the fish's lunges, I feel like a boxer slugging it out in the ring, hoping my opponent will give up before I do. I gain line inch by inch, glad to have an extra, low gear on my reel, only to lose a foot or two at once as the rod is forced down to the folded rag that pads the gunwale. Somebody says it's been an hour now, that I've been playing this grueling hybrid of tug-of-war and arm wrestling. They're pouring water over my head and on the reel. Mostly, the line is straight down, but at times it cuts sideways, spinning the boat. I bitterly regret not receiving the 5½-foot rod I ordered for this trip; this 7-footer gives the fish too much leverage. We pass the hour-and-a-half mark, but I can detect no weakening in the fish. What I've heard about these fish is no longer unbelievable. Four more hours of this is unthinkable. Then, at close to two hours, the rod springs back and I gain a couple of turns. It's off the bottom! The rod tip bucks as I pump in more line. The crew have hung the big knotless net off the side of the boat, like a curtain, and as the pointed rostrum breaks the surface, they push the net underneath the fish with long bamboo poles. But the ray is too far away, and as I lean back to bring it closer, I hear a sudden loud crack and the weight of the fish has gone.

It takes me several seconds to register what has happened. The end of the rod broke, and the resultant jar on the line broke that too: the final punishment for using a rod that was too long. Despite its formidable backbone, my "high sticking" bent its tip too sharply. And with these fish, I now realize, there is no room for error. Something else seemed to go at that moment too, but for now, I just stare at the broken rod, refusing to believe that all that time and suffering were for nothing. We never saw the rest of the fish, but everyone knows it was huge.

The next day, I had another bait taken, but we failed to hook up. The bait came back with a fine honeycomb pattern pressed into its rear half, the characteristic signature of stingray teeth—but also the sign of a wary fish. Then later I hooked something, which over the course of an hour pulled the boat half a mile against the tide. At one point the fish rose thirty yards from the boat and boiled at the surface, but it was not capitulating—just coming up to check us out. This time there were no slips at the boat. With the net pulled around it, cradling it outside the gunwale, the team carefully bound the barb to its tail with a rag, and then we slowly returned to the landing stage where the scientists were waiting. It was a huge female, over six feet across, but with the memory of the lost fish still raw, I was not as jubilant as I might otherwise have been. (The bigger rays are invariably females, the smaller males being easily identifiable by their paired claspers near the root of the tail.)

The next day I brought in another, this one measuring six feet, three inches across. As the team supported it in the shallows, clipping a small notch of skin for DNA analysis and scraping a blob of black mucus from the base of the eight-inch spine for the toxicology lab, we were suddenly aware that there was another stingray in the net, and then another. This female had just given birth, and unlike my first stingray in the Amazon, these newborns were at full term, nearly eighteen inches across, with no yolk sac and fully developed barbs. Before our eyes, these miniature weapons started to lose the protective capsule that prevents internal damage to the mother. Although they were babies, we could see that nothing was going to be bothering them in the river. And it occurred to me that this could be the reason for the mother's immense size: simply to be large enough to harbor such large young.

As we released the mother ship, and watched the tip of her long, whiplike tail disappear, I reflected on the fact that this fish, which Rick estimated at over 350 pounds, came to the boat in just twenty minutes. And I couldn't help wondering again how big the unseen fish had been.

But now was the time to pursue another question: is this giant a true freshwater species? Although a salinity meter had shown that the water here is fresh when the tide is running out, all the recent, confirmed captures have been in the tidal zone of the Maeklong and the last few miles of the strong-flowing Ban Pakong. However, we had heard reports of other captures from locations well inland.

One fisherman told me of a ray accidentally enclosed in a net 100 miles up the Ban Pakong. Something had bumped one of his companions in the stomach, and then they saw it rise in the water before it slid underneath and away. He put it at over 200 pounds. Another man showed me the picture, and tail, of a fish he caught 150 miles up the Chao Phraya at Nakhon Sawan in December 2008. After picking up a live carp on a thirty-hook longline, it resisted the efforts of ten men for four hours, dragging their boat for more than a mile. As I listened to the story, someone showed me mobile phone footage of the fish with two men standing on its back. It certainly looked very big, but was it really 704 pounds, which they said was its weight at the market? It was impossible to say.

Then I traveled to the Mekong, very close to where I'd been arrested. Here fisherman Boon Song told me that a big stingray, six feet across, had torn his net ten years before. When I showed him a picture of the Nakon Sawan fish, he said it was the same fish—and the same size. If this report is true, that's a stingray nearly a thousand miles from the South China Sea. Another fish was reported in July 2008 from the Mun River, a tributary joining the Mekong some five hundred miles inland. This one measured over six feet across and was weighed, in pieces at the market, at 411 pounds.

But the reports of these fish growing to over one thousand pounds remain unproven, so the jury is still out on the world's biggest freshwater fish. In some ways this is an academic question, but it does have wrapped inside it the mysteries of all the world's great river fish, so it's worth asking. Most people would discount beluga and white sturgeon, both recorded at well over one thousand pounds, on the grounds that they are not (normally) full-time river residents. After them comes a disparate shoal of true freshwater species that, in all likelihood, exceed five hundred pounds (arapaima, piraiba, and Mekong giant catfish, although only the last has the paperwork to prove it) and some others that might (Nile perch, alligator gar, wels catfish, Siamese carp [*Catlocarpio siamensis*], dog-eating catfish [*Pangasius sanitwongsei*], and goonch). But which of these has—or had—the biggest specimen at any time, we'll never know. Meanwhile, where the "freshwater" whipray fits into the picture is also unclear, as it is most commonly found in tidal, brackish water and could probably survive in salt water (although, so far, no one has found it there). Unlike Amazon rays, the Thai whipray appears to be still making the transition to fresh water.

And now this gray area has another interloper. One year after my return to Thailand, I heard of another giant river ray whose freshwater credentials are in no doubt. And I started making plans to see if I could catch one of these monsters myself.

THE THAIS SOMETIMES CALL THE STINGRAY *pla rahu*, the eclipse fish, as its shape resembles the dark disc that covers the sun and turns day into night. Eclipses are universally feared, and thus, by association, the stingray is believed to be a bringer of bad luck—and not just in the obvious, cause-and-effect way, when an unlucky victim encounters its spine.

Sometime after the giant *Himantura chaophraya* snapped my rod and escaped, I noticed a hollow in my upper right arm, as if a golf ball–sized piece of muscle had wasted away. On my return home, I showed it to my doctor, who told me that one of the two tendons anchoring the top of my biceps had broken. He referred me to a specialist and said I would likely need to cancel my next film trip, for which all permits had been organized and all kit and crew booked, because I'd need urgent surgery followed by six weeks' convalescence. If we waited too long to operate, according to one website, my arm would lose 30 to 50 percent of its strength.

The news from the specialist was mixed. If I'd been an athlete in my twenties, they would have opened up my arm and tried to re-anchor the tendon. But in my case, doing that wasn't worth it. The good news was that the loss of strength is only 5 to 7 percent, which I can live with. Also, with no tendon, there was now no pain—which was a relief of sorts, as my arm had been aching for several months beforehand. So although I can't be certain that that was the moment when it happened, I now have a hole in my arm, rather like one of the depressions that stingrays excavate in the Amazon shallows, as a permanent reminder of the giant Thai whipray that I lost. And although the two events have become linked in my mind, I don't blame the ray or subscribe to the belief that it is a bringer of bad luck. Nevertheless, when the possibility of a return match with another giant river stingray came up, my interest was tempered by trepidation.

The short-tailed river ray, *Potamotrygon brachyura*, lives in the Paraná-Paraguay River south of the Amazon. According to the Fish-Base website, the species was described back in 1880. But the site gives a maximum size of only three feet and describes it as "harmless." This is at odds with what I was now hearing: stories of a huge, club-tailed beast that terrifies both mixed-race Argentineans and indigenous Guaraní. Although it is short in relation to its body, the ray's tail is covered in thorny spines, which can rip flesh to the bone. Near the tip are one or two barbed prongs, four inches long, which inject flesh-rotting venom. Human deaths, I was told, include a fifteen-year-old Guaraní girl stabbed in the abdomen and a boy pierced in the thigh. Fishermen would rather cut their lines than go near it. As for its size, I was told of a 480-pounder caught in 2008 after a three-hour fight, and one weighing 572 pounds that was caught in 2002. The maximum weight could exceed 600 pounds.

I arrived in the town of Bella Vista after an overnight bus journey north from Buenos Aires through endless flat scrub. The river was far larger than I expected, splitting into multiple channels that extended its width to four miles. But the profusion of low islands meant plenty of promising-looking spots: eddies and slacks where channels merged as well as deep holes where lakes and swamps drained back into the river. I wasn't going to take any chances with these fish, so I'd set up a 5½-foot shark rod coupled with thick 150-pound mono and a 7-foot coated wire leader. To get the line out, I clipped it to a plastic water bottle, using strong elastic bands, and then floated it down the current before jerking it free. It worked perfectly, apart from one thing: sometimes the bottle would dip and bob before I released the line, a sign that the giant gold-colored piranhas, known as *palometa*, that infest these waters had eaten the bait. Other times dorado (*Salminus brasiliensis*), a beautiful, leaping gamefish that resembles a gilded salmon—but in this context, a "nuisance" species—would take it. I clearly needed to change my approach, to get the bait down quickly into the realm of the bottom-feeders.

But even after I switched to an outfit that I could cast (a seven-foot rod with two hundred–pound braid and a shorter leader), the piranhas continued to find the bait, even after dark. Night also brought striped catfish, known here as *surubi*. Although I've handled scores of these, I was holding a small one up for the camera when it kicked and stuck its pectoral spine into the back of my left hand. The pain was excruciating, and I swore and swore. But it was a useful reminder: I could afford no such lapse of concentration when the stingray came along.

I also saw the scars, on feet and ankles. One young fisherman, Tingo, has been stung ten times. He says the pain is like holding your foot in a fire. One encounter was clearly with a very big fish: when he jumped back after being hit, he stepped on another part of its body and got hit again. Later, when he hooked a 473-pounder on a line he had put out for surubi, he shot it three times with a 9mm handgun before landing it. Tingo treated the wounds himself with hot sand. At the town hospital, they first inject local anesthetic and scrub the wound to remove dirt and dead tissue. Then they bathe it in hot water, which breaks down the venom. An older fisherman, Peto, who didn't treat a wound, says it didn't fully heal for six years. The scar, on his left ankle, feels hard to the touch and remains numb to this day. The worst-case scenario, however, if the necrosis sets in, is gangrene. At this stage, amputation may be the only way to save the victim's life.

This all helped to explain the small, dried-out stingray corpse I found with multiple stab wounds behind its eyes as well as the big ray that appeared one day, strung up on the waterfront, with a bloody stump where its tail had been. I measured its diameter at forty-eight inches and, helped by four people, lifted it onto some scales. The needle went round to 194 pounds. With its tail, guts and lost fluid, its live weight would have been about 215 pounds. Despite this animal's reputation—and the fear it inspires—its death seemed such a waste. But perhaps I would have felt less sentimental if I was not simply a visitor here. At any rate, one consolation was that I now had accurate data on its proportions. If I now caught a big one, I wouldn't need to subject it to the stress of being weighed before returning it to the river.

But catching a giant was looking less and less likely. I'd caught a solitary thirty-pounder on my fourth day, but this hardly qualified. How strange that stingrays often plagued me in Brazil, when I wanted to avoid them, but now that I was targeting them, they were oddly elusive. As the days passed, I came under increasing pressure to change my approach, to carpet-bomb the river with baits. But I don't believe this necessarily improves one's chances, and besides, I only had one suitably heavy-duty outfit. In the end though, as a token concession, I set up a second outfit, a light boat rod with eighty-pound mono line.

On my last (tenth) day I went to a different type of spot: a fast, deep run, close to a snaggy bank. Three days before, a dorado fisherman had lost a stingray here, which probably never even realized it had been hooked. I swung a swamp eel out on my big rod and a nine-inch knife fish slightly closer. At 2:05 p.m. the line on the lighter rod moved. I picked it up, felt a steady pull, and then another. On setting the hook, I immediately knew it was a ray. There was a lunge, ripping line, and then it became solid, immobile, and yet animate. We pulled up the anchor and took up position above it. Half an hour later, after no further movement, I was convinced it had swum round a sunken tree. I asked my boatman José to edge across the current a little so I could pull from a different angle. The rod didn't really have enough backbone, but when I locked the reel with my thumb and heaved, I felt a pulsing on the line and then a wrench. Then it was stalemate again—or, rather, the growing certainty that the aches in my back and arms, growing more intense by the minute, were going to be for nothing. If I could lift it off the bottom, the current might take us both downstream beyond the snaggy bank to a slack that lay off a sandy beach. But for two hours our position hardly changed. Then another desperate heave, with José expertly holding the boat still in the current, got it moving again. Looking up, I saw that we were now adjacent to the sand. But the water was still deep. If we couldn't pull it to the shallows here, the ray would continue downstream and we'd never bring it up. For the first time, though, I got the sense that the weight on the line, although heavy, was tiring. The bow of the boat grated against sand, and I jumped out. Then it materialized in front of me: a huge circular shape, humped in the middle and the same color as the sand, veined with a network of dark shadowy lines. I pulled on my stab-proof gauntlets and, taking it by the spiracles, heaved it aground as the tail and skirt thrashed, throwing wet sand in my face. The time was 5:55. Bringing it in had taken nearly four hours.

At fifty-three inches across, I calculated its weight between 250 and 280 pounds—a squashed equivalent of the Queensland groper. But, being in the same genus as the ocellate stingray of the Amazon (*Potamotrygon motoro*) and living six hundred miles from the ocean, there's no doubt that this is a true freshwater species. So it's a record, of some sort, for me. But somehow, despite the numbers, a stingray doesn't count. In my mind, and in appearance, it's still an alien: a sea fish that strayed and then stayed.

I slid it back into the water, where its massive body dissolved, merging once more with the riverbed. All that remained were two dark eyes, opening and closing in a slow, pulsing rhythm. Then they too were gone.

CHAPTER 12

THE LAKE ILIAMNA MONSTER

Canst thou draw out leviathan with an hook?
Or his tongue with a cord which thou lettest down?

Job 41:1

LAKE ILIAMNA IN ALASKA IS North America's very own Loch Ness. For generations the people living on its shores have told of a giant creature that rises from its depths to attack boats, consigning the hapless occupants to its icy waters. But whereas the famous Scottish cryptid is said to be a long-necked creature resembling an extinct sauropod, witnesses are very clear that the Alaskan monster is a fish.

Lake Iliamna is certainly the perfect place for a monster. At seventy-seven miles long and twenty-two miles across at its widest point, with a depth of nearly 1,000 feet, it could swallow Loch Ness sideways (twenty-two miles long and mostly about a mile wide, with a maximum depth of 755 feet). Tucked away between mountains, it's overlooked by a very sparse human population, who don't venture beyond its margins. And with no roads leading in, it's not easily accessible for outsiders. If a monster were living there, it would lead a very undisturbed life. The only thing that might alarm it would be an occasional dark object buzzing across the sky. These are the light planes that, since the 1940s, have been the preferred way of getting around this region. When the bush pilots started spotting things in the water, which broadly matched the natives' descriptions, the old stories gained wider credence.

In these days of the Internet, just a few minutes' research will bring up details of a half-dozen sightings from the air, between 1942 and 1977, by pilots and their passengers. All describe elongated animals between ten and thirty feet long. But a plane flying low at over 100 mph is not an ideal platform for observing secretive wildlife. By the time you've spotted something, it's almost certainly seen you—and possibly heard you too. To avoid losing it, you must circle, but in only one of the reports did the witness keep the animal in view. And in those days before camera phones, nobody got any photographs.

My chance to look more closely into this mystery came in July 2009. This fish would be a perfect story for a *River Monsters* TV episode: a mythical lake monster that appeared to be a fish. As far as the production team were concerned, with their touching faith in my abilities, this would be right up my waterlogged street. But although we'd had some astounding successes on our previous shoots, which normally last just a couple of weeks, wasn't this biting off more than we could chew? Like a giant piraiba with its jaws round an Amazon fisherman, would I end up regretting my overconfidence as I choked on something that, this time, was far too big for me?

I considered the countless man-hours that have been spent looking at Loch Ness, ranging from the twenty men with binoculars and cameras who spent five weeks scanning the water in 1934 for nine hours a day to the acoustic "nets," sonar sweeps, and submersibles of more recent times. Although some sonar readings were interpreted as twenty-foot-long animate objects, there remains no conclusive proof, so the consensus among most scientists is that the monster doesn't exist. But nor has it been definitively disproved (to do that you'd need to drain more than two cubic miles of water), which is why many people continue to find it so compelling. The balance of probability, however, remains on the side of nonexistence. Most "sightings" can be attributed to natural phenomena. Animals such as seals and otters can appear larger than they are if they are in open water—like the giant snake I saw in a Congo tributary in 1991 that shrank to a five-foot gaboon viper after hysterical villagers had launched a canoe and harpooned it. And

I've seen in the Amazon how the wake of a distant boat, itself long passed, can break on offshore shallows in waves that look like a series of dark humps. The water itself, if enclosed, can slosh back and forth when the wind pushes it, thus causing eddies, interference, and standing waves, not to mention the wind-flattened patches in the midst of ripples, reflecting ominous darkness. On top of this there is the psychological dimension. Once a myth becomes established, it forms part of our mental model of the world and alters our perception, the way our brains interpret the fleeting patterns our eyes pick up. To a large extent we see what we want to see rather than what is really there.

I remember during one summer school holiday going to visit my Uncle Mike, a history teacher who lived in a tiny village near Loch Ness. I have a hazy memory of the loch: the same view as the postcards, with Urquhart Castle in the foreground and the water behind. The biggest fish I'd caught at that time was a four-pound pike, and I was far more interested in stories about this predator, which is said to grow huge in the loch, than in the mythical beast that fed the local tourist industry. But even so, the power of the legend still held me and I lingered for a long time half-expecting something to break the surface. Then it was up into the mountains, hiking to forgotten lochans and narrow burns where the trout fishing was open to all and where I waved a borrowed fly rod ineptly and unsuccessfully. The biggest fish I caught was a five-inch salmon parr, but it beat Nessie watching, which didn't really interest me because it wasn't a fish and because I knew it was something I would never see.

So what were my chances on Lake Iliamna? I reminded myself that I had something of a track record for seeing and filming things that other people hadn't, such as the Amazon saw-backed lake monster and goonch underwater in their natural habitat. But here there was very little to go on—no grainy images on film or video to computer-enhance. There was, however, an extensive oral history, and the obvious first step was to tap into this.

The normal way to get around Alaska is by float plane; they use planes like other people drive cars. Waiting to take off from Anchorage,

I was not totally relaxed about this given my previous experience with light aircraft, and a preflight chat with a regular passenger was only partially reassuring. "You go in through Lake Clark Pass," she said. "It could be sunny this side, but you go in and it's snowing. You've got to turn an L-shaped corner in total white-out. But you can't turn round either, because it's so narrow. So now they've got these webcams there, so they can check the weather before they fly."

We approached the mountains over tidal mudflats and wandering creeks, passing three oil platforms in Cook Inlet. I was facing backward, toward our strapped-in kit, and for the sake of my neck, I had to content myself with looking mostly out to the side. But already I could sense that the snow-covered peaks ahead were higher than our 2,500-foot altitude, as the valley we were following closed in on either side. Soon there was sheer rock alongside, slipping by in an eerie slow motion that belied our roaring speed. All around were graphic reminders of gravity: glaciers sliding down from the peaks way above and vertical chutes of born-again water.

We landed in Port Alsworth, halfway down Lake Clark, which is linked to Lake Iliamna by thirty miles of river. This small settlement is situated beside a sheltered inlet, where float planes can land on calm water regardless of the wind's direction, so it's the perfect base for Lake Clark Air, which covers the Iliamna area.

Legendary bush pilot Leon "Babe" Alsworth, who gave up logging his flying hours after 48,000, founded the original air-taxi service here. He also saw the Iliamna monster in the 1940s. His son, Glen Alsworth Sr., a soft-spoken man with a white beard and twinkling eyes, now runs the company, and I buttonholed him in between flights to get more details of that sighting. "This day it was absolutely glassy water calm," he told me. "And my father was flying across the lake in his float plane. And he noticed two large fish near a reef in shallow water. . . . So he circled them to try to get an idea of how big they were, and he judged them to be the same size as the floats on his aircraft—probably more than fifteen feet long."

But there was more: "As the fish began to move from the shallow water . . . he looked down into the deep water, and there was a school of perhaps a hundred fish. To him they looked small, but when these fish joined them from the reef, they were all the same size. . . . It was a shoal of huge, huge fish."

Glen Sr. has never seen such a sight himself, but in 2008 he saw an animal that he reckoned was between eight and ten feet long. The wind was blowing offshore, and it was swimming in the shore's calm wind shadow in about fifteen feet of water at the edge of the drop-off. At first he thought it was a seal, but its tail was moving side to side. Glen Sr. is highly experienced at spotting fish from the air for sport-fishermen, but this was none of the normal species, and it was much bigger. As the plane turned for another pass, the fish moved into deeper water.

But on the same flat-calm day when Glen Sr.'s father spotted the giant fish he also saw something even stranger. Approaching the shallower southwest end of the lake and flying into the sun, "He could see on the surface of the water what looked like huge octopus. He could see these large, round kind of animals, or something that was underwater but lying at the surface. And as they would fly over them, they would sink, they would go down, they would start descending in the water. And initially he passed it off as some type of illusion . . . but he saw a *lot* of them." His passenger also saw them, a schoolteacher he was taking to the town of Levelock. Babe Alsworth estimated that the arms of these creatures had a spread of nearly one hundred feet. "Whatever they were, they were very large, and there were many of them," said Glen Sr.

Then came another surprise: the stories aren't restricted to Iliamna. Back in the same era, one of their aircraft technicians hooked something very large in Lake Clark. The man was in the habit of fishing a set line for lake trout and had suffered some break-offs. He kept upping the strength of his line, but the same thing happened. Eventually he forged a giant steel hook in the workshop, baited it with half a salmon, and attached it to a length of aircraft control cable. He then secured this to a heavy tree stump washed up on the lake shore. The next day a neighbor, looking out at the lake, spotted a tree stump moving in the water, against the wind. At first he worried about his sanity—that is, until he heard the explanation from the equally incredulous mechanic.

Hearing this, although it happened more than a half-century ago, I couldn't resist putting out a large bait myself. Wedging my rod upright on the shore, I took a fillet of salmon out by inflatable kayak and released it beyond the drop-off in thirty feet of water. It was my first Alaskan night outdoors, but in the Arctic summer, just six degrees south of the Arctic Circle, it never really gets dark, something that contributed to the unreality of what I was doing. I flattened the seats in the beached kayak and lay down inside it, but the wind and lapping waves that rocked it didn't allow me to sink into the near-sleep state in which I'm oblivious to everything except the urgent scream of the ratchet. I kept having to check that I hadn't drifted out—with mist obscuring all around, and a thousand feet of water underneath me. When morning came, the line still hung slack.

The next story I heard was from Bill Trefon, a native Alaskan of the Dena'ina tribe who lives on the shore of Lake Clark. One day in 1957 his parents were out on the lake when there was an impact and their motor stopped. Bill's father pulled up the motor to inspect it, and while he was doing this, his wife saw a large tail break the surface behind the boat. But this wasn't the most extraordinary thing. "There were teeth marks on the propeller," said Bill.

His mother said that, based on the size of the tail, the fish must have been ten or twelve feet long. The largest known predator in the lake is the northern pike (*Esox lucius*). Perhaps the prop had acted like a fishing lure and a pike had reflex-hit because of its flash and vibration. If so, this would be highly unusual behavior: you'd expect the mass and movement of the boat to deter it. But a wake actually attracts certain aggressive predators such as marlin (expecting to find propeller-minced small fish?), which will hit skittering teasers right up against the transom.

I'd heard there are big pike in Lake Clark, but I wanted to put this to the test. The weather had turned exceptionally sunny, so my guide,

Glen Alsworth Jr., took me fish spotting in the air. In summer, pike move into shallows, so we circled a weedy creek across the lake where we saw some loglike shadows. The next day we went there in the boat, and I missed a take right in the weed stems on a surface-fished rubber frog and then caught a two-pounder on a bucktail jig, a weighted three-inch strip of white fur that kicks just like a small fish if you twitch it along the bottom. But I hooked nothing big. So we came out into deeper water, a bay that a ten-foot cliff topped with bushes partially bounds. Underneath this, right against the rock, was a classic ambush position, not just for picking off small fish but also bonus items, such as nestling birds falling in from above. From fifteen yards out I dropped a spinnerbait repeatedly into this zone, without result. We'd now drifted past the most promising area, so I sent a last-chance cast back along the rock face, and halfway in there was a sharp wrench. In the clear water I soon saw that it was a pike, which we beached on a small patch of waterlogged bank and measured at forty inches. Weighing maybe twenty pounds, this was a very respectable pike. A thirty-five-pounder would be the fish of a lifetime. But even the largest pike in the most uncertain historical reports, such as the ninety-pounder netted in Ireland in the late 1800s, wouldn't measure more than six feet. So the fish in Bill's story was not likely a pike. But what could possibly bite a moving propeller and survive?

Both Lake Iliamna and Lake Clark are connected to the sea, so one possibility is a marine animal that has wandered inland. To check this out, we flew over the shallowest part of the Kvichak (pronounced Kwee-jack) River, an area known as the braids, where the river splits into numerous small channels. In many of these channels we could see the bottom, but others appeared to be six or eight feet deep, which could potentially be enough water for an animal like a beluga whale.

Belugas are toothed whales, like orcas and sperm whales, and look rather like oversized Amazon pink dolphins, with a bulbous forehead and flexible neck but without the long beak. They grow more than fifteen feet long with a weight of over three thousand pounds, which fits the bill almost perfectly in terms of size. What's more, there is a well-known population nearby in Cook Inlet, and they are known to move into estuaries in summer. Being air-breathing mammals, there's no reason why they couldn't swim into fresh water if they wanted. In fact, in 2006 a dead eight-foot beluga was found nearly one thousand miles from the sea beside the Tanana River, a tributary of the Yukon River, near Fairbanks in central Alaska. As the biologist who identified it said, nobody in their right mind would want to drive this far with a decomposing carcass in order to perpetrate a hoax. Instead, there's speculation that it could have simply been following its food: the salmon that run upriver to spawn. So seventy-five miles up the Kvichak to Lake Iliamna would be a breeze. But the idea that the Iliamna monster might be a beluga comes crashing down as soon as we apply more scrutiny. Being an air-breather, the beluga would have to surface at regular intervals, and being brilliant white, it would be easily visible in the clear water— not to mention its habit of making loud squeaks and whistles. Its color is also at odds with witness statements, which also maintain that the tail movement is side to side, not up and down. So this white whale is not the Moby Dick of this tale.

If bull sharks were this far north, they could easily get into the lake and remain hidden there. But the coastal seas here are too cold for them; the nearest bull sharks are off Baja California. However, there is one shark species up here. Salmon sharks (*Lamna ditropis*), as the name implies, follow runs of salmon, sometimes very close inshore. This abundant food source enables them to pack on the pounds, reaching over ten feet in length and weights over five hundred pounds. This fast-swimming, stocky-bodied shark is able to keep active in these subarctic waters by virtue of a remarkable adaptation, which it shares with the related great white shark. Unlike most fish, it can keep its body temperature higher than that of the surrounding water. However, it lacks the bull shark's special ability to enter fresh water. So it has a cast-iron alibi. Another potential suspect is ruled out.

Flying over the lake one day, Glen pointed out a group of large animals below. Without anything to give a sense of scale, estimating their size was difficult, but I can confidently say the bigger ones were around six feet long and close to three hundred pounds. Lake Iliamna is one of just a handful of freshwater lakes in the world with breeding colonies of seals (the best known is Lake Baikal in Russia). The animals we saw were hauled out on a tiny island, and the total population is estimated at over two hundred, but it's hard to imagine these giving rise to the monster myth.

Running out of likely suspects, I decided to take a more indirect approach. A large animal needs an abundant food source to sustain it. Without this, any idea of a mythical monster is a nonstarter. The Kvichak's run of sockeye salmon (*Oncorhynchus nerka*) is reputedly the largest salmon run anywhere in the world, with over ten million fish returning every year to spawn and die. Apart from anything else, this gave me the opportunity to catch my first salmon, the "king of fish," after almost fifty years chasing everything else in fresh water—and this was something I was quite excited about. My background as an angler is decidedly "coarse" rather than "game." That is to say I am a maggot drowner, a plunker of worms, a dirty-fingered mixer of stinky concoctions that I lob into the path of unsuspecting fish that stand no chance when presented with real food, if the most vocal adherents of fly-fishing are to be believed. Conversely, fly-fishing is said to take extreme levels of skill because you are trying to deceive the fish with something that is inedible. This distinction takes us right to the essence of "Fysshynge with an Angle," as it used to be called in the fifteenth century before that special bent piece of metal became known as a hook. All angling is about putting something with minimal food value into the water and pulling out a potential meal, a conversion that seems all the more miraculous when the bait has no food value at all—a trick that would seem to require the highest levels of human guile to make it work. But, as with most things in life, other factors are seldom equal. "Game" fish have the misfortune of being tasty to eat so they don't get the chance to wise up to the extent that nontasty species do, which are returned to scrutinize a hook another day. At any rate, until now I had only heard and read about the sublime difficulty of deceiving and landing salmon. Now was my opportunity to evaluate this for myself.

Flying over a hummocky landscape, we spotted a straw-colored grizzly bear beside the river below, a good sign that the salmon were there, although we couldn't see the fish themselves, which can turn the water black at the peak of the run. We landed on a small windswept lake nearby and took a winding path to the river. The bear had gone when we arrived, but fresh paw prints were a reminder to stay on our guard. We were only sixty-five miles from where, six years before, bears had killed and partially eaten the self-styled bear conservationist Timothy Treadwell, the subject of Werner Herzog's documentary *Grizzly Man*. So before we started fishing, Glen gave me and the crew a safety briefing. If a bear confronted us, we were to face it and hold our ground, presenting the broad mass of our combined five bodies—in other words acting much like a rival bear would do: avoiding conflict by showing that we were bigger. If this didn't work, we were to back off slowly. But it seemed to be academic. There were no salmon-scooping bears anywhere to be seen, which was quite disappointing. There was only the river and patches of low shrubs alongside.

The received wisdom about salmon is that they don't feed in rivers. But the truth isn't quite this clear-cut because anglers (of the "nonsporting" variety, notably in Ireland and Wales) catch them on prawns and worms. And they will of course take flies, although most salmon "flies" resemble small tropical fish more than insects. Curiosity is often given as the reason: what the heck is that shiny red and yellow thing? But the only reason most fish will check something out is to see if it is edible, so why would a nonfeeding fish be curious? With salmon, a fly or spinner or spoon, if presented close enough, must trigger the remnants of a feeding reflex. But this is not so with the sockeye, which is unique among the eight species of salmon (seven Pacific and one Atlantic) in not taking flies. This is put down to the fact that, when at sea, it is less predatory than other salmon, sucking up crustaceans rather than striking small fish. So what was I doing setting up a fly rod? Glen explained that there is a way around this difficulty, and the key lies in the sheer number of fish.

We had waded out to a small gravel patch at the head of an island, and every few minutes a pod of dark shapes pushed upstream alongside us, about two rod-lengths out in a couple of feet of water. Glen gave me a small streamer fly to tie on and then a piece of split-shot. "Put that about four feet up your line, then cast upstream," he instructed.

I took some time to get the hang of it. Fly-casting with a piece of lead on the line is not very effective or elegant, especially with a stiff downriver wind. I settled on shooting the line out with a backhand flip, watching the lead plop into the water just a few feet out. But that was all the distance I needed. After a bit of practice and adjusting the weight, I would see the fly and lead hit the water four feet apart and then feel the lead ticking along the gravel bottom. The idea is for the line between fly and lead to sweep downstream a few inches off the bottom and intercept the fish coming up. A salmon, opening its mouth to breathe, feels the line and bolts, thereby sliding itself down the line to the hook. Mostly the fish will be hooked near the angle of the jaw, but the point will have penetrated from the outside, although sometimes it will catch inside the mouth, giving the impression, probably incorrect, that the salmon actually took the fly.

A bear had appeared a little way upstream from where we had crossed. Peeping out from the low bushes, it peered down into the undercut margins, moving with the utmost stealth. No bait on his fish hooks, I reflected, but deadly all the same, impaling the flank of his surprised prey. Shortly another bear materialized, further upriver. This one was using different tactics, charging into shallows and flailing the water with his hooks. After a couple of attempts, a fish was kicking in its jaws. Then another bear appeared, working the opposite bank adjacent to us. This one was moving upstream with its snout and eyes scoping underwater, but, despite making a few lunges, it didn't catch anything.

Eventually the time came to try my method. After casting ahead of a couple of pods without making any contact, I finally felt the line check and lifted the rod, but the fish rolled to flash its flank and the fly skittered up to the surface. One more fish managed to bump off the hook, but the next time there was a satisfying weight on the line as a red shape tore off down-current. On the light eight-pound leader I was worried I wouldn't be able to bring it back upstream, and the water cut too deeply alongside the island for me to follow. But at length I managed to bring the fish up the quieter water at the side into a small slack at the head of the island.

This was a momentous catch for me—and on camera too! But a camera lens, for all that it can magnify and sharpen physical detail, diminishes the emotional dimension and renders it flat in every sense. All that the viewers see, in the words of the first director I worked with, Gavin Searle, is "just a bloke stood there with a bent rod." Even the appearance of a large fish, stripped of its significance, will leave the viewer cold—mere "fish porn" as it has been called. To retain the emotional component, you must open a window to the angler's soul, and the only way to do this, within the limits of technology, is through words: narration in the heat of the moment. But fishing is experienced and performed through the brain's right hemisphere, a domain of patterns and colors and abstract feelings where words don't exist. Finding and ordering words in retrospect is one thing, but if you can find and compose anything at the time, what comes out is a chaotic, impressionistic, abstract tumble—which actually serves the purpose perfectly.

These are the moments when the world shrinks to a single frail thread stretched between two opposing wills. So the thing that appeared next to the fish, a pole-camera that James or maybe Alex wielded, was an unwelcome intrusion but one that I have learned to live with. Duncan the cameraman was also next to me in the water, pointing the main camera down at the fish to show it from my point of view. And what a shocking sight it was: no bright bar of silver but instead a green-headed, hump-backed apparition whose deep red flanks told the story of its improbable life. The pigment first acquired from gobbling down crustaceans in the distant ocean and then concentrated in its fatty tissues was now surfacing in the leathery skin as those fat deposits burned. Some say that this breeding livery intimidates rivals, along with the hooked lower jaw and curved not-for-feeding teeth of this aquatic Quasimodo. Behind the angle of the jaw, a pugnacious eye stared back at me. The sockeye's name has nothing to do with this but rather is an Anglicization of *suk-kegh*, its name in the Native American Salish language, which means red fish. And its redness is truly startling, even more so than that other "red fish," the Amazon arapaima.

A movement in my peripheral vision to my left made me reflexively turn my head. A brown shape had come out of the bushes on the island and was lumbering down the bank toward us. It was just ten feet away. The others heard my squawk and we splashed out of the water and re-grouped to face it. But the bear wasn't concerned about us. This fish, displaying itself at the surface so tantalizingly, so unlike its furtive fellows, had captivated its attention as well. Not wanting a bear on my line, I pointed the rod at the fish, wound down tight, and took a couple of steps back to snap the line. But this had run the fish aground, and it didn't have time to right itself and swim away before the bear was upon it.

Apparently satisfied, the bear disappeared back into the bushes. But almost immediately it was back. This time we had no protection payment to give it, and it kept coming.

"You guys plug your ears," said Glen, as he put a .50-caliber round in the water beside it. That did the trick, but it was time to go. The bear was young and it needed to learn that not being wary of humans was not going to be a good idea in the long run. Nonetheless, I'd seen enough. The presence of the bears and their monstrous size—up to 1,400 pounds for a mature male—was evidence enough of the fecundity of this water. The food chain here stretches out to the far Pacific, a conveyor belt of nutrients that fertilizes these otherwise barren mountains: not only the seasonal glut of adult salmon and their corpses, but their eggs and the young that swarm in these waters before descending to the sea. On another occasion I went by boat to a river mouth at the eastern end of Lake Iliamna, and the sonar screen was so solid with fish that the beam couldn't see through them to find the bottom. Seeing this, I thought about the solid, muscular *tambaqui* fish of the Amazon, which gorge on rubber seeds during the annual flood and then eat nothing for half the year. Although it's an alien concept to modern humans, alternating feast and famine is common in nature and some animals do very well on this regime. With the bears here demonstrating this point so visibly, it's hard to rule out a large creature doing the same invisibly, under the waters of Lake Iliamna.

One person who is sure there is something down there is Robbin LaVine, an anthropologist studying subsistence fisheries on the lake. Just a couple of years earlier she had been in a float plane, about to touch down, when she and a colleague saw a dark shape in the water beside two small islands. Glen took us up so she could point out exactly where she saw it. In this area of the lake there is a shallow marginal shelf, fifteen to twenty feet deep, which, from three hundred feet up, is clearly visible as a light-colored band beside the dark blue deeper water. As we circled and approached, I marveled at the visibility. I could see pods of salmon, like furls of iron filings drawn to the magnetic poles of the river mouths. Robbin says she observed the animal for a good thirty to forty seconds. Far too big to be a seal, she said it was "distinctly fish-like" with a long, broad head and large pectoral fins, giving a profile somewhat like an arrowhead. She said it wasn't on the surface: "It almost looked like it might have been stirring up something on the bottom, although there were no clouds of silt." Her colleague thought he saw a flash of pink, which made him think it might have been feeding on salmon. She estimated the fish was the length of one of the aluminum skiffs used on the lake—at least fifteen feet.

Hearing her description, the monster came into sharper focus in my mind. From being a hazy entity, it now suddenly became clear, and when I cross-referenced it against my mental database . . . yes, I had a match! It was a fish that I knew only from pictures, but now I had to see one in the flesh. But to catch it from this thousand-square-mile lake in water hundreds of feet deep would surely take a lifetime. The only way I was going to be certain of the monster's identity was to leave Lake Iliamna and cast a line somewhere else.

ABOUT 1,500 MILES DOWN THE PACIFIC COAST of North America from the mouth of the Kvichak is the mouth of the Columbia River, flowing between the states of Washington and Oregon in the United States' Pacific Northwest. Some 100 miles upriver is the city of Portland, and a little upriver from there but below the Bonneville dam is a hole in the bottom that is ninety feet deep. From a boat anchored at the upstream end of the hole, just off some fluted cliffs that looked like they might have been shaped with a jelly mould, I dropped a dead herringlike shad into the water—a little over a foot long with bright silvery flanks. On the other bank was a beach that shelved away into deep water much like the margins at Lake Iliamna where Robbin saw her fish. But unlike Iliamna, this water was moving very strongly. To hold the bait on the bottom, I'd put on a pound of lead, and if something took the bait, I'd be fighting the combined weight of fish and water. On the plus side, however, the moving water would take the scent of my bait way downstream, unlike in still water where the flavor diffuses into a small cloud that is restricted to the immediate area. I waited in tense anticipation, knowing that something could be following that scent trail right now.

For a long time all was quiet, but then came the knock on the line. There was a pause, and then another knock, and then . . . yes, the line was running out steadily and decisively. As I engaged the drag and wedged the rod butt into my stomach, the rod took on a frightening bend and a huge weight accelerated downstream, making me double up, like a blow to the guts. The pitch of the ratchet rose from fast click to continuous squeal as I yelled above it to cast off from the anchor buoy. This was a borrowed rod and reel, and I wasn't sure how much line I had, although I'd been told it was two or three hundred yards. But the bright yellow braid was pouring off the reel at a frightening pace. With horror I realized that the spool containing what was left of it, as well as shrinking in diameter, was also changing color as the bare spool or backing appeared underneath it.

With only a few turns to go, I learned it was backing, but I had no idea what or how much, so I frantically loosened off the drag and watched the last of the main line disappear through the rod rings and into the water, followed by thin mono that looked only about thirty-pound strain. But at least the boat was moving now, and in a couple of minutes I had the main line back on the reel and was putting pressure back on. The fish was hanging deep and made a couple more long charges, and at one point the line cut up through the surface, making me think the fish was going to jump, but at the last moment it sounded again. We engaged the motor and tried to steer it toward the shallows where we could jump in and secure it, but the fish refused to come up the drop-off, powering away every time it sensed the light of the surface layers or the reduction in water pressure around it or the grating of the bottom against its belly. But the distance that the fish was going back and forth was getting shorter, until the line length and angle told me that the magical moment when imagination and reality converge was near. I shifted my focus, hunting up and down beneath the surface, and suddenly, there it was: a long shape, streamlined as a missile and with the prominent pectoral fins that Robbin kept mentioning.

The creature before me was a sturgeon, said by some to be the biggest freshwater fish in the world. But many would take issue with this because most sturgeon are not full-time residents in fresh water. Like salmon, they are anadromous, migrating to the sea to feed (more food there) and then returning to rivers to breed (a safer nursery for young). However, they are the biggest fish found in fresh water. The largest of the twenty-odd sturgeon species is the beluga sturgeon (*Huso huso*), which lives in the Black Sea and Caspian Sea as well as the surrounding rivers in Russia and central Asia. Historical reports include a twenty-four-foot fish, weighing 3,250 pounds, from the Volga estuary in 1827 and another from the Dnieper estimated at 3,400 pounds. The FishBase website gives a maximum published weight of 7,040 pounds, which is over three tons. My fish was a white sturgeon (*Acipenser transmontanus*), the biggest North American species. (The word "beluga" also means white, although these fish are not the brilliant white of the beluga whale, whose name shares the same Russian origin.) The fish now in front of me looked gray in the water, or "dull aluminum," in the reported words of pilot Babe Alsworth. When it surfaced, the water blur cleared to reveal an intricate granular pattern of small white discs sprinkled on a gray-brown background with a hint of blue. The leathery skin was scaleless, but running down the middle of each flank was a row of diamond-shaped bony "scutes," and another row followed the ridge of its back. This was what left the "bite" marks in Bill Trefon's parents' propeller—not when the fish attacked the boat but when they motored over the basking fish. And something else now fell into place. Robbin had told me about a fisherman who found a strange bone in the form of a large circular dish on one of Iliamna's many islands. When she asked where it was—thinking that DNA analysis might prove useful—he was unable to relocate where he had hidden it. But I'd found it here. Behind the tapering snout on each side of the head, protecting the gill chamber, was a bony disc about a foot in diameter.

My fish was nine feet long and would have weighed around 300 pounds—at the bottom end of the size scale for the fish seen in Iliamna. (We didn't get an accurate weight because local regulations forbid lifting large sturgeon out of the water, as this can damage their internal organs.) But they grow much bigger than this. In the 1970s a legendary sturgeon nicknamed "Big Moe" was sometimes hooked, but never landed, below the McNary dam. The wide-eyed anglers said this fish was at least twenty feet long. In 1893 a 2,000-pounder was reportedly caught. This was when commercial fishing on the Columbia was at its peak. The year before, the total catch was five and a half million pounds, the average size being seven feet (150 pounds). Going by some other fish that were both weighed and measured, the 2,000-pound fish would have been fourteen or fifteen feet long.

But commercial fishing on this scale was unsustainable, and by 1898 it had almost wiped out the Columbia River's sturgeon. Only after fishing was closed for a decade did they start to make a comeback. In the 1940s small sturgeon were showing up in salmon gillnets. In 1950 the government introduced strict regulations that forbade the taking of any fish over six feet long. At the other end of the scale, all sturgeon measuring less than four feet must be returned (thirty inches for those non-commercial fishermen who don't practice catch and release). The results of this policy are tangible. As well as my catch, some fish around the thirteen-foot mark have been reported in recent years, and these fish would have cleared a thousand pounds. And in early 2008, when sonar showed what appeared to be a huge pile of rubble beneath the Bonneville Dam, prompting panic among engineers, this turned out to be a solid "ball" of sturgeon, which the operators of the submersible that was sent down to investigate estimated to comprise around sixty thousand individuals. Maybe in time the mythical leviathans of the past will, after all, be reincarnated.

In the meantime, although the white sturgeon's massive size isn't in question, there remains the question of how they might sink boats. Sturgeon are secretive bottom-feeders, commonly vacuuming up sedentary food items such as shells and crustaceans. Instead of jaws crammed with teeth, they have a strange protrusible mouth on the underside of the head, behind a curtain of four dangling feelers. To retrieve my barbless hook, I rolled the fish partially on its side and put my hand in this toothless chasm. It was like a rubbery oversize sleeve that I was able to extend about a foot from its "stowed" position. Even without jaws to seize larger prey, I could now see how a big sturgeon could easily inhale a live shad or even a salmon just by the suction created when this tube is deployed and opened. Because of the position of its mouth, however, it would have to roll its body to direct this suction, unless its prey was directly underneath it. And thinking about this, I remembered the strange, twisting movements of the fish that Robbin saw. . . .

Its behavior is, in a way, predatory and aggressive, but there's a world of difference between nailing a salmon on the lake bed and attacking a boat. But a crop of eye-popping reports from the Suwannee River in northwest Florida bridge this credibility gap. In the summer of 2006 a flying four-foot gulf sturgeon (*Acipenser oxyrinchus desotoi*, a subspecies of the Atlantic sturgeon) knocked unconscious a twenty-three-year-old jet skier, Blake Fessenden, who only survived because his girlfriend, on another craft, arrived and held his head out of the water. Another sturgeon victim that year was thirty-two-year-old Dawn Poirier, who was in a coma for fifteen days and had to have half her face reconstructed. Among nine injuries reported in 2007 was one fatality, when a boat swerved to avoid a jumping sturgeon, thereby throwing two passengers into the water, one of whom drowned.

Nobody knows why some fish jump. Dominance display, group communication, and getting rid of parasites are the normal suggestions. In the days when I used to camp beside English lakes, I saw and heard bottom-feeding carp do it a lot, usually crashing down on their sides. And I'm told the white sturgeon of the Columbia River do it as well, which would be quite something if you happened to be underneath it. In the enormity of Lake Iliamna, such a misfortune would seem extremely unlikely, until you consider that some fish jump when alarmed.

Sometimes, too, the best defense is attack. Picture a fish basking near the surface and suddenly a strange black shape appears right overhead. Whatever that shape is, it's invading body space with no regard for the normal niceties of territory and dominance. In 2009 I received an e-mail from a man who was out on Lake Chelan one day, a dammed arm of the Columbia. "We came across a monster as long as our boat, 18 foot. It got mad at us, like a jaws movie. It was faster than us and put up more wake, with a 55 HP Merc opened up. . . . It does have old Indian stories about it, but only two old men believed us, saying they'd seen it too."

But are they really in Lake Iliamna? White sturgeon are said to inhabit coastal waters from central California right up to Alaska. But bottom-fishing halibut anglers diligently sample Alaska's coastal waters, and they never catch sturgeon. And no one would miss a ten-foot fish running up the Kvichak—unless the sturgeon went up at night, like cagey Himalayan mahseer entering a shallow clear-water tributary. But there are anecdotal reports: of one caught in Bristol Bay; of another spotted a few decades ago in the Igushik River, which runs into Bristol Bay; and of others allegedly in the Kvichak. Either their range has shrunk or these are strays—or both. Certainly sturgeon worldwide are not as widespread as they once were. Seeing a sturgeon in a British river would be like spotting a UFO, but there are cast-iron cases of their presence in the past.

For instance, on July 28, 1932, Alec Allen was fishing Gilbert Pool on the River Towy, near the Welsh village of Nantgaredig, when his line caught on something that he at first thought was a log. But then it started moving upriver. Unable to leave the pool because the water had recently fallen, the thrashing fish leapt into the shallows, where it straightened a gaff before a rock dropped repeatedly on its head subdued it. The fish was hauled onto a horse-drawn cart and taken to a nearby farm, where it was identified as a common Baltic sturgeon (*Acipenser sturio*), measured at nine feet, two inches, and weighed at 388 pounds. This still holds the distinction of being the largest fish ever caught on a rod and line in a British river, although technically it was not a "fair" capture because it was not hooked the mouth but rather in the skin of the head. Because sturgeon have been a royal fish since the time of Edward II (1284–1327, and gruesomely murdered in Berkeley Castle beside the River Severn), a telegram was sent to King George V, who apparently wasn't at home. So the fish was sold to a fishmonger in Swansea for two pounds and ten shillings (£2.50); the caviar inside it would have been worth £25,000 in today's money. By all accounts Mr. Allen didn't talk much about his catch in later years, but when he died twenty-five years later, his ashes were scattered, in a ceremony attended by no priest, on the pool "where I caught leviathan."

Another sturgeon, known as the Croesyceiliog fish, broke three nets and tipped over two coracles near Towy Castle in June 1896, but it was eventually recorded at eight feet, four inches and 320 pounds. The captor, "Billy Boy," sold the fish to "Slippy Dick." In the River Severn, sturgeon were commonly caught in salmon nets until the 1950s, including a fish reportedly weighing over 500 pounds that was taken from Lydney to London's Billingsgate fish market in June 1937. Further north, a sturgeon of 460 pounds was reported from the Yorkshire Esk, and in 1956 the trawler *Ben Urie* netted a 700-pound fish, ten feet, five inches long, off the Scottish Orkney Islands. The sturgeon's subsequent decline can probably be attributed to intensive sea fishing, pollution, and blocked migration routes, but we can't be certain whether the species ever successfully bred in British rivers. To be fair, these fish more likely were strays. Even those renowned navigators, salmon, occasionally swim up the "wrong" river; in fact, the figure is at least 10 percent. But this actually signifies greater perfection, from the long-term survival point of view, than a 100-percent homing rate. Scientists believe that having a small percentage that "get lost" helps the salmon to recolonize territory lost because of a changing climate, such as an ice age advancing and receding.

The most celebrated lost sturgeon of recent years was a nine-footer weighing 264 pounds that was netted in Swansea Bay, off South Wales, in 2004. A message was duly sent to the Queen, who declined the offer of a fish supper and said that the captor, Robert Davies, could "dispose of it as he saw fit." But despite this royal go-ahead, sent by fax from Buckingham Palace, camera-wielding scene-of-crime officers from the Devon and Cornwall constabulary interrupted the sale of the fish at Plymouth fish market. After all, Baltic sturgeon are a protected species in the UK, which is very odd when you consider that individual sturgeon turning up in British waters are non-native vagrants, and the species has probably never bred here. Even so, Mr. Davies was looking at a maximum penalty of £5,000 or up to six months in prison. (He would have been in the clear if, instead of selling it, he'd given it away or eaten it himself.) The story then took another twist when, right after the sale, the fish disappeared. As the net was closing in on the sturgeon's buyer, there was a phone call, and the fish, by now called Stanley, was taken into police custody at "an undisclosed location." The situation had been resolved by offering the fish to London's Natural History Museum, which was delighted to acquire this large, rare fish. But here, the curator of fishes Oliver Crimmen made an observation that let everyone off the hook. He was struck by the short, blunt snout of this fish, and after further tests, he identified it as an Atlantic sturgeon from—final double-take—North America (*Acipenser oxyrinchus oxyrinchus*). (Interestingly, this catch supports the theory that Baltic/British sturgeon are a recent offshoot, dating back just 1,200 years, from North American sturgeon rather than a subpopulation of European sturgeon, which have been isolated from their western Atlantic cousins for some sixty million years.)

There's one other thing that sturgeon share with salmon. Both have populations that buck the general trend and don't migrate to the sea. Even with the loss of rich marine feeding grounds, they still manage to grow to maturity and successfully breed. In northeastern North America, from Maine to Ontario and Newfoundland, several lakes contain a landlocked subspecies of the Atlantic salmon. In Europe there's the entirely freshwater huchen (*Hucho hucho*), alias Danubian salmon, which has been caught to 127 pounds, and in Asia there's the non-seagoing taimen (*Hucho taimen*), which has been recorded up to 231 pounds. In North America the once abundant but now rare lake sturgeon (*Acipenser fulvescens*) of the Great Lakes, Hudson Bay, and Mississippi ecosystems survives without a marine phase in its life cycle; and there are some eighteen landlocked populations of white sturgeon, mostly because of dams. But there's one population of white sturgeon that was naturally cut off from the sea. The Kootenai sturgeon, named after the river where they live, were cut off from the sea when glacial deposits from a retreating ice sheet created impassable waterfalls in the river's course. Despite this, they managed to breed and sustain their numbers for ten thousand years, evolving into a distinct genetic strain of white sturgeon—less solid in body, as might be expected, but otherwise thriving. (Only now, after the construction of the Libby dam in Montana, have these sturgeon stopped breeding due to reduced water flow, which is causing siltation of the clean gravel beds that sturgeon need for spawning.)

Could something similar have happened in Iliamna? At its western end, the lake is confined not by mountains but instead a flat glacial moraine, over which the Kvichak now meanders to the sea, fifty miles away and just forty-six feet below the level of the lake. Before this outwash deposit formed, what is now the lake was likely once open to the sea. And if so, it's perfectly possible that a population of sturgeon became isolated there. (Although the Kvichak is technically navigable, its shallowness and clarity would rule against sturgeon using it as a regular highway.) Once such a hypothetical population is there, all it needs to survive is an adequate food source and a place to breed. The prodigious runs of salmon fulfill the first requirement. In fact, why waste energy getting food from the sea if that seafood comes to you? For spawning grounds, the areas where feeder streams run into the lake ought to provide a perfect combination of deep-enough, safe water as well as clean, well-oxygenated gravel.

Although this scenario is only a "thought experiment," in my mind it makes a pretty convincing case for declaring this a mystery no longer. What's more, this conclusion also appears to settle another mystery: the likely identity of the world's biggest freshwater (nonmigratory) fish. All we need now is for somebody to catch one. . . .

There's one more thing that makes me think the Iliamna monster is a sturgeon. While filming near the village of Nondalton on the river between Lake Clark and Lake Iliamna, we met up with three lads fishing in a boat who had seen the first series of *River Monsters* and were curious to know what we were doing here. I said we were investigating the monster, and asked if they had any ideas about what it was.

"Yeah, it's a sturgeon," one of them said.

Now I find myself idly wondering about those twenty-foot-long objects that sonar detected in Loch Ness, moving between mid-water and the bottom. There's also a story from the 1930s of a woman who saw a large creature swimming up the five-mile-long River Ness toward the loch. She described it as looking like a crocodile with tusks. Now, if you had never seen a sturgeon before, think how you might describe a large animal with a pointed snout, bony plates on its back and long, dangling barbels. Somebody should go there in the summer months and cast a dead salmon on very strong line where one of the feeder rivers comes in, either off Invermoriston or in the mouth of the River Enrick near Castle Urquhart. The latter location is opposite General Wade's Military Road, but I'm not taking that as any kind of omen. After taking six years to catch a goliath tigerfish and another six for the arapaima, I think I'll leave this one for somebody else.

CHAPTER 13

SNAKEHEAD

Packed with relentless monster action on water and dry land,
Snakehead Terror proves you could be next on the menu!

Publicity for *Snakehead Terror*, 2004

THEY CRAWL ON LAND! They breathe air! They eat animals, and they've killed people! And they're taking over the waterways of the United States! What are they? Snakeheads, of course. Just the name provokes an involuntary shudder.

Snakeheads made US national headlines in 2002 when northern snakeheads (*Channa argus*) were caught from a pond at Crofton, Maryland, just twenty miles northeast of Washington, DC. Some of the fish were two feet long, already half their maximum size, with razor-sharp cutting teeth and markings reminiscent of a reticulated python. But the two-inchers were more scary. This meant that this fish, normally a native of China and one of the largest of the thirty-odd snakehead species, had successfully bred. Right next to the pond was the Little Patuxent River. If there was a flood, the fish could spread to there, and then they would really be on the loose. Maybe they could even get there without a flood, thanks to their suprabranchial organ, a breathing chamber above the gills, and their alleged ability to colonize new waters by wriggling over land. They had to be stopped.

Mindful that this species, which survives harsh Asiatic winters, could potentially colonize much of the United States, wildlife officials took the drastic step of poisoning the pond with rotenone. They killed six adults and more than a thousand juveniles. The emergency was over.

The mystery of how they got there was cleared up a little while later. A man originally from Hong Kong had bought a pair of the fish from an Asian market in New York in order to make a medicinal soup for his sister, who was ill. But by the time the fish arrived, she had recovered, so he kept them in an aquarium. It wasn't long, however, before they were eating twelve goldfish a day, so he decided to evict them.

But in south Florida the discovery of snakeheads came too late. In 2000 fisherman Bob Newland caught a fish that he didn't recognize and took it to the state's exotic fish lab. Here, fish specialist Paul Shafland didn't recognize it either. Only after plowing through a tome of world fishes did he have a positive ID: bullseye snakehead (*C. marulius*).

"After that he wanted to know exactly where I caught it," Bob told me, as we bank-fished a canal near a busy highway. "I said I caught it on a golf course in Tamarac. And he said, 'No, I need to know what *hole* you found it on.'"

Shafland hoped the fish would be confined to just that one pond so he could quickly eradicate them. But when his team sampled the surrounding canals using electro-fishing boats to stun the fish to the surface, they found them there as well. "South Florida is a maze of interconnected canals," he told me. "We couldn't have created a more ideal habitat for snakeheads."

I saw that for myself when I went fishing with Alan Zaremba, a guide who normally takes clients fishing for peacock bass. These fish are also not native to Florida but instead come from the Amazon. Unlike snakeheads, however, they were introduced officially and are hence classed as "exotic" rather than "invasive." This partly comes down to fish snobbery: the fact that they're considered desirable "game" fish— like trout, which continue to be spread around the world despite biologists' concerns about their impact on native species. But more to the point, peacock bass are not able to breed in cold water, so there's no risk they'll spread. And there are no stories that peacock bass will kill you.

Alan's top snakehead bait is a rubber frog. This is used in conjunction with a special kind of single hook, which has the point precisely aligning with the shank and the bend shaped rather like a keel. This is threaded into the bait so the point nestles invisibly in a groove in the frog's body. Thus mounted, it can be cast among weeds and branches without fouling, but the action of a snakehead chomping down on the soft bait exposes the point. With my briefing over, Alan quietly maneuvered me into position using the electric trolling motor. I cast beyond some lilies and then, with the rod held high to keep the frog on the surface, brought the bait chugging back toward me. On about the third retrieve, passing a gap in the pads, the surface opened and the rod yanked around. I wasn't expecting this at all, but somehow I managed to do everything right—hustling the fish out of the weeds and into the open water and then alongside the boat. In the clear water I could see what it was, so I gripped its lower jaw with a metal grip, rather than my fingers, and swung aboard my first snakehead.

I'd seen pictures of other snakeheads, but this one was a real stretched version: about four pounds of fish extending over two feet. A rosette pattern of scales on top of its head added to the serpentine effect, and the mouth was wide and toothy beneath large eyes. Each jaw had a single row of teeth, which act as spikes for pinning prey, but this is only half the story. When the fish shakes its head from side to side, the effect is like a saw, cutting large prey in half. The body color was nondescript brown on the back and flanks, shading to a lighter tone on the belly. The only punctuation was a couple of black flecks on each lateral line, edged with white, and the eye spot on its tail, which was black ringed with orange, from which it gets its name. It's a feature it shares with its new neighbors, peacock bass, which will sometimes hang near the surface with their head end sloping down, in which position this marking looks exactly like an eye to any heron or other avian spear fisherman that fancies taking a jab at it. And it probably serves the same decoy function in the bullseye snakehead, as they often lurk very close to the bank. After only an hour or two of fishing, I could tell exactly the kind of place where they would be—gaps in weeds, around sunken branches, under trailing bank-side vegetation—although sometimes in a perfect-looking spot there'd be nobody home. If they were there, they'd strike on the first pass, but after my early success I was now missing fish after fish and cursing my hair-trigger strike-reflex, which invariably pulled the bait out of their mouth. And unlike a peacock bass, which will get more and more wound up until it hooks itself, a missed snakehead won't hit a lure again. Alan explained I had to override this and drop the rod on the take while winding up the slack that this creates—and *then* strike. In other words, I'd probably connected with the first fish precisely because I wasn't fully alert.

The bullseye snakehead normally lives in Southeast Asia. Lt. Pat Reynolds, who investigated the case of this illegal alien, found live snakeheads in the first Asian store he walked into and traced the supply line to New York City via Miami. But this didn't explain their presence in the wild. One theory cited the Buddhist custom of giving captive animals their freedom, but Reynolds suspects that a Florida "entrepreneur" had the idea of establishing his own local supply. Since then, federal law has prohibited the importation, transportation, or possession of any of these "injurious" fish anywhere in the United States. Aquarists who used to keep them say it's easier to buy a gun than one of these fish.

But although the Florida canals are stuffed with snakeheads, there's no evidence that they're the ecological disaster that many fear, although all biologists would prefer that they'd never arrived in the first place. Although it's true that native Florida species now share their home with invasives, Paul Shafland has conducted research that shows that the total biomass of native species has remained more or less unchanged over the last decade. In other words, snakeheads have not muscled out the native species (as filter-feeding Asian carp have done in the Illinois River) but instead have somehow managed to live alongside them in a more complex ecosystem. (A similar situation seems to exist in the Potomac, where there's now an established population of northern snakeheads that anglers are catching to over ten pounds. Because it's not practical to poison 380 miles of river, we can only assume that these are here to stay.)

There's also no evidence from the United States that snakeheads are a direct hazard to humans, although to be honest I didn't see anyone swimming in the Florida canals and couldn't imagine anyone wanting to. To get to the bottom of their fierce reputation, I traveled to Thailand, to the mountainous region near the border with Burma, where two large lakes, Khao Laem and Sri Nakharin, have been formed by damming tributaries of the River Kwai. As soon as I asked, I started hearing tales of extraordinary aggression: a child mauled, a man rammed in the leg, a spear fisherman who had his mask smashed. Another fisherman, who was hose-diving in Khao Laem, breathing air from a compressor on a boat, had the tube ripped from his mouth and drowned. Another died after his throat was ripped open.

The fish behind all these stories was the giant snakehead (*C. micropeltes*). Already a few members of this species have turned up in the United States, thought to be released from aquaria after their owners, who bought them as pretty red tiddlers, got tired of smashed tank lids and being bitten when they cleaned the glass—or when they found out that keeping them was illegal. As yet, however, there are no signs that they have found one another and bred. . . .

Giant snakeheads can exceed four feet and forty pounds, which is certainly big enough to do some damage. To be convinced, though, I needed more than secondhand stories. So when a man named Sombat showed me his scar, it was a major breakthrough. Three years before, he had dived underneath his floating house to fix one of the bundles of bamboo on which it floated. As he was working, he saw a snakehead approaching with its pectoral fins flared—like an elephant spreading its ears as a last warning before a charge. The next thing he knew, it was savaging his leg, and he scrambled out of the water. At the hospital, staff refused to believe that the tooth marks, the size of a dog bite, were those of a fish. After stitching him up, they gave him a rabies shot.

Sombat had been minding his own business, but most attacks are not motiveless. There's a big industry on these lakes based on collecting snakehead fry and then growing them in pens for later sale. When giant snakeheads are young, they form dense shoals, just a few feet across, which the fishermen net, having located them from the dimpling they make on the surface when they come up to breathe. As air-breathers, they can then be kept at very high density—unlike other fish, which would die in such conditions. This would be about the easiest fishing anywhere but for one thing. You first have to deal with the parents.

Everyone said the most experienced fisherman on Khao Laem was a man named Khun Dar. I went to his floating house and found a slight, soft-spoken man who filled me in on the finer points of hunting *pla chado*. He told me that when you approach a fry ball underwater, you do not need to look for the parents; they will find you. Generally the male corrals the young while the female patrols the perimeter. These observations, I realized, are actually more detailed than any that scientists have made because his livelihood—and his life—depend on them. He confirmed that snakeheads have a threat posture, facing you head-on with fins flared, but you mustn't shoot at this time because this is a small, hard-boned target. You must wait until the fish turns side-on and then spear it in the flank.

If you get it wrong, the worst-case scenario can be very bad indeed. A Burmese man who had crossed into Thailand to fish failed to return to the surface after diving toward a fry ball. His wife, waiting in the boat, dove in search of him and found his body. He had speared the fish in the head, but it had continued its charge and, in so doing, thrust the back end of the man's metal spear through his mask and into his face. Then, according to fisherman Khun Lang, who told me this, the fish's continued struggles forced the spear out the back of the man's skull.

Although this was a freak incident, the aggression of giant snakeheads is very real. Back in Florida, at Palm Beach Atlantic University, ichthyologist Ray Waldner had told me about the extreme nature of snakeheads' parental care, and this is the reason he still fears for Florida's native species: because snakeheads could in time out-reproduce them. In the breeding season in Southeast Asia, rod-and-line fishing mostly seeks to provoke this aggression, not any desire to feed. Khao Laem, most of which is a national park, is a maze of bays, inlets, and backwaters that are surrounded by misty pinnacles of forested rock, and the rod fishing, just like spear fishing at this time, is all about finding the fry balls. If there's a wind-chop on the water, these can be almost invisible. You find yourself looking at a certain place but don't quite know why. Then you think you see an orange tinge in the water, the color of the very young fry before they grow beyond two or three inches. At this point, you need to paddle into casting range and be ready for the next dimpling, which should be near the last place you saw them if you've managed not to scare them off. Then you cast a noisy surface lure beyond the fry ball and bring it back right through the middle of them. . . .

In theory, this provokes a savage strike from one of the parents, but on Khao Laem, the snakeheads know all about fishing lures, so mine were ignored. My only hit was from a ten-inch fry, at this size more subdued in appearance, with a black stripe down its side. I wondered if this shoal had perhaps been orphaned, but then a larger rise disproved this notion.

Frustrated by my lack of success, I switched to casting blind, systematically exploring likely looking spots along the shoreline. Halfway into one inlet, I saw an abandoned floating hut. Remembering Sombat's story, I sent a cast toward it, and it dropped a fluky six inches short. Scarcely had I started the retrieve when a fish smashed into it and then crash-dove into weed. Paddling closer, I managed to disentangle it, and minutes later I was admiring a small (three-pound) giant snakehead. Things were looking up. But when I returned to the floating hut that was our daytime base, the person acting as our film monitor explained that we hadn't in fact received permission to fish yet, so I'd have to stop for now. For the whole of the next day we sat in the rain, waiting for a permission that never came. This inaction went on and on until we realized we would have to abandon fishing altogether.

Fortunately this wasn't the complete disaster it could have been. Pulling in a giant snakehead on a line from the safety of a boat might have been a risk to my fingers, but for our director Steve Gooder, this had always seemed like the soft option. Steve wanted me to swim into a fry ball, with Khun Dar as my bodyguard, in order to witness real snakehead aggression at first hand. On top of that, he wanted me to carry a minicamera, as this could be the first-ever footage of its kind.

This was an exciting idea, but it also made me uneasy. Observing fierce fish underwater is one thing; provoking them with your presence is another. But I agreed that doing this would give the film an extra dimension, and it was the only way we could test the likely truth of the stories we'd heard. We duly located a fry ball, which seemed to be resident in one particular bay, secured Dar's cooperation, and planned to roll into action the next morning.

That evening, however, our film monitor announced that she was returning to Bangkok. We could do no more filming here. Not being able to fish was one thing, but without this scene, we had no film. We would have to come back—God knows when—for an expensive reshoot, possibly having to hire the fishing guide that our film monitor kept recommending. But Steve refused to be defeated. We'd go to Sri Nakharin, which is not a national park, and do it there. Without hesitation, Dar, barefoot in shorts and T-shirt and carrying only his mask and spear, agreed to come with us. But I thought we were wasting our time, and on arrival at Sri Nakharin, my opinion appeared to be vindicated. Unlike Khao Laem, this lake has very little shelter, and a strong breeze had whipped up big waves. This meant that finding a fry ball would be impossible. On top of that, the weather had stirred up the water. Instead of several yards' visibility, we had barely a few feet. Even if we found any fish, going after them could be crazily dangerous.

Teaming up with some local fishermen, we divided into two boats and started quartering the water. Against all expectations, in the afternoon the other boat located a fry ball and called us over. Beaching our boat, we walked along the shore, scouring the surface. Then Dar pointed. At first I couldn't see it, but then I did: a small patch where the surface texture was momentarily different. I would have to go through with this after all.

While the film kit was prepared, I lay on my back and did some breath holds. Dar dives most days, so I was unsure of my ability to stay down with him. To make things worse, my rising apprehension was raising my heart rate and increasing my oxygen consumption. I tried to control this by calming my mind, sending my thoughts away to a quiet place. I wanted to do this thing but also I didn't. Ideally, I wanted to be sitting in comfort watching back the footage from the snakehead's territory, having fast-forwarded the process of going to get it or, better still, having skipped it altogether. Actually that wasn't true. This was not unlike the topsy-turvy feeling I used to get when lacing up my alloy-studded boots before eighty minutes of exhaustion and pain on the rugby field when I was a teenager: a mixture of fear and something else that catalyzed that fear into a kind of psychic food. And somewhere in here surely is an explanation for the universal human need for an adversary, whether human or abstract. If the pulse never quickens for anything, then there's little point it beating at all.

It was time to go. Dar was on the bow of the small boat, and I boarded behind him. He signaled to the man paddling—forward, this way, stop—and then slipped into the water. But as I prepared to follow suit, he submerged and was gone. I belly-flopped after him and kicked with my fins, but the murky water had swallowed him up. Pushing through a forest of weed stems, the camera cable dragging behind me, I could barely see beyond my outstretched arm and no longer knew which way to go. I started to have visions of a five-foot metal rod flashing out of the gloom. It was time to come up.

But I hadn't missed the shot because Dar hadn't made contact. We found the fry ball again, some way off now, and went down a second time. But again I lost Dar, and again Dar failed to find the fish. The next time, I resolved not to lose him and stuck so close that his feet were kicking my mask. Suddenly he stopped and I drew alongside, and I saw him looking around with his neck arched and eyes wide. Then I saw a movement, diagonally toward me, of black-and-white striped shapes. And when I looked back toward Dar, just a heartbeat later, I saw no discernible figure but instead a confusion of movement rising in the water. Instinctively I knew and kicked for the surface, where I saw him arrive moments later, not holding the spear itself but rather the grip in the middle of its thick rubber strips—the sign that it had been fired.

The spear's breakaway point, secured by two feet of cord, had passed through the snakehead's back muscle, just underneath the long dorsal fin. A flesh wound only, from which this tough customer would easily recover. Having been forced to confront the fish in this way, I was overwhelmed by this improbable twist: that both fisherman and fish would survive. Held in the water after being freed from the cord, it rested quietly in my hands and tilted up to sip some air. As it started to flex, I took one last look at its broad black-and-white flanks, abstract patterned like the map of some secret land. The eyes, like black marbles, told me nothing, as it flicked its tail and melted back into the water.

CHAPTER 14

RIVER SHARK REVISITED

Then he began to pity the great fish that he had hooked.
He is wonderful and strange and who knows how old he is, he thought.

Ernest Hemingway, *The Old Man and the Sea*, 1952

IN JANUARY 2009 a small team of scientists in South Africa made a discovery that sent such shockwaves through the scientific community and beyond that those waves rebounded on the team's leader in the form of anonymous threats.

What they had found was the largest bull shark ever recorded anywhere in the world: over thirteen feet in total length (four meters exactly) and weighing an estimated one thousand pounds. But its immense size was not the only thing that caused such waves. What intrigued other biologists was that it was in an area where they had never before recorded the species: two hundred miles south of its normal range, in water thought to be too cold for the species to survive.

But what caused the wider stir was something else. This water is also populated by jet skiers, kite-surfers, and holidaying bathers, and it is flanked by luxury homes and condominiums. In the popular imagination, this earthly paradise should have been free from such hellish beasts for one fundamental reason: it is up a river.

For some biologists and fishermen, the bull shark's ability to swim up rivers—way beyond any estuarine saltiness and into pure fresh water—is well known. And this is something that no amount of hand-wringing about real estate values or wanting to shoot the messenger can do anything about. But the reason *why* a bull shark was in the Breede River was a mystery. Was it a freak occurrence or did it have company? And why was it so astoundingly huge? To try to get answers, the team returned to the river the following year. Their interest was not only academic. Although most sharks are harmless to humans, bull sharks are one of the few species, alongside tiger sharks (*Galeocerdo cuvier*) and great whites (*Carcharodon carcharias*), that are confirmed man-eaters. In other words, was this a human tragedy waiting to happen?

In the hope of shedding light on this dark subject, they had brought three acoustic tags and a hydrophone. Each tag would enable them to track a shark until the tag's miniature battery ran out after about three months. But first they had to catch a shark. This was where I came in. With my experience of catching large fish from rivers and, more specifically, river bull sharks in Australia, I was ideally qualified to join the investigation.

From Cape Town, the film crew and I drove four hours east along the coast through parched empty countryside to the sleepy town of Witsand at the river mouth. White-painted houses gleamed against a cobalt sky like a picture-postcard. A bar of windswept sand reached across the river mouth, leaving only a narrow gap on the far side where the river joined the Indian Ocean. This setting couldn't have been more different from the jungles and mountains that are my normal fishing grounds. And seeing the fishermen wading up to their waists to collect prawns and cast flies, I realized that this investigation was different too. My fishing success or failure could make the difference between life and death.

In some sport-fishing circles, a shark is "caught" once you've touched the wire leader, which you then cut as close to the shark as possible, trusting that in time the hook will rust out, especially if it's not stainless. Similarly, if you want to attach a thin plastic "spaghetti tag" with serial and phone numbers, you'd normally do this remotely, using a long stick. But fixing an acoustic tag is more hands-on: we would need to restrain the shark in the shallows or on the bank while we also took accurate measurements, samples of any parasites, and a small fin clipping for DNA analysis.

The fish caught in 2009, by South African Angler Hennie Papenfuss after three fishless days, was a heavily pregnant female. Although some shark species lay their eggs in a protective case—the so-called "mermaid's purse"—most retain them in the body. Bull sharks take the process one stage further, with the yolk sac turning into a type of placenta that is embedded in the uterus and supplies the embryo with nutrients from the mother. It's remarkably similar to the mechanism in mammals, and was first observed in sharks by Aristotle, in the fourth century BC. Coming into the world at between twenty and thirty inches long, bull shark pups have a significant head start on most other fish.

After tagging and releasing the big female, the scientists took to the tracking boat, lowered the hydrophone into the water, and rotated it until it they picked up the "ping" from the tag. The plan now was to follow it, day and night, in continuous shifts for two weeks. But four hours later it was still lying in the same place. The team's leader, Meaghen McCord, began to worry that the fish might not have recovered from its long struggle on the line. If this was the case, they'd remain in the dark about what this shark had been doing here, although for some people living beside the river, its death would have been good news.

Then, suddenly, it was no longer there. The tracking boat swept up and down the river, dipping and rotating the hydrophone every five hundred yards, but all they heard was crackling static. Finally, they picked up a signal in the surf zone, outside the river mouth. Maybe the carcass had been washed out here? But the signal's source was moving. Maybe its recent experience had told it that the river was not a good place to be, or maybe the moving water here was just a good place to get reoxygenated.

What happened next surprised everybody. The shark reentered the river, and when the team had to pack up fifteen days later, it was still there. During this time it was found to patrol a beat some fifteen miles long, up and down on each tide, twice daily—a total distance of fifty to sixty miles a day. The furthest upstream it traveled was twenty miles from the sea, which is beyond the influence of the tide, and where there is no trace of salt in the water.

The scientists' hypothesis, based on its continued presence, was that it was in the river to pup. Compared with the sea, rivers contain fewer predators that could prey on the young. For a start, there are no other sharks and possibly no male bull sharks, which won't hesitate to eat their own kind. But set against that, a small bull shark isn't as comfortable physiologically in fresh water as a big one. It has a higher surface-area-to-volume ratio, so it has to expend much more energy expelling water from its tissues. Giving birth to their young in a river would only make sense if the pros exceeded the cons.

To find out more, we needed another shark. I had come well equipped with my own big bull shark gear, which was based on what I had previously borrowed from Terry Hessey in Australia, for shore fishing in the Brisbane River mouth. This comprised a custom-built 5½-foot shark rod, an 80-pound-class reel holding nearly half a mile of 80-pound mono, and PVC-coated wire rope in strengths up to 1,300 pounds. But the information I now got hold of meant that I could have left all this at home.

Witsand used to be a big port for commercial fishing vessels, but nowadays only a handful of boats are left. Eugene Beukes skippers one of these, and he told me that occasional Zambezi sharks, as bull sharks are known in Africa, have been turning up here for decades. To prove that this was no fisherman's tale, he showed me a brown-and-white photograph of his father with a 532-pound female caught in 1963. In those days the commercial boats used to fish in the river for dusky kob, a fish the color of old pewter that can grow to over 100 pounds. Once in a while, when a fisherman was pulling in his line, suddenly there would be less weight on the end and in would come just the kob's head, cleanly cut behind the gills. If this kept happening, it made a serious dent in the fisherman's income, so one year, after bringing in sixteen kob heads, Eugene's father baited a wire trace on a handline. He landed the shark after a one-hour battle and didn't boat any more incomplete kob that year.

Cobus Wiid, a sun-tanned wiry man in his early sixties who grew up here, told me something similar. "The people of Witsand always refer to *the* shark," he said. He remembers another fisherman, his neighbor Johan Engela, who caught a 352-pounder in the mid-1980s after having several fish removed from his line. "There were no more incidents after this shark was killed," he said, referring to the time the plastic bait container hanging off the back of his boat was grabbed that same year.

Snaffling fish from an angler's line is something that pike sometimes do in English rivers. But these reports indicated something more regular and systematic. The team had put the word out among local fishermen, asking them to report any incidents, but for a long time they heard nothing. Then, a week before we arrived, word came of two fish that had been taken. Our informant had seen the shark responsible and estimated it at seven feet long. The time had come to put a bait in the water—but there was a problem.

These were intelligent sharks. They were clever enough to identify a food source that they didn't have to chase around, and they were clever enough not to be fooled when that same food source was attached to a thick wire leader. (The drag of this would also make the bait swim less naturally.) The year before, the scientists had tried to recapture the big fish in order to attach a more sophisticated tag, but the shark had ignored baits right on top of it. In addition, a local farmer had put up a quarter-million-rand bounty (about $30,000) on the fish, after which fishermen had been spotted on their way to the river with heavy shark gear—but nobody caught anything. However, Meaghen had since been given a leader that she'd been told should work, that a man who had caught a Zambezi shark further north had made. Just by looking at it, I could tell that this angler knew what he was doing, and I agreed to keep the details of its construction confidential, for reasons that will become apparent later. But, essentially, I was going to be fishing much, much lighter than I had expected, which I wasn't altogether happy about.

Normally I gear up for the largest fish I am likely to encounter. There are some who consider this approach "unsporting" and crude because landing average-sized fish can be too easy. Fishing light, the argument goes, requires more skill. But although this has some truth in it, these critics fail to take account of the fact that deceiving a fish on fine tackle is easier. At this crucial point, the angler with heavy gear is the one who suffers the self-imposed handicap. Thick, springy nylon line can be a nightmare to cast if you have no other way of getting it out, and it drags more in the current, making bait presentation more tricky. But I don't see the point of hooking a very large fish if there's a good chance that I'll then lose it, trailing a length of broken line. So fishing light here—in strong, tidal water full of corrugated iron and wood debris, the remains of seventy-odd jetties washed into the river by recent floods—went somewhat against my principles.

January in South Africa is high summer, but on the river the weather is windy. Our first job was to get bait, but the team's seine net pulled up nothing suitable. We dispersed with light rods and a small supply of thumb-sized mud prawns, but nothing bit. This is often the way when fishing for a predator, be it an Amazon catfish, a goonch, or a goliath tigerfish: a lot of your time is consumed struggling to catch small fish. And we needed something soon if we were to try for sharks today: the short period of slack water at the bottom of the tide would soon be upon us. When the tide started to push again, presenting the bait in a natural looking way would become increasingly difficult. Skipper Mark Woof anchored the boat at a place called Rooiwalle, Afrikaans for "red wall," where the river widens at a bend with a steep bank overlooking it, and after catching nothing ourselves, we were relieved when team member Paul van Nimwegen pulled alongside with a prime silver-flanked baitfish.

The fish, which was spotted and making grunting noises, is known locally as the spotted grunter. It was nearly two feet long, deep bodied, spiny finned, and about four pounds in weight. I nicked the hook lightly into its back, lowered it into the water, and let the slackening tide take it slowly downstream. Ten feet up from the bait was an orange balloon, attached by a thin rubber band, which would allow the bait to swim freely in the upper layers but break away if a shark took so the shark would not feel any drag, which could alarm it. Then I briefed the film crew. For once I didn't have an issue with boat noise, as, by all accounts, the sharks here actually zero in on noise, much like Amazon pink dolphins. So everyone could drop cables and drink cans as much as they liked. I would even join the fun, splashing the surface with the rod tip, the same way you do when fishing for piranha. If a fish hit the bait, the important thing was to remember that I was using a circle hook and override the reflex to tighten up immediately. To make sure the shark had properly taken the bait, I would wait for a count of twenty before slowly engaging the drag. This gradual increase in tension would then pull the hook from wherever it was in the mouth or throat to instead lodge in the corner of the jaw. The last thing we wanted—for our sakes or the shark's—was a deep hook-up.

We settled in to wait. The water ran brown and sluggish now. I was fishing off the stern with the balloon bobbing just fifteen yards away—if the sharks are attracted to the boat, why fish a long way off? I soon noticed the stern was no longer pointing downriver; it had swung nearly ninety degrees and was now pointing to the far bank, indicating that the tide was on the turn. Then, a movement caught my eye: a rapid dip of the balloon, creating a coronet of jumping water around it, like an exploding raindrop. The line was no longer pointing at the balloon but instead curving off to the left, and my spool was starting to turn, gathering speed.

"One! . . . two! . . . " I started. We'd been in position barely half an hour, and after an initial pause of disbelief, the crew scrambled to action stations. The line was going out at a frightening rate, and my heart was in my mouth as I slowly pushed the drag lever forward. This seemed to have the effect of making the fish run even faster, and I yelled at Mark to hurry up with the anchor in case I ran out of line. The fish was heading for a protruding branch, and I didn't seem to be making any impression on it as we started to follow with the motor. But as I gained line, it turned away to the left, into what looked like clear water. My relief was only momentary: a message then came up the line telling me this fish was about to escape.

I had about eighty yards of line out, but it was not running directly to the fish. A horrible grating told me that it had swum round a sunken snag. The line could go through at any second. To take pressure off the line, I loosened the drag, and after a frantic attempt to visualize what was going on, I directed Mark to take a curving course to the left, around the perceived position of the snag. With huge relief I felt a live weight again—the line was clear! We could now work closer to the fish and get more control over where it went. But as I wound line onto the reel, my heart sank again. A piece of line surfaced that looked as if it had been shaved by a razor, and then another and another. What had started out as eighty-pound breaking strain now had several weak points that could be just half that—or even less.

The fish now changed its tactics. Having failed to secure its freedom through speed, it now hung deep, very close to the boat, occasionally surging away for a few yards and then allowing me to gain line back— but never allowing me to lift it up. Each time the damaged line grated through the rod rings, I winced. I needed to get it in quickly, but too much pressure would cause the line to break. Somebody told me the shark had been on for an hour. I remembered Eugene telling me that his father once lost a shark after nine hours. The next day it washed up on the shore, and he realized he had been fighting a dead weight, literally, for most of that time. Sharks are negatively buoyant, having no swim bladder. They get their lift from their large pectoral fins, which act like wings when the shark is moving forward. But when they stop swimming, they sink. A couple of times now I'd seen a knot peep above the surface, the Bimini twist where a short length of double line started just above the trace. In other circumstances this would have given some hope. A normal shark trace is strong enough to pull the last few yards in by hand, but not this one. And besides, the knot was no longer in sight.

We then entered a zone that was stuck outside time. I heard some-body say that another hour had passed, but nothing was different. The same few yards of line were repeatedly and laboriously gained and then taken back again as my hunched body repeated the same moves—now

207

straightening a little, now crumpling as if from a punch. The locked muscles in my back pleaded with me to end this brutal dance. I tried to shut them out, to stay focused on the wrenches and lunges of my invisible foe. A late reaction could cause the shaved line to part. But a voice inside my head, getting ever-louder, told me there would be no shame in that. Sooner or later, it was the only outcome, so why prolong the agony? Besides, this was all about getting a shark for the scientists. The sun was now sliding down, and we'd never be able to deal with this shark in the dark. This was make-or-break time. We resolved to grab the double line the next time it appeared, but the first few times we managed this, it was wrenched out of our hands.

I noticed power lines hanging above us. Our slow sliding had carried us five miles upriver. The bottom here shelves up to shallows off the north bank, and the shark reacted by running for the channel. We made our way above it, and there was the knot again, and the leader swivel this time. I backed away from the side as gloved hands pulled on thick mono and then the final six feet of wire: two cheese-wire-thin strands loosely twined. The shark was just below the surface, but they couldn't reach round its great girth to fasten the tow straps, so we made the decision to use the gaff. This was the only way we'd lift the head enough to get the strap around it. But although barely punctured in the thick hide of its chin, the shark reacted by going into a spin, twisting itself free. I thrust the rod into a spare pair of hands, grabbed the gaff, and tried to secure the fish a second time. I felt the wooden handle twist and start to splinter. If it went, the wire leader could garotte someone. I hung on with all my strength while the strap was looped behind the shark's winglike pectorals and tightened. Only now could we widen the circle of our attention to the body behind that fearsome head. At this point Meaghen's comment was so graphic that we had to delete it from the soundtrack.

We towed the shark to a mudbank and heaved it ashore by its tail. Tags went in and the hook came out from where it was neatly lodged in the corner of the jaw. Then we walked it into the river, waist-deep to the drop-off where we launched it into deeper water.

With a total length of 9 feet, 9½ inches (2.99 meters), this shark was one of the biggest male bull sharks ever recorded anywhere in the world. By continuing the curve on weight-for-length charts, Meaghen estimated its weight at around 525 pounds. To understand the biology behind bull sharks surviving in fresh water is one thing, but to see a fish this size come out of a river is quite another. Perhaps this is why only now did something else fully sink in, something Eugene and Cobus had told me. Even though a Zambezi shark had killed a lifeguard further up the coast the year before and a great white had carried off a bather further south, just as we were setting out for South Africa, here in the Breede River, bull sharks have never attacked a human being. This raised another *why?* The fact that this shark was a male and that no small sharks were ever caught—like the three-footers I took from the Brisbane River in Australia—seemed to rule out that they were using this river as a nursery. Everything now said that they were coming here to feed, which made the fact that they were ignoring people, given their track record elsewhere, a real riddle.

But it turned out they weren't ignoring people. When the tracking boat followed this fish, the position of its signal indicated that it was regularly approaching people as well as boats in the water. This unseen ten-foot beast would get within just a few yards before veering off. The previous year's giant female had done the same thing. Despite the cloudy water, they seemed to identify the noise source as human and then decide it was something they didn't want to eat.

The next day another shark took, but after an hour, it bit through the leader when it rose to the surface and then did a rolling dive, thereby wrapping itself in the line and bringing the leader across its teeth. Paul had had the leader in his hands twice but hadn't been able to hold it. The next day I had another take, landing the fish after two and a half hours. This one was a couple of inches shorter than the first fish, but it was more solid bodied. It took just six feet from the boat after I'd pulled the bait in to be near a grunter that Mark was bringing in. Previously I'd been throwing stones at the balloon to get more attention. We thought this fish had also rolled up the line because it wasn't pointing to its nose, but this turned out to have an odd explanation. The hook had somehow caught in the fourth gill slit and was holding by just a small sliver of skin. It was the only time I had ever seen the turned-in point of a circle hook catch anywhere outside the mouth. So this was not, strictly speaking, a fair catch, but that was academic to the scientists, who had another fish to tag and follow. The team was divided on what to call this fish. The two nominations were "Paul" after our expert deck-hand who brought it in and "Duncan" after our director who, in a Hitchcock moment, was the only person available to lend a hand. In the end we opted for a mutant hybrid of these two and called this nine-foot, eight-inch male bull shark "Pumpkin." (Meaghen had christened the first Jeremy.)

With two sharks now tagged, the data was coming thick and fast. The first thing that struck everyone was how much ground the sharks were covering: patrolling a regular beat some five miles long. This made it harder for me to fish because we didn't want to recatch a fish that was already tagged. But when I fished outside this beat in water the hydrophone had swept and found to be "all clear," I had no takes. From Meaghen's original guess of maybe fifteen sharks in the river, we began to revise our estimate down. I returned to the proven spots, but the two fish seemed omnipresent. The only way to be sure they weren't around was to transfer the hydrophone to the fishing boat during the brief slack-water period when a bait could be presented. One windy day we could hear a very faint beep through an ocean of static, coming from about five hundred yards away, near a couple of other boats, and I was hoping the surface chop would cut down its hearing range. But suddenly Meaghen warned me that it was getting nearer. By the time I'd asked her how fast and wound in the bait, the signal strength was ninety-eight: it was right underneath us.

I didn't catch any more sharks, although I did lose one as I tightened up after a take and the line cut on something underwater. My guess from this is that there were perhaps only two or three sharks in the river at the time. Knowing this, some people might argue that removing the sharks would be a realistic strategy to ensure human safety. But our observations clearly reveal that this would be misguided—and could have disastrous consequences.

When I came to the Breede River, I never imagined that what we would find out, in just two short weeks, would take the investigation so far forward and actually give likely answers to the big questions about sharks in this river. Our capture of two large males and the fact that no small sharks are ever caught pretty much rules out that bull sharks are using the river as a nursery, as a place to release their young. Instead, they seem to come here during the warmer months of the year primarily to feed. But this is not normal bull shark feeding behavior. Here they are feeding in a very specific, intelligent way. Rather than wasting energy chasing free-swimming fish, they are taking it from anglers' lines, like plucking fruit from a tree. This is like a form of protection payment. They take a percentage of the anglers' catch and, in return, they leave humans alone.

This is truly a remarkable coexistence—but it is also very fragile. Specifically, there are two things that could threaten it. The first is a decline in numbers of grunter, its normal prey. This is already starting to happen thanks to some anglers being creative in their interpretation of regulations. To avoid ambiguity, this should be two grunter per boat (or, better, none) instead of two for everybody in the boat. Humans find grunter tasty too, but this regulation would be easier for fishermen to swallow if the reason were made clear.

The second necessary measure is to protect the sharks: forbid all fishing for them. Both the sharks I caught were observed to go back to their normal routine of taking grunters from anglers' lines, but if anything happened to make them wary of their normal prey, they could revert to normal, opportunistic bull shark behavior, namely checking out any living creature they come across. Regular attempts to catch them would be sure to do this. As we have learned, they won't be hooked on heavy gear; however, on light gear they are extremely hard to bring in. Just a few break-offs could be enough to have them changing their diet. It would be the classic unintended consequence, so common when humans interfere with nature, but in this case it's one that the application of forethought can help avoid. It's also a classic illustration of the best way to deal with fear: instead of wanting to destroy the thing that you are afraid of, the answer often lies in simply understanding it.

CHAPTER 15

BOL KATA

VEN: Now, *Piscator*, where will you begin to fish?

PISC: We are not yet come to a likely place, I must walk a mile further yet, before I begin.

Izaak Walton, *The Compleat Angler,* 1653

AT THE END OF A SWELTERING DAY in the tropical lowland forest of Papua New Guinea (PNG), Francis Sambin takes off his clothes and gets into waist-deep water at the edge of the mud-brown Sepik River. As he takes a cooling wash, something bumps against him. He brushes it away, but the next moment sharp teeth are clamping and then tearing his genitals. He is so severely mutilated that he bleeds to death. It is 2002, and the local Pidgin language, based on a simplified version of English, gives the mystery perpetrator a graphic name: *bol kata*.

Sometime later, washing in the same stretch of river, Nick Sakat feels something touch his leg. He kicks it away, but it fastens onto his foot and pulls him toward deeper water. Terrified and confused, he makes a grab for a moored log raft—his family's washing platform—and manages to drag himself onto its surface. There is nothing in the native fauna that makes a bite mark like the gushing wound in his foot, a mark that resembles, in shape and size, the imprints of human teeth. He can only think it is an underwater spirit—an invisible person.

From the capital of PNG, Port Moresby, there is no way to drive to the Sepik. Having loaded our thousand pounds of equipment, six of us board a single-engined P-750 XSTOL, a fast-climbing workhorse of an aircraft originally designed for skydiving, which hoists us to twelve thousand feet, following the coast, and then cuts inland toward the island's mountainous spine. Below, the vegetation that covers the valleys and ridges is unbroken. I look for signs of human habitation, but there are none, not even a thread of smoke. As the land climbs toward us, the clouds change from a low broken layer to a pavilion of unsteady pillars, through which we pick our way.

After landing to refuel at Goroka, a cleared and populous valley ringed by mountains, we reweigh ourselves and take off again. The moment our wheels leave the ground we're flying at 5,200 feet, and we climb steeply through the thin air toward a jagged dark line that is intermittently visible above us through rising billows of cloud. Crossing the ridge, we enter a zone where the clouds are more substantial than the earth below, which rises and falls, a little further away each time, until it flattens into a wide coastal plain, which we turn and follow west.

From where the Sepik's branched tail leaves the mountains, a straight line to its mouth would measure 250 miles. Between these two points, the land drops just a hundred feet, a gradient that is scarcely perceptible, except to water. But the Sepik obeys gravity on its own terms, looping this way and then that to investigate far-flung curiosities as it goes. From above, its signature is confident and expansive, with extravagant loops and curlicues that give away its deeper character. In my role as aerial graphologist, I try to read what the river is telling me, and immediately I see that all is not well. The river's identity is not clear and distinct but instead confused with that of the land, which gives back a partial reflection of the sky. The annual flood has not yet receded, which is going to make finding anything in the water doubly difficult.

The other thing that might not help, on top of this thirty-year flood, is the Sepik's notoriety as prime crocodile habitat. It has one species of freshwater crocs as well as much larger salties, the same species found in Australia. The human relationship with crocs is complicated. At the village where we set up base, on the banks of a large lake (a *raunwara*, or round water) in the floodplain, a fisherman, Ramsin Tero, tells me how his twenty-four-foot dugout was attacked from below, splintering its stern. He escaped by climbing a tree that was standing in the water.

He said the massive animal was a *masalai*, a spirit that, although dangerous to individuals, preserves the environment on which humans depend by keeping open the narrow channels that link the lake to the river. Further downriver, people believe that they are descended from crocodiles and hold initiation ceremonies at which young men are symbolically reborn as crocodile men, identifiable by the scalelike patterns of raised scars on their backs and shoulders that are created by a painful process of rubbing ash into cut skin. Others hunt the crocodiles to sell their skins and penises. But when I go out at night with crocodile hunter Alphonse Mava Sanye, I'm surprised by how few crocodile eyes reflect our flashlight. They'd be easier to find if the water was down and more contained, but even then I'm told their numbers are noticeably down lately. This is attributed to a thinning of the floating weed that used to cover most of the lake, in which the crocodiles make their nests. I'm told this change dates from about the same time that Francis Sambin was attacked.

Above the surface, this place could be the Amazon were it not for the mountainous horizon above the trees, the solidity of the stilt-house supports, and the appearance of the people—black skinned and curly haired. The lake is black water, like strong tea. To start getting an idea of what's down there, I put together my tiddler-catching rod, a six-foot wand with six-pound line loaded onto a miniature fixed-spool reel, and I flick a small cube of coconut flesh from a moored dugout into the margins in front of the village. After a few minutes the line twitches and runs, and I bring in a silver-scaled fish about six inches long. A small catfish follows, known here as *nilpis* (nail fish) on account of its dorsal and pectoral spines. A bit later I bring in something a bit bigger, elongated and brown with a big mouth and spiky dorsal fin. I ask Wapi, a boy fishing with a heavy handline by the nearest house, "*Wanem dispela kain pis?*" He tells me it's a *bikmaus*, and some men on the bank get very excited because they never catch this on a hook. Suddenly I have a bit of cred as a fisherman, but this is only because I'm using much finer gear than they do. And this, I'm quickly reminded, also has its down side, as the next fish, although not very big, breaks the line.

Actually, it *bit* through it just after I glimpsed it on the surface: a bright flash of silver with a splash of red. I blink, trying to recall the image. It looked like a red-bellied piranha, which might not be such a surprise if this was Florida or even southern England, but there can't be too many fish-tank hobbyists with imported species around here. I rummage in my bag of terminal-tackle odds and ends, and I tie a larger hook to a few inches of a flexible silvery leader material that incorporates strands of superfine woven wire. To achieve an enticingly slow sink of the bait through the water, I add a bubble of expanded polystyrene, but things underwater have gone quiet. Then I miss a couple of takes. I cast toward a half-submerged bush, and after a long wait my answer to a line twitch is in turn answered by a bent rod. As I grab the leader and swing the fish aboard, I do another double-take. The color scheme is similar to a piranha, but it looks more like a pacu (*Piaractus brachypomus*), another Amazon inhabitant, which is sometimes confused with the red-bellied piranha. In fact, unless I'm very much mistaken, it *is* a pacu.

This is another species that gets liberated from domestic aquaria—not because they eat the other occupants but because they grow into potential tank-busters, capable of smashing the glass if they're spooked. Once released, they seem to survive in unfamiliar surroundings better than piranhas. Two anglers each caught foot-long specimens from California's Lake Don Pedro in 2009, and a man has told me about a twenty-pounder he spotted in Florida. (According to a map on the FishBase website, the only US states where they *haven't* turned up are Alaska, Idaho, North Dakota, New Mexico, and Maine, although to breed, the initial "stock" would need to be numerous enough for them to find one another.) They've also crossed the Atlantic: one recently turned up in southwest England in the East Okement River, a tributary of the River Torridge. But the pacu in PNG, it turns out, were introduced officially in the late 1990s in order to supplement a very thin selection of native freshwater fish. Because the falls in sea level that accompanied ice ages never linked PNG with the Asian mainland (which at times extended as far as Bali), the spread of most freshwater fish was blocked. So the thinking behind this introduction was to supplement the existing food source, which would give the added benefit of taking some of the hunting pressure off the crocodiles.

Pacu are tasty, solid-bodied fish, and I've caught a few in the Amazon, where they also go by the name of *pirapitinga*. Although they are a valuable food fish in their home waters, they tend to be overshadowed by their larger relative, the much prized tambaqui (*Colossoma macropomum*). During the high-water season, tambaqui enter the flooded forest and gorge on high-protein nuts and seeds that fall into the water. Rubber seeds are their particular favorite, and they crack these open with crushing teeth. Because of this, they're one of the few species that can be reliably caught on a line in high water, but the locals guard their fishing spots jealously. When the water goes down, they're caught using nets, and it's normal to find their stomachs completely empty at this time, as they live on their reserves for half the year. Because of their desirability and high price, tambaqui have attracted the attention of fish farmers, but without their normal 100-percent organic diet, they're not the same.

The pacu is a scaled-down version but with similar vegetarian habits. As intended, it has found favor as a food fish in PNG, where they call it *ret bros* (red breast). Fishermen tell me that, in high water, they catch them on fruit, cast near fruiting shrubs, usually on handlines. To try this for myself, I go to an area of flooded lake margins where green fruits the size of marbles hang from low shrubs, and I plop these onto the water using my single-handed rod. In most places I catch nothing and attribute this partly to my less-than-stealthy approach: instead of a small dugout that slips quietly between the close-packed trunks, I'm with the crew and their kit in a huge forty-footer that has to be noisily manhandled around corners. But in time I catch a few, each about a pound in weight. It's incredible to see how they've become so established. As a new protein source, the introduction appears to be a clear success story.

But Alphonse the crocodile hunter is not a fan. He says pacu are responsible for clearing the floating weedbeds where the crocs nest. He claims they chew the delicate roots. On a couple of occasions I see ripples made by something nibbling the tips of reeds where they trail in the water, but I can't see what it is. Now that I'm looking more closely, I see that many reeds have ragged tops. There are apparently some hungry fish around.

But there seems to be an absence of predators. I put a wire leader on the bait-caster rod and cast a variety of lures around the lake margin. In the Amazon you might expect a peacock bass, aruanã, red-bellied piranha, or even surubim catfish to respond to this. But here, I get nothing. There are certainly carnivores down there though, as the small fish that the women collect from their nets in the mornings often have small pieces missing. One day Wapi brings a good-sized catfish for me to see. It's a couple of feet long and about fifteen pounds, and it's the biggest fish I've seen here. But although it has a large mouth that's capable of engulfing small fish, it has no teeth—only the rasping pads that are standard issue to most catfish. It's not the ball cutter.

The only thing with teeth that would do the job is the pacu, but according to all authorities, this is a vegetarian, so it doesn't have the temperament or inclination. I did meet a fisherman who had his finger bitten, but this was while he was unhooking one. It was his thirteenth fish of the day, but because it weighed over thirty pounds, he didn't feel unlucky, despite having to paddle home one-handed. But this doesn't really qualify as an attack. And I've not myself seen anything remotely approaching that weight. In one village I visit, however, they say big pacu are not unusual—about two feet long as far as I can gather. They catch them on dead Java carp, another introduced species, on lines thrown out from their houses. The pacu come into this area late at night when the village has quieted, and a makeshift bite alarm, made from a bag of stones hanging on the line, wakens the fisherman. I can't wait to try this, but they say it doesn't work now—only in the dry season. But they do suggest I try small *live* fish. They give me some in a bucket, about the size of a finger, and I cast one out at the junction of two channels. After about an hour I strike a take and retrieve a bitten remnant. I reason that a big pacu will manage a whole bait, but when I finally connect, the fish is an unexceptional one-pounder. It is nevertheless a highly significant catch. By the standards of our vegetarian director Duncan, or anyone else for that matter, this fish ain't no vegetarian.

Perhaps I should have known. In the Amazon I've caught a couple of pacu on small subsurface lures and witnessed half a dozen more, all about five pounds. I've also caught a couple of nonvegetarian tambaqui, one on a whole nine-inch fish. But these were over a period of more than ten years, so I'd mentally filed them under "freak captures." All were in the dry season, when nuts and seeds aren't available, which suggests hunger might cause more opportunist feeding. And in PNG, which, despite superficial similarities, is not the Amazon, it's possible that the pacu goes hungry year-round. (Although I didn't catch any on lures here, I did have one chase a fruit I was retrieving and then take it when I paused. My Amazon lures, however, were definitely mimicking fish rather than a motorized nut—or at least I think so.)

Maybe I should have tried something bigger. Long ago I saw a picture in a fishing magazine of a foot-long, multisection pike lure called a "wibbly-wobbly banana." I remember this now, because Alphonse has just told me that he once found a hatchling crocodile inside a pacu he'd caught. But he also tells me that a crocodile bone placed in a fire will divert storms that might otherwise devastate a village. It also repels "magic men" who approach the village at night, making sounds like birds.

As it happens, I hook my biggest pacu on a white cube of coconut flesh, right in front of the hut where we're staying, from a moored dugout. The six-pound line sings painfully as I strain to hold it from trailing branches, and I wince as it grates around the supports of Wapi's house. Pound for pound, its big brother the tambaqui is one of the strongest fish there is, and the pacu can't be far behind, so on this gear my chances aren't good. At length I get it away from the snags and into open water, but its strength seems undiminished. After a while, it boils at the surface and I can see its deep flank. Each run is now taking less line, down and out and then slowly back to the surface, until it's lying still on its side and I can just reach the leader. As I swing it aboard, the 2/0 hook partially opens and then loses its hold.

Solid and deep bodied, the fish must weigh eight pounds. It's as big as any they've seen here lately but well short of the fifty-five-pound maximum quoted for the species. (Tambaqui can reach ninety pounds, but even weights halfway to these figures are exceptional nowadays.) Its small scales are iridescent, showing hints of violet, green, and pearl. The fin area is large, including the characteristic small adipose fin, which marks it as a characin. But what truly defines this fish is its mouth. It looks like an overweight European river bream with badly fitting dentures. Looked at head on, the almost straight row of teeth at the front of the lower jaw appears eerily human. But they are molars, not incisors, with ridges that work against cusps embedded in the upper gum. In front of the teeth is a rubbery lower lip for manipulating food along with suction. When opening and closing, the tooth surfaces stay squarely aligned to one another, although individual teeth have a degree of float, all of which makes for a very effective nutcracker operated by powerful jaw muscles. There's no doubt they could cause a very painful wound to a person.

We've put the word out that we want to talk to ball-cutter victims, and one day a canoe arrives from a village downstream. One of the men is Nick Sakat, who tells me in his gravelly voice about the terror he felt when his foot was grabbed. There's a young girl who was bitten on the buttock while playing near her mother, who was washing plates. The girl instinctively swiped at the fish and flipped it out of the water. She says it was a pacu. Now she washes very quickly and never stays long in the water. Another man, Patrick, dove into the water and felt a sharp pain in his scrotum. Thinking he'd stabbed himself on the dorsal spine of a catfish, he climbed onto a floating raft, from where he saw a large fish homing in on his dripping blood and then circling at his feet. Patrick said he was very afraid, and he was adamant that this fish was a pacu.

Finally I meet Francis Sambin, not dead as the newspaper and Internet reports stated but instead fully recovered thanks to treatment at a medical center. He thinks he inadvertently chummed the water by washing his dinner plate before getting in himself, something he's careful not to do now.

It seems an open-and-shut case. The locals all agree now that the ball cutter is the pacu, a normally vegetarian fish that, finding itself in a new, nutrient-poor environment, is giving expression to latent carnivorous tendencies. "Good meat, problem fish," as Alphonse puts it. Or a bit of a *bagarap*, as they say here. But the biologists who introduced the pacu say the accounts of pacu attacking humans are fabrications. They don't suggest an alternative culprit though. So you're left wondering: who is invoking spirits now?

CHAPTER 16

ELECTRIC EEL

The extraordinary noise made by the stamping of the horses made the fish
jump out of the mud and attack. These livid, yellow eels, like great water snakes,
swim on the water's surface and squeeze under the bellies of the horses and
mules. A fight between such different animals is a picturesque scene....
Several horses collapsed from the shocks received on their most vital organs,
and drowned under the water.

**Alexander von Humboldt, *Personal Narrative of a Journey
to the Equinoctial Regions of the New Continent,* 1825**

IT STARTED AS A NORMAL DAY'S WORK for the six *vaqueiros,* Brazilian cowboys, out checking animals on the ranch in the northeastern state of
Pará. In the middle of the afternoon they came across a donkey struggling in the waters of the Rio Vermelho, trying to make its way to land.
Three of the horsemen rode in to rescue it, but before they reached it,
their mounts reared up and threw them into the water. One of the men
was a very strong swimmer, but accounts vary about the other two.
What's certain is that all three disappeared beneath the surface, and by
nightfall their companions had seen no further trace of them.

Watching aghast from his horse on the riverbank was Reginaldo Fer-
nandes Neres. Although a strong swimmer himself, he felt powerless to
help, as he feared he would become a victim too. But after some time
had passed, he summoned the courage to get in the water. Although the
horses had been walking in shallows, the men were thrown into deeper
water: "It was black water, about twelve feet deep. I couldn't see anything
on the bottom. I just felt with my hands, but I didn't find anything."

The next morning a search party turned up with boats. They fired up their outboards and circled the area, and by the end of the day the wash from their propellers had dislodged two corpses. They found the final body the next day. One of the boatmen was Hermes Alves da Silva. He told me that all three men had clenched fists, gripping handfuls of weed, a detail that Reginaldo also mentioned. The bodies also had patches of black discoloration. "A bit like burn marks, but without the skin being broken," said Hermes.

Normally we expect monsters in deep water; in the shallows we feel safe. In the Amazon, there are two large predators that ambush prey in shallow water. Black caimans can sometimes be seen at periscope depth, with the gnarled head appearing like a piece of waterlogged driftwood. The rest of the time they lurk like submarines, the nictitating membranes over their eyes acting like goggles as they look up into the air, ready to launch themselves at a dog on the edge of a floating house or, perhaps, something more substantial. Anacondas are likewise masters of invisibility, remaining submerged for long periods or just breaking the surface film with their nostrils in the midst of some bankside weeds, as they wait for hours for the thirsty animal that will feed them for the next few weeks.

But neither of these was responsible for the cowboys' deaths. The victims of caimans and anacondas are normally never found unless the predator is disturbed. In that case the killer will have left a clear signature. The teeth of a big caiman make deep punctures, and an anaconda's needlelike teeth cut two crescent-shaped wounds. In the case of an anaconda, there might also be signs of partial digestion, as this predator sometimes regurgitates its prey, and possibly broken bones too, inflicted during the slow, crushing suffocation. These bodies had no such marks.

This left one possible perpetrator. Unlike other monsters, it has insignificant teeth and very little muscle. But the *poraquê* is greatly feared because it has invisible powers. The poraquê is otherwise known as the electric eel (*Electrophorus electricus*), a creature with a unique aura in the Amazon and in the wider consciousness because of its ability to kill at a distance. At least with a goliath tigerfish or bull shark you can see what you're dealing with, and if you don't come into direct contact with it, you're safe—but not this animal. Teeth are easy to understand but an animal that generates electricity is beyond the power of most of us to comprehend. We're all told by anxious parents not to take hair-dryers or other mains-powered appliances anywhere near the bathtub because the combination of electricity and water is lethal, but here's a power source that *lives* in water, in open defiance of the laws of physics—it's a sci-fi fantasy made flesh. Thus, the fear of poraquê is the fear of the supernatural.

There are actually hundreds of fish species that make use of electricity in some way, over and above the transmission of nerve impulses. Sharks and rays detect weak electrical fields in the water, and these lead them to prey. Others, such as knifefish (so named because of their blade-like bodies, which taper to a pointed tail) generate their own electricity, creating a field around them that becomes distorted by external objects. By reading these perturbations with electro-receptor organs, these fish can navigate and communicate with others of their own species even in pitch dark. The voltages these fish produce are tiny—too weak for a human to feel. But an elite few species have taken things one stage further, using electricity as a weapon.

Despite its English name, the electric eel is not an eel at all. It is not related to true eels and has no marine stage in its life cycle. It is, in fact, a type of knifefish. These belong to the same superorder as catfish, carp, and characins, whose main common feature is the weberian apparatus—the tiny bones linking the ears to the swim bladder that give these fish their super-sensitive hearing. But it is the poraquê's eel-like shape that is the key to its powers. Its tail makes up 80 percent of its body length, and almost everything in this part of the body, beneath the backbone, is electric organ (of the nonmusical kind). This is modified muscle tissue that, instead of converting the stored energy in blood sugar to mechanical energy, converts it to electrical energy.

At the microscopic level, this organ (actually three separate organs, each with a left and right half) is composed of vast numbers of flattened electrocytes—minibatteries—that are stacked like poker chips down the length of the body. One of the organs, the Sachs organ, produces only low-voltage discharges of about ten volts for electro-location. But the voltage the other two organs produce is much higher. Each electrocyte produces only 130 millivolts when stimulated by a nerve impulse, but when large numbers are connected in series, the voltage starts to add up. Thus, a small eel can produce 100 volts, but a four-footer, whose electrocytes number in the hundreds of thousands, can produce 500 to 600 volts. This is the maximum voltage normally quoted. But a bigger eel will produce an even higher voltage. I've heard stories (from Peru) of electric eels growing to twenty feet, but the consensus of scientists is closer to eight feet. One of my aims was to catch an eel close to this size and measure its output, and in order to chart this unknown territory, I'd brought a voltmeter. Perhaps not surprisingly, some people I told about this before going to Brazil thought this was taking curiosity too far.

These discharges are normally used to stun small fish and amphibians, both of which are then sucked in and swallowed, going quickly past the delicate membranes at the back of the poraquê's mouth that it uses to absorb oxygen from air gulped at the surface, an ability that enables it to survive in poorly oxygenated water.

But a human being like me is hundreds of times bigger than its normal victims. Nevertheless, in the records of the forensic science office at the town of Marabá, also in Pará state, there is a case in which an electric eel is cited as the cause of death. The victim was a twenty-one-year-old farm laborer, Francisco Conceição Souza, who drowned in waist-deep water. An internal examination revealed no medical condition that might have caused him to faint or lose consciousness, so the pathologist, Dr. Ivo Panovich, concluded that a shock from the electric eel paralyzed the man, thereby causing him to fall in the water where, with no one able to pull him out, reflex breaths resulted in a fatal inhalation of water into the lungs. To see *"peixe elétrico"* (electric fish) written on an autopsy report sent a shiver through me. In this context the fish's capabilities were much more than an academic curiosity. Perhaps more than any other fish, the poraquê makes water an alien element because it makes empty water an invisible extension of its body, where you can trespass without intention and pay the price without warning. Despite the strangeness of this notion, it was something I had to fix in my head to make sure I didn't end up on Dr. Panovich's slab.

Visiting the farm where this fatality happened, I spoke to Fernando da Silva Nunes, the boy who witnessed it. He said that Francisco, newly arrived at the farm, wanted to go fishing in a small pond nearby, a scoop in the ground just thirty feet long by fifteen feet wide. Fernando warned him against this, as an electric eel had shocked him there, but the man brushed off his concerns. Arriving at the pond, he waded out to his waist, leaned forward so his arms were in the water, and swept his woven palm basket along the bottom. After lifting the basket out and finding no fish inside, he repeated the procedure with the same result. On the third dip, only his hands and wrists had gone beneath the surface when he cried out and fell face-down into the water. Moments later, Fernando saw an electric eel encircling the man's chest. After trying to pull it away with a stick, Fernando ran to his house for help, and when he returned with his uncle and grandfather, there was no sign of Francisco, so they thought he might have gotten out. But when they hit the water with a stick, something rose to the surface: the head of the missing man, lifted up by the poraquê, which was still coiled around his body.

This creepy detail brought to mind something the German explorer Alexander von Humboldt had written. Humboldt wanted to examine some electric eels, but the Indians in the Venezuelan Llanos refused to fish for them in any normal way. Instead, they employed a novel way of discharging the eels before catching them with harpoons tied to long pieces of dry cord, bringing them in "only slightly wounded." To do this, they herded thirty wild horses and mules into a muddy pond and then forced them to stay there by beating them with sticks when the eels started to shock the trampling animals in self-defense. Several of the horses collapsed and drowned. "They attack the heart," observed Humboldt, and on reflection, this is probably what happened to Francisco. From the eel's point of view, a large creature was attacking it, and its initial shocks paralyzed the skeletal muscles. But it would have still detected electrical activity from one part—the heart—meaning that its attacker was still alive. So it delivered further shocks to this region of the body to extinguish this final sign of life.

Using a long stick with a hooked end, the men finally pulled Francisco's body to the side, still wrapped in the eel's embrace right up to the moment it grounded in the shallows. With the corpse lifted clear, they then dragged the bottom and hauled the fish ashore, where it shocked one of the men when he struck it with a machete. They eventually killed it with a wood-handled hoe and hacked it into three pieces. The combined length of the pieces was just over six feet.

This desire to exact revenge or to make the water safe is understandable. Fishermen routinely carry out preemptive executions of caimans and anacondas. But one story I heard, in which villagers drained a lake with buckets after a boy had been fatally shocked there, was a bit hard to believe. Then one day the crew and I called in at a roadside shop, whose owner had lost her son to an electric eel some years before. The owner wasn't there, but a young woman customer told us an eel had shocked her dog just two hours before and then stated, "Everybody's gone to drain the pond."

The place was barely a hundred yards away. At the edge of a field we entered some scrub and followed a short path to a felled tree that bridged a narrow ditch some twenty-five yards long and eight feet across. Below us, around the water's edge, were about twenty people, mostly men and boys. Some were sweeping and jabbing the water with long poles. Others had plastic buckets and were forming a chain to tip water into another pond nearby. As we paused on the bridge, a thick serpentine form broke the surface underneath us, heading up the pond, and everyone yelled, "There it is! Kill it!" A moment later the water erupted just short of the far end. One of the men had a pole like a shepherd's crook, with twelve inches of angled-back side-branch at its far end, and I now saw this swept down and jerked back. Someone at my side shouted, "Don't kill it!": we wanted to see it alive. But this lynch mob was deaf and purposeful. There was only one way this was going to end. Next time the victim could be a child, and what alternative could we offer? A long-handled billhook was already slicing the air on its way to the writhing black form.

Hacked halfway through, bleeding and twitching, the corpse was taller than any of the men there. But more impressive was its girth. Behind the respiratory chamber in the head, electric eels have a very truncated gut cavity, with the vent opening shortly behind the gills. This creates a distinct hump behind the snout that, on this specimen, was as thick as my thigh, and it tapered only slightly to the tail. Its impressive profile was also due to the long anal fin, running all the way from the vent to the tail. When alive, this can ripple both forward and backward, enabling the fish to swim without flexing its body. Its color further accentuated its bulk: almost black on the back, shading into olive green, with a bright orange throat and red spots on the flanks like glowing coals.

Having seen this huge fish and convinced now of their ability to kill humans, I was increasingly apprehensive about grappling with a live poraquê in the wild. So I thought it best to start with a small one in an aquarium. With the Brazilian-born ichthyologist Dr. Jonathan Ready at my side, I donned thick rubber boots (rated to 7.5 kilovolts) and gloves (1,000 volts) and lowered a plastic-handled probe into the water. The probe consisted of two copper strips, at opposite ends of a clear plastic rectangle, that were connected by wires to a receiver unit that converted electrical pulses in the water into sound. At first we heard only isolated deep-toned blips, but when I moved the probe toward the fish, the speaker emitted a sound like a small motorbike trying to start. Assured that this was just the Sachs organ emitting low-voltage pulses for electro-location, I dipped a bare finger in and verified that this was indeed below the threshold for me to feel. Then, with finger safely out—because their shocks can be felt up to three feet away in water— we prodded the fish and heard the speaker rasp a short, angry buzz.

The next stage was getting it out of the water, which Jon did using a cotton pillowcase and two twigs as a makeshift dip net. Tipped onto a plastic sheet, the two-foot-long fish flapped feebly while we touched a copper terminal to each end—nothing like the writhing of a true eel, which still has all its tail muscle. The tiny eyes seemed to accuse us. What were we doing, two grown men in protective clothing, holding down such a puny creature? But the terminals were linked to a bank of LEDs, which flashed repeatedly as the eel discharged, indicating a pulse of at least one hundred volts. Without insulation, handling even this small fish would have been like sticking our fingers into a mains socket: it could have floored both of us.

Having seen now what these fish were capable of and being reassured that the gloves and boots gave adequate insulation, at least on a small specimen, I was as ready as I would ever be to go after a big one in the wild. But where should I start? Normally one might get a lead at a fish market, but fishermen don't fish for them and people don't eat them, although those that are caught accidentally are sometimes rendered down for their oil, which is said to "contain electricity" and is believed to ease rheumatic pains when rubbed into the skin. (I've also met fishermen who treat cuts with anaconda fat, the original "snake oil.") But I'd already seen and heard enough to give me a clear pointer. Now was the dry season, and the best places to look were shrinking, drying-out pools in the river floodplain. This is where electric eels breed, the male making a foam nest from his saliva, into which the female lays up to seventeen thousand eggs and where the firstborn larvae cannibalize the later-developing eggs and embryos. It sounds almost as unlikely as their reputed taste for vitamin-rich *açaí* palm fruits, which they cause to fall during the flood season by shocking the trees; or the Tupi myth that the ancestral poraquê received its powers when it was struck by lightning; or the fact that you can sometimes stumble upon this monster in tiny water bodies where you'd never find a big fish of any other species.

I'd heard about a small pond on a cattle ranch where poraquê had been seen, but getting a boat there, several miles from the river, looked like being a problem. I had visions of us doing a reenactment of Werner Herzog's epic movie *Fitzcarraldo*, in which hundreds of people drag a riverboat through the jungle. Brazilians, however, pride themselves on their ability to *dar um jeito*, to find a way. This is a special kind of lateral thinking, usually involving a bending of the rules. In this case the answer was a tractor driven by Milton Pereira de Freitas that swung an aluminum skiff out of the river, suspended by a rope from its loading arms, and set it down on a trailer. An hour later, after a bumpy ride over dried-out swamp, the trailer was reversed into the lake and we were in business.

The lake was a winding thirty-foot-wide ribbon, and we slowly paddled down the middle with the receiver in the water. But the speaker emitted just ambiguous crackles and hums, nothing like the clear messages in the tank. Perhaps they were not on the move and were instead taking a siesta. I dipped another device into the water, a transmitter of low-level pulses, to maybe get a conversation going, but there was no response. So at midday I resorted to a bait on a line. Near the lake was a shallow ditch, and taking Milton's bamboo fishing rod, I baited up with a small piece of cut fish and flicked it just beyond the marginal weeds. On the third or fourth cast the line jagged sideways, and my firm strike swung a silvery blur onto the bank. According to Milton, the slippery, gap-toothed traira is a preferred food of the poraquê, and also a favorite of his for eating sashimi-style, so we decided to catch a few more. I was also enjoying this back-to-basics fishing until the line got snagged next to a branch in the water. Having pulled to no avail, I shuffled out along the branch, with the water halfway up my canvas "ninja boots" (bought in Thailand, and the perfect footwear for deep mud), and I reached down the line with a stick. But I still couldn't free it.

"Just break the line and put on another hook," Milton called.

So I pulled, and something started to move. A tangle of mud-clogged roots appeared, and in the middle of it was a sinuous gray form. Somehow I jumped vertically clear of the water and managed to come down on the bank while not letting go of the line. As the gray-brown fish squirmed in the grass, Milton chuckled, "It's a *mussum*. They're good bait for jaú, but you don't often catch them on a hook."

Regaining some dignity, I held the fish, a marbled swamp eel (*Synbranchus marmoratus*), in front of the camera and reflected on my good fortune that it hadn't been a poraquê. If I'd been shocked, at least there were other people around with rubber boots and a wooden-handled plastic hook for pulling me out, as well as a portable defibrillator for stopping a heart that has been shocked into spasm prior to restarting it with cardiopulmonary resuscitation (CPR).

Word then came of a place where the pools were almost disappearing, as the heat of this extra intense dry season baked the land far drier than in normal years. Walking through a parched landscape of singed trees with a farmhand named João, I spotted a pool in the distance, scarcely twenty feet in diameter and partially shaded by a small tree. On getting nearer, we saw the surface bubbling with four-inch armored catfish, sipping air. Then something that looked like a tree root slid out of the shade and into the body of the pool. Six feet long and snakelike, with the whole of its back out of the water, it could have been an anaconda, especially as the water, which was actually liquid mud, obscured any markings. But it moved without making lateral loops, and on a few occasions it went instantaneously into reverse. What's more, its mouth was regularly pushing clear and opening, after which bubbles appeared from behind its arched head. I had found my giant poraquê—but how to get it out?

There seemed little point using a bait, as our aim was simply to see it out of the water. João suggested capturing it cowboy-style—by lasso—which seemed fitting. I found a forked stick and rigged an open noose to its Y-shaped end. João then prodded the monster's tail with another stick and it started swimming straight toward me. I'd been expecting to chase it round the pond for half an hour but, on dropping the noose right in front of it, managed to snare it on the first attempt.

With it safely clear of the water, we slid it into a shallow groove I'd made in the damp mud, in the shade of the tree, and then donned gloves and boots. Even in bright daylight, we could see it firing the LED panel, and each time it did so, its body tensed like a muscular contraction. We then connected the voltmeter to measure the strength of the discharge—finally, the moment of truth. But the damn thing, which had worked fine back in the UK, must have gotten damaged in transit.

With difficulty, keeping our knees clear of the damp ground, we then lifted the fish for the camera—a confirmed killer measuring 5 feet, 10½ inches and living in six inches of water.

Only after we'd returned it did we make a discovery that was even harder to take in. Underneath the tree, hard against the bank, was a knot of about twenty more, all between two and three feet long. From time to time the knot would flex and a mud-coated head would push into the air. One fish, off to one side, was in mud that had almost solidified. Although I told myself that these were simply fish waiting quietly for rain, at a reflexive level I found the sight repulsive. And it graphically underlined what I already knew even before I had seen them here: that if anyone had happened to walk into this puddle, to try and scoop up the small catfish perhaps, they could have suffered the same fate as Francisco.

And I'm not surprised that Reginaldo, the cowboy, doesn't have the courage to get in the water any more, even though the chances of falling foul of this fish are normally very small. He thinks his three companions encountered a shoal of them that were running up the swelling river. If the men had arrived five minutes later, they would still be alive today.

CHAPTER 17

SAWFISH

The Saw Fish is also a beast of the Sea; the body is huge great;
the head hath a crest, and is hard and dented like to a Saw.
It will swim under ships and cut them, that the Water may come in,
and he may feed on the men when the ship is drowned.

Olaus Magnus, *History of the Northern Peoples*, 1555

THIS IS ANOTHER STORY with its origins in the Amazon but its conclusion far from there, on another continent. That day in 1993 when I saw the stuffed seven-foot bull shark hanging in Casa Dragão, the fishing tackle and hardware store in Manaus, there was something even more unreal there. It was about a yard in length with a profile like a chainsaw, except that each saw point was nearly three inches long. This was the rostrum of a *peixe-serra*, a sawfish, an animal I had been vaguely aware of from my youth from drawings in encyclopedias and comic books, where its other-worldly bulk usually menaced knife-brandishing skin divers. I remember looking at its bizarre outline and wondering if this was a real fish at all or whether the illustrator had misheard *sword*fish and made this creature up. Then, more recently, I saw it was the conning-tower symbol on U-96, the German submarine featured in the movie *Das Boot*. This cartoon sawfish had a big cheerful smile, which was disturbingly at odds with the fact that this real-life U-boat sent twenty-eight allied ships to the bottom of the sea in World War II. So the real-life animal was clearly stealthy and lethal. But I'd still never seen a picture of a real one, and until now I'd had no idea that this giant swam up rivers.

As with most large species, the knowledge about its maximum size shades into an area of doubt. Oviedo, who chronicled the Spanish conquest of Central America, wrote, "And they are huge fish, and I have seen them so big, that a pair of oxen with a cart had a full load with one fish." Much more recently, on November 25, 1922, the *New York Times* reported the capture of a sawfish from the Bay of Panama measuring twenty-nine feet and weighing more than two tons (4,301 pounds). Its captor was the adventurer Frederick Albert Mitchell-Hedges, whose book *Battles with Giant Fish* reports an even more monstrous beast, measuring thirty-one feet and weighing 5,700 pounds. Unlike other fabled captures, however, these are accompanied by photographs. One shows a trilby-wearing Mitchell-Hedges, pipe clamped in mouth and "companion" Lady Brown at his side in a full-length dress and immaculate hairdo, standing by the tail of the fish and hauling on a rope that is attached to the tip of its rostrum so that it rears up in the picture's foreground to an apparent height greater than that of the couple. It's certainly a huge fish, but from this end-on perspective, with its dramatic foreshortening and low viewpoint (the horizon cuts Mitchell-Hedges at below waist level), getting a clear measure of its length is not possible. Furthermore, the modern consensus is that this colorful man was not a totally reliable witness. His autobiography, *Danger My Ally*, has him tearing around like an Edwardian Austin Powers, being kidnapped by Pancho Villa in Mexico (with whose gang he later held up trains), hanging out with Trotsky in New York, being invited to spy for the British Secret Service, and discovering a crystal "skull of doom" in a Mayan ruin. His finding of this artifact has established him, for many, as the real-life inspiration behind the Indiana Jones stories, but later evidence suggests that the skull came from nineteenth-century Europe and that he bought it from Sotheby's, the London auction house. So although the weights alongside his photographs of stingrays, sharks, and jacks appear realistic, perhaps the dimensions of these saltwater-caught sawfish need to be taken with a pinch of the stuff.

Descending from these mind-boggling figures, though, we appear to reach an area of agreement. The FishBase website has the green sawfish (*Pristis zijsron*, pristis being Greek for saw), which has the longest rostrum of any living sawfish, growing to twenty-four feet, and the large-tooth sawfish (*P. perotteti*) growing to twenty-one feet and 1,300 pounds. This latter species was the one in the Mitchell-Hedges photograph and in the Manaus shop.

And this brings me back to that fearsome weapon that, in the flesh—if that's how you can refer to an ancient desiccated assemblage of cartilage and teeth—exerted the same gruesome fascination as the spiked crushing mass of a medieval mace. I remembered seeing these in my childhood on family visits to English castles, and now this heavy, toothed prototype from the animal kingdom stopped me in my tracks—and, as before, I found myself not wanting to imagine in too much detail the damage it could inflict. Certainly its potential has not been lost on others. In the Pacific islands of Kiribati, tribesmen used these ready-made weapons to slice open up the abdomens of their enemies and to puncture the brachial artery inside the elbow joint, thus causing fatal bleeding. They also used them against supernatural enemies: they believed that concealing one in the thatch above the entrance of a hut would guard against evil spirits. More recently, intruders broke into a caravan in Queensland, Australia, and hacked the occupant's arms and back with a sawfish rostrum.

Already forming in my mind, inevitably, back in that shop was the unvoiced question: what would it be like to see one of these fish, perhaps the most fearsome and massive beast to inhabit any river, not dead and dismembered, but alive? But even in the light of my other harebrained fishing schemes, this was surely off the scale, evidence that I'd finally lost the plot. Even handling goliath tigerfish would seem like child's play next to this flesh-ripping animal. But even so, there could be no harm in opening a mental file . . .

I looked in *Game Fish of the World*, the last word on large, exotic species, published in 1949, whose contributors included Ernest Hemingway. Alongside the chapters on arapaima and goliath tigerfish, there was not a single mention of sawfish. But other sources were more forthcoming. Paul Le Cointe, director of the museum at Belém, at the

Amazon's mouth, wrote in 1922 that to catch sawfish "of good size" around Óbidos, 500 miles upstream and well beyond the 250-mile tidal zone, was not rare. Around the same time, the Manaus newspaper *Jornal do Comércio* reported a fish measuring six and a half feet and weighing 132 pounds (two meters/sixty kilograms, possibly excluding rostrum/ entrails) that was caught on a line off the town of Manacapuru, fully 900 miles up the main river. As I got to know Amazon fishermen, I quizzed them about the peixe-serra. A few had seen or caught bull sharks, and some had heard of sawfish, but nobody I spoke to had ever seen one. They apparently had vanished in just a couple of human generations.

It was a similar story in Central America. Thomas Thorson, the noted bull shark researcher, wrote in the mid-1970s that largetooth saw-fish were "plentiful" in Lake Nicaragua, reaching fourteen feet in length and over five hundred pounds. He estimated that commercial fishermen were removing between 1,500 and 2,000 fish a month, a truly staggering quantity of fish. But between 1970 and 1975 the average size had noticeably declined, so that few fish were now reaching breeding size. "Action to protect the sawfish of Lake Nicaragua is overdue, if not already too late," he wrote. Three decades later some friends of mine came back from a tarpon fishing trip to the Rio San Juan, which drains the lake, to report that the sawfish have disappeared without trace, just like the once-plentiful bull shark of this unique freshwater habitat. (The river's giant freshwater tarpon are still there though, growing to over two hundred pounds. Perhaps their reluctance to feed on anything containing a hook has saved them.)

Mainly living in bays and estuaries—although all species can survive in fresh water—sawfish also used to be caught in US coastal waters, ranging from New York to Texas. But the rostrum is easily tangled in fishing nets. Thanks to this, and the loss of habitat to development, the days of commercial fishermen considering sawfish a pest are long gone. George Burgess, the director of the Florida Program for Shark Research at the University of Florida, is fighting a rearguard action to save the ones that are left, mainly around the state's southern tip. But over one hundred attempts to catch sawfish for study in the first half of 2009 using nets and trotlines yielded no fish. Killing or removing sawfish is now illegal here, but this may be too little too late.

On the other side of the Atlantic, off the coast of West Africa, over-fishing has driven sawfish to local extinction. This was not done by African fishermen but by European vessels whose governments cut deals with local politicians.

Worldwide, the International Union for Nature Conservation (IUCN) lists all sawfish species as critically endangered (CR), the last category before extinct in the wild (EW) and extinct (E). So I thought this was a fish I was never going to see—that is, until I got the chance to join a research team in Australia, using my line alongside their nets to try to capture sawfish for tagging and tracking.

Dr. David Morgan of Murdoch University in Perth was originally doing species surveys of Western Australian rivers when he came across the freshwater sawfish (*P. microdon*) in the Fitzroy River, which runs for 455 miles between the Kimberley Plateau and the Great Sandy Desert. In July the landscape is baked, and I arrived to find this water-way scarcely resembling a river at all. With no discernible flow, it was a shrunken, fragmented thing hiding between great beaches of heaped sand. Even our shallow-draught "tinny" had to be dragged between some of the pools. But above my head I could see great loose branches wedged in the trees, evidence of the river's Jekyll-and-Hyde character. Nonetheless, I still found it hard to picture it raging, nine miles wide with monsoon rain under cyclone-lashed skies. As we drove the straight roads over scorched plains, past bulbous boab trees and the odd thun-dering road train, our veteran Aussie cameraman Rory McGuinness recalled helicoptering into Fitzroy Crossing with relief workers in 2002, when the river rose more than forty feet.

Along with this annual cycle, the river also experiences, at its mouth, some of the largest tidal movements in the world: great inhalations of sea water that raise and lower the level here by as much as thirty-nine feet twice daily. An unwary fisherman who beaches his boat in King Sound to go throw-netting for the popeye mullet that swarm the mar-gins on the rising tide may turn to find his uncrewed vessel receding from view. With twenty-foot saltwater crocs in the water, swimming after it is not a sensible option, but the crocs might find you anyway when the water covers the mangroves. By the same token, the falling tides and shifting mudbars can leave even experienced skippers stranded. Twice a day a twisted metal structure rears above the water south of Derby and reveals itself as the remains of the *SS Colac*, a 1,479-ton steamship whose engines failed on September 17, 1910. After sitting for a few hours on a huge sandflat, this temporary landmark then vanishes once more as the rising waters rip and eddy.

Dave reckons these extreme conditions could be instrumental in sawfish survival here. Biologists think that the gravid females drop their live young (thirty inches long, with sheathed saws) in the estuary, whereupon these are pushed into the river on the tide. Then, in the wet season, they just keep on going, away from the estuarine predators. As well as salties and bull sharks, these include the northern river shark (*Glyphis garricki*), a fish superficially similar to the bull shark but with some distinct differences, in particular its smaller eyes, larger second dorsal fin, and more acute-pointed teeth. Although fearsome looking and growing to possibly ten feet, this, like the sawfish, is a rarity. Only twenty have been recorded from here in the last ten years. Nevertheless, while the science team put out nets in the shallows, in the brief window of slack water, I put out an eight-inch mullet for a *Glyphis*, surely the ultimate in forlorn hope, even for an angler. All was quiet while the tide turned, and then a run in the shallows led to a big swirl on the surface when I tightened up. This turned out to be a threadfin salmon (*Eleutheronema tetradactylum*), which is not a salmon at all but actually an elongated perch with a deeply forked tail, a mouth that opens to the diameter of its body, and bizarre finger-length tendrils trailing between its pectoral fins, as if it has somehow incorporated a gene or two from an insect. Although prized for their taste, mine was too small to keep, so back it went, followed by a recast into the deeper water of the basin where we were anchored.

The next time the ratchet whined, I connected to a much heavier fish, which plunged powerfully next to the boat once I had managed to shorten the line. I couldn't see anything through the opaque water, but a gray body and high dorsal fin breaking the surface told me it was a shark. Then I saw that the hook was just nicked into its left pectoral fin. I was using a circle hook, so its hold was probably very tenuous. Luckily, I was using a light-action rod that gave gently to the fish's lunges rather than resisting stiffly, but even so, we had some nervous moments before Andrew, the boat's skipper, managed to get both hands firmly around its tail. The hook fell out as we boated it, just as graduate student Jeff Whitty declared a positive ID for a *Glyphis*. We measured it at fifty-two inches, quickly put a numbered plastic tag in its dorsal fin—in case it should ever turn up again—and then released it. Before I knew it, the needle was back in the haystack.

Once up the river, away from the estuarine predators, the sawfish pups' safety is only relative. Ninety miles upstream at Camballin barrage, an abandoned irrigation dam that completely blocks the passage of fish in the dry season, I caught some small catfish on camp supper leftovers and swung one out on a handline into the pool below the barrier. Like many catfish, you have to handle these ones very carefully because of the three multibarbed spikes sticking out of their bodies—one on each pectoral fin and one on the dorsal fin. In the Congo the one-inch pectoral spine of a small dead catfish impaled the end of my right-hand ring finger, and the pain was almost unbearable. So the thought of putting one of these fish in a human mouth doesn't bear thinking about. But fish have different notions, and our aboriginal rangers assured me that these spiky catfish are a good bait. Sawfish tend to be more active at night, so we'd unrolled our waterproof canvas swags on a low beach, staying well back from the water as a token precaution against the saltwater crocs that have been seen here. Before zipping myself inside, I loosely fixed an empty drink can on the line, and within minutes it went scuttling across the sand, catapulting me to my feet. On tightening my grip around the line, I felt a fast-moving fish, swimming first this way and then that. In the light of my headlamp, a dorsal fin cut the water, but I could see no toothed rostrum. After a couple of minutes I slid a bull shark onto the sand, a stocky but disconcertingly flexible yard-plus in length, and I caught two more in quick succession. No matter how familiar I am now with the bull shark's osmotic control, to see them in such abundance in completely fresh water still doesn't quite compute.

There was also something about this place that was both disturbing and reassuring, something about a saw-snouted monster from the dawn of the Cenozoic and sharks from the far Jurassic swimming under the reflection of a concrete dam. Underwater was not just another world; it was another time. And at night by this river you can feel the closeness of that other time, restrained by such a flimsy rippling skin, and almost imagine that time and this time dissolving into each other to form something else that's outside of it all. And indeed they do, in a way, when the drink can rasps its message across the millennia and I pick up the line to feel the weight of time itself.

At nearby Myroodah, the scientists deployed their net in some shelving shallows, and shortly after dark something swam into it, pulling a couple of net floats under. I went out to investigate with them, in a hurry because a croc had been checking out the net earlier. Lifting the top cord, I felt a sudden strong kicking and, in the light of my headlamp, saw a flailing rostrum. The body behind it looked over six feet long—too big to bring into the boat, so we gathered both ends of the net and towed the fish to shore. Grounded in the shallows, I could finally see the whole fish. The rear half was just like a shark: sleek and elongated with an asymmetric, long-upper-lobed tail, and two high dorsal fins, although the body on which they were mounted was more flat-bellied and triangular in cross section than cylindrical, as befits a bottom-hugging lifestyle. But forward of the first dorsal fin is where things got interesting—and strange—as the body flattened and widened, merging smoothly with winglike pectoral fins. Two holes near the front of the head opened and closed, like black eyes blinking, and in front of them the real eyes, unblinking, regarded us, their horseshoe-shaped irises edged with gold like tiny jewels. Forward from there was just a tangled mass of thick monofilament: graphic evidence of how vulnerable these fish are to any kind of net. Normally, gill nets are selective, to a certain extent. Only fish of a certain size get stuck, whereas smaller fish pass straight through and bigger ones bump into the meshes without their heads getting caught. But sawfish will get their rostrum teeth tangled in anything trailing near the bottom, and their thrashing only entangles them more. Seeing this fish so comprehensively trapped, the global decline of sawfish became all too understandable. Even if they aren't targeting sawfish (their fins are in demand for the disgraceful Asian "shark fin" market), most commercial fishermen aren't going to waste time and risk injury disentangling a live fish, only for it to swim back into their nets at a later date. The use of a wooden club is a matter of simple economics.

Disentangling takes time and care. With Dave holding the tail and body, I carefully worked the net free of the rostrum teeth using a screwdriver, leaving the rostrum tip until last. To free the final teeth, I was told to hold the end of the rostrum between thumb and forefinger, coming from the front, and to let go as soon as the net was clear. Then, giving its front end a wide berth, I moved in to straddle the fish's back, a position that is safe from the rostrum unless the fish manages to flip onto its side and flex its body, which it can double into a full circle, thus touching its rostrum tip with its tail. A person trying to wrestle it in this position would risk getting a face full of rostrum teeth. Fortunately though, the fish telegraph their intentions by tensing before they kick, so you know when to hang on more tightly. But this seven-footer just calmly sat there and allowed us to get on with measuring and tagging. Although its back was in the air and its mouth was resting on sand, its spiracles were under the surface, and these simple flap valves on the top of its head were supplying clean water to the gills. I was struck by how similar this arrangement was to that in rays, to which sawfish are more closely related than to sharks, despite the sharklike rear half of the body.

To attach the numbered tag, we punched a small hole in its cartilaginous dorsal fin and put the small disk of tissue thus obtained into a tube of alcohol for later DNA analysis. There are roughly half a dozen sawfish species worldwide, but the precise number is not agreed upon. The "freshwater" sawfish of Australia, Southeast Asia, and the coasts of the Indian Ocean is very similar in appearance to the largetooth saw-fish of the western Atlantic, and they may in fact be the same species. Finally, a pinkie-sized acoustic tag was fixed to the second dorsal fin. This would transmit location and depth information to strategically placed hydrophones along the river's course, anchored black capsules that are periodically retrieved in order to download their electronic memory onto a computer. "It's a chunk of change," said Jeff. "But the data's more valuable." Of particular value is the fact that fish movements revealed by this high-tech system are not influenced by the presence of a tracking boat.

One clear finding so far is a strong correlation between the strength of the wet season and the numbers of new sawfish pups that make it up into the middle reaches. Our visit followed a particularly low flood season, and there were very few new recruits to the river's sawfish population. Even though yard-long sawfish can swim in four inches of water, the chances are that most didn't make it much beyond the tidal zone, so they were likely polished off by the more abundant predators there. This new insight explains the team's concern about a proposal to divert the Fitzroy's "surplus" monsoon water south to supply the human population of Perth. If nobody else would miss it, the sawfish certainly would.

Once they reach the size of this netted one, however, sawfish can hold their own. This fish had the whole tip of its right pectoral fin missing: a crescent-shaped cut some eight inches long and still not completely healed—bearing witness to a nonfatal encounter with a bull shark. It also had crocodile tooth-marks in its head and flank, but these had bounced and slid across its tough hide, failing to penetrate. There are also reports of sawfish injuring people in self-defense when cornered in shallows or caught in a net. I even read in a newspaper archive that a flailing fifteen-footer off Darwin managed to hole a wooden fishing dinghy, and this certainly gave me pause for thought as I prepared to go after one with a line.

Most line fishermen in these waters are after barramundi (*Lates calcarifer*), a scaled-down Nile perch lookalike that is prized for its flesh and dramatic, leaping fight. A couple of times at night I almost jumped out of my skin as this predator nailed a surface-swimming baitfish from below, making a sound like a rock falling in the water as it snapped open its cavernous mouth. But anyone fishing with live- or deadbait on the bottom, rather than a lure, may hook a sawfish. And, sadly, some fishermen will kill an accidentally caught sawfish and throw it up on the bank to rot rather than attempt to unhook and return it. We found three yard-long sawfish dead beside one pool—a significant dent in a precarious population. Therefore, targeting them with a rod or hand-line is illegal. But because I was working with the scientific team, hunting specimens for them and under their supervision, I had the rare chance to experience this legendary creature on the end of a line.

But I almost didn't want to. Catching a fish is normally a very private thing for me, and somehow catching my first sawfish under camera lights with a scientific team standing by to process it didn't excite me as much as the prospect of a solitary encounter. And failure is normally private too—perhaps that was it. Then I snapped out of it. The unique circumstances were in fact all part of being here. I took my mind away for a moment and reminded myself that fishing is about challenge, and that challenge should be welcomed and sought, not feared and avoided. It was time to finish the chapter that had started so strangely all those years ago in the middle of the Amazon.

For a couple of hours, as the riverbank dimmed into moonlit dark, both lines hung lifeless, and I fished with little confidence. Then, suddenly, one line was running out. But when I engaged the drag and tightened, nothing was there. And there was no more activity that night. The next night I moved to a different spot, from where I could cast into an eleven-foot hole. Again, baitfish were scarce—just a handful of tiny mullet. Shortly after dark I missed a screaming run but somehow lost the bait. But when the next four-inch mullet was taken, I connected to a heavy fish. Out in the dark I could feel it scything from side to side, punctuated by heart-stopping jags as something raked the leader. It felt a bit like a stingray, lashing the line with its barb. But although Australia has big river rays—previously believed to be the same as those I'd caught in Thailand but just recently shown to be a separate species—I somehow knew this was a sawfish.

Although I could tell it was a good-sized fish, on my heavy gear it tired quickly. Inside a couple of minutes it was aground on the mud-and-rock bank at my feet, its rostrum in the air. What to do now? One swipe could sever the taut line even though my hard fluorocarbon leader had lasted the fight so far. I yelled into the darkness for help, and soon Travis, one of our aboriginal rangers, was there, coolly hooking the final two tusks with his second and third finger to immobilize the rostrum. Then the whole team was there and we pulled the fish onto the mud for measuring and tagging, all the while keeping a constant eye out behind us for crocs in case one came to investigate the commotion. With the data logged, I then had the chance, while squatting astride the fish with my hands lightly holding its head, to savor the moment.

Here at last was the fish that had been swimming around in my head for the better part of twenty years. At seven feet long and with that double row of fearsome tusks glinting in the flashlight beam, it was certainly a monster in terms of appearance and size. But in my whole time here I had found no evidence of this creature ever using that weapon willfully against people. Even so, humans judge others, both human and non-human, by appearances, and our first reaction is to recoil from such outlandish beasts. It's not a measured intellectual response but a visceral one, and it helps us to survive in a hostile world. But sometimes we get it wrong, and in the case of the sawfish I had been as guilty as anyone of being misled by my preconceptions. Maybe I wanted to believe that it was a homicidal flesh ripper and I was disappointed to find that it wasn't because that in some way diminished my capture. But in truth I liked the twist to this tale, and as I let it go, I felt we somehow now shared our own private joke. Sure, if you're a mullet or a bony brim, you should be very afraid. But from the human perspective, this animal is a gentle giant—more sinned against than sinner.

This one, three or four years old, was just a juvenile, not yet quite ready to descend to the sea to start breeding. Once in salt water, the picture is, if anything, even more hazy. Sawfish don't turn up very often off the Australian coast, but when they do, the sizes can be astounding. In 1926 a Sydney newspaper reported an eighteen-foot, two-inch fish harpooned in coastal shallows. Malcolm Douglas, croc hunter turned celebrated conservationist, once found a massive one in an illegal net in King Sound, though the fish was eventually left high and dry by the falling tide, with Malcolm and his mud-trapped companions unable to free it in time. (He also told me of the time he watched a sawfish feeding, slashing a shoal of mullet with its rostrum ablur and then circling back around to suck in the hacked and mutilated fish. In captivity, they've been seen to eye up individual fish before cocking sideways and hitting their target with a movement like a karate chop.) In 1985 Owen Torres, a retired pearl diver of Aboriginal-Filipino-Sri Lankan-pommy descent, caught a fish bigger than his seventeen-foot boat while up Willie Creek near Broome, although he never saw a single sawfish during all his time underwater. And in the same year a coastal fisherman I spoke to got a twenty-three-footer caught in his barramundi net.

My mind returned to those fish Mitchell-Hedges caught, and armed now with the length and weight of my fish (seven feet long and seventy pounds), I did a back-of-envelope calculation. Most unreliable reports (such as those for fifteen-foot arapaima and sixteen-foot wels catfish) give weights that are far too low for the fish's length. But Mitchell-Hedges's weights are spot on. So perhaps I'm more inclined now to believe his report of a thirty-foot fish weighing over five thousand pounds.

I pause for a moment and try to turn those cold numbers into a mental picture of a real, live, swimming animal, but my imagination, which I am used to sending into the unknowable depths, cannot summon or find it. Even though I've now touched a live seven-footer, a sawfish the size of a boat is too big and unreal to fit inside my head. Maybe a two-and-a-half-tonner is still out there somewhere, but I doubt we'll ever know for sure. Given the state of the world's sawfish population, such giants will likely never return.

CHAPTER 18

CAPTAIN COOK'S MAN-EATER

To stick your hands into the river is to feel the cords
that bind the earth together in one piece.
Barry Lopez, *River Notes,* 1979

WHEN CAPTAIN JAMES COOK made his second voyage to what is now New Zealand in the mid-1770s, a man named Taweiharooa told him about snakes and lizards that grow to enormous size: "eight feet long, and equal to a man's body in circumference." Furthermore, these animals "sometimes seize and devour men." But there are no snakes in New Zealand, and there are no large lizards. So what could these sinister creatures have been?

When Cook made his wind-powered voyage from England in *HMS Resolution*, he went via the southern tip of Africa and the Southern Ocean, taking nearly nine months. When I went to New Zealand in March 2010, I had a much easier time of it. I left London's Heathrow airport in an Air New Zealand Boeing 747 one afternoon and touched down in Auckland, on North Island, twenty-six hours later, having briefly stopped to refuel in Los Angeles.

From six miles up, if there's not too much cloud, you can see where you are. Sometime before landing in LA, I looked down through darkness and saw the bright grid of Las Vegas as the setting sun poured molten red light over the western horizon. Most of the other passengers

246

dozed or watched films. Then a series of bright stepping stones led to our destination.

But the journey's second leg was entirely over ocean, a wide empty space where navigation has to be done by instruments. Sensors embedded in the aircraft feel the gentle pull of the earth's magnetic field while others hear whispered signals from satellites. Others monitor the weight of remaining fuel while an electronic brain continually recalculates its position relative to the programmed destination. In Cook's time, as now, a vital navigational instrument was an accurate and reliable timepiece. Even without this, he would have been all too aware of the slow passage of days and nights on his voyage. But when you hurl a human body-clock at 500 mph through the earth's time zones, it goes completely to pieces. If this is in an east-to-west direction, fleeing the sun, it stretches time, lengthening both day and night. So although outside was dark, inside I was awake. On the screen in front of me I watched as we crossed the International Date Line and passed instantaneously from March 13 into March 15. This vanishing of an entire day was something that my tired but wakeful brain couldn't comprehend. But the place on the map where it happened, the Kermadec Trench, south of Tonga, is home to far greater mysteries.

The indigenous people of New Zealand, the Maori, arrived by sea from Polynesia only seven hundred years ago—a much more recent colonization than that of Australia, which was fifty thousand years ago. One clue to the identity of Cook's beast comes from Maori folklore, which is full of mythical beings called taniwha (pronounced *tun*-eefa). These shape-shifting creatures are notoriously hard to pin down. Maori elder Te Pare Joseph told me they are spirits that protect places, and if they are not acknowledged properly, by placing the correct offerings, they can be dangerous to humans. Sometimes they inhabit a harmless-looking log or a rock, but when these slippery customers come more into focus, they commonly take the form of a giant eel.

Like the serpent in the Garden of Eden, the eel in Maori legend is a mischief-maker, an emissary from heaven who was banished to wander the seas and rivers after pursuing its own agenda of cuckoldry and seduction when on a mission to Earth.

The most obvious characteristic of all eels is body shape: long and thin, just like snakes. This could give rise to mistaken identity, particularly as most observers wouldn't want to get too close. To improve propulsion, both dorsal and anal fin are greatly elongated and fused with the tail to form a continuous paddle around the rear half of the body. Most eels are marine, such as the congers and morays that lurk in reefs and shipwrecks, but sixteen species are found in fresh water, in temperate and tropical river systems around the world, except those draining into the eastern Pacific and south Atlantic. So there are no eels in South America, western North America, or West Africa (although, confusingly, some unrelated long-bodied fish are commonly called eels).

Along with their body shape, the main characteristic of freshwater eels is behavioral. Every year there are two mass migrations: of adult eels swimming downriver on moonless nights to the sea and of elvers, their tiny young, swarming in their multitudes in the opposite direction. This is something that humans have been aware of, and exploited, for thousands of years. Eel spears, traps, and bones have been found beside Lough Neagh in Northern Ireland from the pre-agricultural Middle Stone Age of 6,000 BC. Archaeologists have discovered a five thousand–year-old eel-fishing camp in Nova Scotia. The Maori, too, have been trapping and spearing eels for centuries, smoking the surplus from the seasonal glut to see them through the lean times in between.

For recreational fishermen, however, the eel has the distinction of being the fish that most of us don't want to catch. I remember them with anything but fondness from my early days. Foot-long "bootlaces" swallowing the worms and maggots intended for other fish and tying themselves and the line in knots. Unhooking them was the devil's own job, as they were impossible to hold still and coated our hands with slime that took forever to remove. Bigger eels, however, attract a select band of devotees. The British rod-caught record is eleven pounds, two ounces, and good-sized ones are sometimes caught accidentally. I once caught a yard-long three-pounder from an old dammed lake when night-fishing for carp with earthworms, and I thought it was a much bigger carp for the first few seconds until I realized that there was a very different feel to this fish.

This was a European eel (*Anguilla anguilla*), a species that had mystified naturalists for centuries. Aristotle, in the fourth century BC, noted that they migrate to the sea in autumn. But where do they go then? And where do they come from? If you observe most freshwater fish long enough, sooner or later you will see them breed: carp churning up lake shallows or salmon thrashing in gravelly redds after their heroic journey from the sea. But nobody had ever seen eels breed. The idea took hold that they arose from "the entrails of the earth"—spontaneous generation. The Italian naturalist Francesco Redi was the one who, in the seventeenth century, first published the correct basics of the eel's life cycle: that the eggs are laid in the sea and then the elvers ascend rivers. But nobody had ever found eggs inside an eel. Sigmund Freud, when he was a student of anatomy, was one of those who looked. The time he spent staring at eels—firm, smooth, muscular—while he dissected four hundred of them possibly influenced the future direction of his career.

The breakthrough came in 1897 when the Italian biologist Giovanni Grassi announced the capture, from the sea near Sicily, of a male eel carrying sperm. He also discovered something else: swarming in the sea were transparent creatures, shaped like willow leaves and known as *leptocephali* (Latin for "thin heads"), which everyone else assumed were simply small, strange fish that didn't grow very big. But Grassi suspected they were the larval stages of something else. He noted that the number of vertebrae—115, give or take 1 or 2—matched that found in freshwater eels. On keeping some under observation in an aquarium, he subsequently observed the metamorphosis of thin-head into eel.

However, all the thin-heads that Grassi found were fully grown, about three inches long and almost on the point of metamorphosis. Because there were no smaller ones here, they must have come from somewhere else, but nobody knew where. Danish scientist Johannes Schmidt was the one who finally discovered the eel's breeding grounds, three thousand miles from Europe in the Sargasso Sea, a deep, still patch of water north of Puerto Rico and east of Florida. He did this by towing fine nets in different areas of the north Atlantic until he located the region where the smallest thin-heads were found. These were one-fifth of an inch long (five millimeters), and for the purposes of general textbooks, the European eel's life cycle is now a closed case—except nobody, to this day, has ever observed eels breeding in the wild.

The first eels that ventured into fresh water are thought to have evolved in the ocean near present-day Indonesia. This population split and dispersed on the changing ocean currents as the proto-continents drifted toward their present positions. But why these eels ended up spending most of their lives in fresh water is another mystery. Rivers are no-go areas for most sea fish, but like bull sharks and rays, eels were able to make this transition. And once inland, there must have been some advantage to make them stay. Perhaps they found better food supplies or more hiding places or fewer predators.

New Zealand is home to three species of freshwater eel, the largest of which is the longfin eel (*Anguilla dieffenbachii*). This is said to be the largest freshwater eel in the world, a sliver of information that has been in the well of my memory for many years. And, on reflection, there's every reason why this should be true. Adrift on the fringes of the shifting continents, New Zealand is ecologically unique, having been beyond the spread of mammals until humans arrived. So huge flightless birds, including the quarter-ton moa (*Dinornis robustus*), came to dominate the land, and only the supersized Haast's eagle (*Hieraaetus moorei*) hunted these—until the Maori arrived. Underwater, the picture is similar, with few native species. So the interloper from the sea has become the top predator, with nothing to hunt it as it slowly grows, waiting for its call back to the sea. But could this flesh-and-blood fish be the creature behind Cook's report of an eight-foot-long devourer of men?

There are recent stories that seem to support this. In 1971 eight-year-old Carol Davis was paddling in a stream near the small town of Maheno when an eel grabbed her ankle and started pulling her toward deeper water. Eels can swim backward, so it must have felt like a dog attached to her leg that only let go when the girl's older sister came to her aid.

I heard another tale from Brian Coffey who, in the 1970s, was an ecologist working with a dive team doing maintenance on the Arapuni dam. Working with lights in one hundred feet of water, they would often see a huge head looming out of the murk, or part of a snakelike body, but never the whole animal owing to the poor visibility. Although large eels are invariably female, they christened their shadowy companion "Horace" and amused themselves on long saturation dives by occasionally tugging a workmate's fin or bumping him on the shoulder. One day two divers were decompressing, ten feet down, clipped to the grill over the turbine intake, when one of them saw the eel's tail against the dam wall . . . and whacked it with his hammer. Understandably, the eel bolted, colliding with the other diver, Ian Sutherland, and breaking two of his ribs. The severity of this injury confirmed Horace's monstrous size—until the next day, when she was found dead on the surface. Her head was indeed very large, but her body, although nearly a foot across at its thickest point, was only four feet long. "She was a fat slug of a fish," said Brian. "She was probably the only big eel in there."

He speculates that she was imprisoned in the lake, unable to follow her migrating instinct. So she stayed there and kept growing. This could be why some eels reach a very large size: old-style dams or steep banks block their way to the sea, allowing no easy exit. However, even for eels that aren't imprisoned, there is no set size or age at which they migrate. Some stay in fresh water long after their contemporaries have left. I asked Brian if that was the biggest eel the divers saw. He said that in Lake Wanaka, before it was fished commercially, they'd spotted eels with the same body mass as themselves.

Another diver, Clint Haines, was searching for a friend's boat propeller one hundred feet down on the bottom of Lake Rotoiti near Nelson on South Island when a "huge" eel swam toward him. Within moments others joined it, one of which grabbed one of his dive fins. Panicking, he dropped his flashlight and kicked for the surface. His wife, who was waiting in a boat above, says the eels pursued him to the surface, and Clint was screaming to get out of the water. He had come up so fast from deep water that he collapsed with the bends. Mr. Haines had seen forty-pound eels caught from the lake and estimated these fish were about eighty pounds.

For my first look at a New Zealand longfin, I went to the Manga-whitikau cave system near Waitomo, in North Island. Here, in near-total darkness in a river that runs through subterranean tunnels in the limestone, lives an individual known to Te Pare as "the caretaker," but that is more popularly called Gollum. Normally the only illumination comes from dim constellations of glowworms on the cave roof, so you'd expect a bright flashlight beam on the shallow clear water plus the vibrations that six people dragging film kit make to cause some alarm to anything living there. But the effect was exactly the opposite. A black shape a yard long slid through the shallow water to meet me, clearly in expectation of my offering. The water was so clear, she appeared to be gliding through air. I could easily see the pronounced dome of muscle on top of her head that all large longfin females have, the reason for their vicelike bite and a feature that disappears prior to their final migration, when they stop feeding. I dangled a finger-sized strip of goat meat in front of her, and she appeared to locate it by smell rather than vision before sipping at it and then taking it with a loud slurp. This was a great opportunity to get some underwater footage, but the next time she approached she ignored the meat and went for the camera, biting the lens and chewing its strap. Perhaps she was responding to minute electrical currents and thinking it was some kind of rival or competitor on her patch. Interestingly, there were other eels down there, but none in what appeared to be her territory apart from one that I saw pulling itself tail-first into a cranny between loose rocks a good six inches above the water line. As it did so, I heard echoes of Cook's words: "He said that they burrow in the ground." Clearly the big one was not used to upstarts in her patch, so we removed the camera and tried to regain her confidence, and eventually we had her crawling half out of the water onto the base of a smooth low stalagmite. She seemed to be curious about me, as though there was some kind of intelligence there, and I wondered how she experienced her world and what swimming to this place along an underground river had been like.

After three days in North Island, the crew and I got up at 5 a.m. and caught a flight to Christchurch on the South Island. From eighteen thousand feet, the geology of the land is made clear in a way that it isn't at ground level. Erosion has sharpened the mountains into serrated ridges, between which the rivers flow, gnawing away at the rock and depositing it on the flat coastal plains. Looking down, I thought of the elvers making their way against current and gravity, intimately penetrating the land like a swarm of parasites.

But they are a gift to the land. Although their life cycle is a mirror image of the salmon's, which grow to adulthood in the sea and then fertilize the rivers with their dead bodies, eels still bring nutrients from the sea, packed into the bodies of multitudes of elvers. As is the nature of things, most of these will not make it to the top of the food chain. In the past the Maori harvested them, as they were a vital protein source, and they are still fished today. I went to see fishermen on Lake Ellesmere who dig blind channels to trap migrating adults, which can be handled safely because they've stopped feeding so they don't bite. The fishermen's catch is exported to Europe and Southeast Asia, and although eel numbers are way down on historical levels, New Zealand is about the only place left in the world with a viable eel fishery, thanks to taking conservation measures in good time. All longfins over nine pounds have to be returned. Once they reach the sea, though, their peregrinations are as mysterious as those of the European eel, but biologists think they breed over a thousand miles away, south of Tonga, from where the ocean currents bring the young back home.

Not far from Lake Ellesmere, in Christchurch, is the National Institute of Water and Atmospheric Research (NIWA) and the laboratory of Don Jellyman, their principal freshwater fish scientist. He showed me recent pictures of the biggest eel he'd seen in a long time: a "feeder" measuring four feet, eleven inches and weighing just under thirty-one pounds that was trapped from a stream running into the lake. In part, the maximum size of any fish species depends on how long they live—

and eels are extraordinarily long-lived. I watched as Don dissected out a tiny flake of bone from inside an eel's head, an otolith, or "ear stone." These lie in nerve-lined cavities and give the eel information about its orientation and movement. Equally significantly, they grow throughout life, producing clear growth rings, where growth stops each winter, that are visible under a microscope. The oldest eel that Don has aged was 105 years old. He doesn't dismiss the possibility of them growing to eight feet and a weight of over one hundred pounds.

This dissection also yielded information about the eel's diet. Inside its stomach was another, small eel, already well digested. But the surgical gloves on my hands were not worn for reasons of squeamishness. A splash of longfin blood on the lips or eyes can cause inflammation, and only three teaspoons, if it were injected, has enough toxin to kill a person.

From Christchurch we drove across the southern Alps to Hokitika on the west coast, on the trail of the biggest living freshwater eel known about anywhere in the world. Four years before, so we'd heard, one of the longfin eels in the aquarium here had been netted and measured at over seven feet. This is close enough to the dimensions Cook gave to substantiate that part of his report, and it would potentially look like a devourer of men to anyone in the water. My job was to get in the tank and verify its size, hopefully without confirming its liking for human prey. This would mean netting it again and this time weighing it, which wasn't done last time.

The circular tank was some ten feet deep, and my first surprise was the sheer number of eels in it. Instead of one fat individual lying on the bottom, there must have been more than fifty, mostly in and around a large tree root. In the center a stone-clad column housed the filter unit, and a close look revealed portions of eel tail protruding from holes in this where, despite its underlying structure of bolted steel mesh, they had forced entry. Accurately gauging the size of the eels that were visible through the curved, distorting glass was difficult, but they were undoubtedly large and thick bodied. I put the longest ones at five feet, which meant the big one must have been hiding.

While the crew prepared lights and worked out camera angles, I lay on my back and did some breath-hold exercises, working up to three and a half minutes, followed by one breath-hold of two minutes while walking around. I tried to relax mentally, to push away thoughts of being nipped out of curiosity, of teeth catching in neoprene, of a panicked fish pulling further into cover . . . but I knew my pulse would shoot up under water, cutting my time right down to thirty or forty seconds. On top of that, the water was icy. When I lowered myself in, the cold went right through my three-millimeter wetsuit and knocked the breath out of me, making my body immediately demand extra oxygen. I tried to breathe evenly through the snorkel while scoping out the eels from the surface, and then—no point delaying any more—I made the most complete exhalation possible, followed by a deep intake from the diaphragm, and dove down.

Immediately I felt uncomfortable. Despite my fascination with fish, there is something about eels that disturbs. I think it could be the fear of anything snakelike, which is hard-wired into all of us. The thought occurred to me that I was going into an underwater nest of vipers, but I pushed it aside and tried to look for the big one—or, rather, the big girl, I reminded myself. Somehow the knowledge that these were all females made the situation feel less threatening, although I didn't pause to question the logic of that. For their part, the eels regarded me with curiosity, turning toward me when I approached but drawing away when I got too close. Three of them, Medusa-like, had their heads and half their bodies protruding from the root mass. With subsequent dives I gained confidence, but the cold was working through me. From this viewpoint I could see what wasn't visible from the outside: that several eels were hidden between the boulders of the perimeter wall. One of these looked bigger than the rest, with its head looking out from one hole and its tail sticking out of another. I wondered how territorial these fish were, whether the bigger individuals muscled the others out of the best, most secure lies. This could explain why I hadn't seen the big one. And if a seven-foot eel can stay hidden in a small tank of clear water, how would you ever find such a fish in the wild?

After running to the shower, where I gushed hot water inside my wetsuit, I asked one of the aquarium workers when the big eel had last been seen. Not since it had been netted, he said. It had some kind of growth on its head, so they hadn't put it back. I had been hunting a phantom. As for its size, he directed me to one of the other staff, who couldn't remember.

"But it was significantly bigger than these ones," I prompted.

"Not really," she replied.

So where had the reported seven-footer come from? Nobody knew. I'd found a real case of spontaneous generation.

But we still had the net and my 230-pound scales, so we decided to go after the biggest one we could see. This turned out to be "Number 7," so called because of a pronounced downward kink in her neck, like an arthritic grandmother. Seeing that she was lying in an open area of the bottom, I dove down and scooped her head into the meshes, but her broad tail wouldn't fold inside, so I supported it in the crook of my arm as I surfaced, hoping she wouldn't wake up to what was happening and reverse out. Hands above me took the net's handle, and there she was, lying quietly on the damp mat that we'd laid out—before grabbing the edge of our wooden platform with her tail and pulling herself back in the water. But by then we had the data we needed: a length of exactly five feet, and a girth of eighteen inches, giving a weight of thirty-five pounds—an impressive fish, but well short of the size we were hoping for.

Although the seven-footer had vanished on our approach, we then heard stories of "huge eels" in some dredge ponds nearby from the days of the gold rush. But there was no time to check these out because we had a flight to catch. At the check-in desk they told us not to hand back our hire vehicles just yet. Because of low cloud, there was some doubt whether the incoming twenty-seater would be able to land. At length, we took off through squally clouds, climbing steeply to clear the Alps. But the worst lurching and rattling came on the other side when we flew between windswept clumps of cloud with the flat coastal plain beneath us. One of our crew heard the passenger behind him praying.

The next stop was Invercargill at South Island's southern tip, where I met Vic Thompson, the manager of an eel processing plant that sends eels on aerial journeys as far as Billingsgate market in London. The biggest eel he has seen out of the water was a fifty-two-pounder, squeezed into one of his fyke nets when he was a commercial fisherman. But he's seen two shapes in the water that were bigger than that: one that he first thought was a log that took a bait his uncle fished and nearly pulled him in the water, and another close to the length of his ten-foot boat. He's also seen eels attacking sheep, overpowering them in a stream where the banks were too slippery for the animals to escape. The eels burrowed into one sheep's anus, ripped out the intestines, and ate the internal organs.

At Vic's suggestion, we met at a creek near his plant just before dusk. Finally, I was getting my rods out—a whole week after arrival. I set up a very simple rig: a forty-pound main line with a running lead on a weak link that was stopped by a rubber bead and a barrel swivel, with the hook attached to eighteen inches of fifty-pound wire. I opted to use a circle hook because these normally catch in the edge of the mouth, with a crushed-down barb for easier unhooking. I nicked this in a small mackerel strip, keeping the point clear, and swung it toward some trailing branches on the opposite bank. With Vic chumming the pool's inlet with abalone guts, the first run came very quickly. I let it go for a few seconds, but as soon as I closed the reel and tightened, the fish fell off. My lack of cursing puzzled the crew, but I assured them I knew what I was doing. A bigger fish would take the bait properly, whereas a small one would just hang onto it, so this method would select the bigger fish and avoid the messy business of unhooking small ones. For once, the practice bore out the theory, with a handful of smaller eels dropping off and a couple of bigger ones being slid up the bank, although at less than three pounds, these were not as big as Vic had been expecting.

Vic also taught me how to "bob," a traditional way of fishing without a hook that he had used as a commercial fisherman. At first I wasn't convinced, considering it only marginally more likely to succeed than the lamb intestine method Claudius Aelianus described in the second century. (You put a reed tube in one end and dangle the other end in the water. When an eel grabs it, the fisherman blows "with all his might" and inflates the eel.) To make a bob, you wrap a strip of fish or meat in wool. It works because the eel's tiny teeth get tangled in this— and because its predatory instinct makes it reluctant to release its meal. Normally the bob is fished on a piece of strong cord that is attached to a stiff pole. When you feel the eel take, you allow it a few moments before hauling it unceremoniously onto the bank. I also cast out a bob using a rod and reel, and I found that, if I pumped in the line in a smooth and businesslike way, I could land a good proportion of the eels that took.

But although the eels were numerous and voracious, they were still a long way from man-eating. In order to devour a human in the way that a giant piraiba or jaú catfish could, by swallowing whole or part-swallowing, an eel would need jaws wider than a person's shoulders, and this would mean a very large animal indeed—a good deal longer than eight feet. A more likely scenario would be a number of eels acting en masse. Having heard now of them attacking live sheep and humans as well as having filmed them spin-feeding, crocodile-fashion, on a deer carcass, imagining them killing and eating a human wasn't such a huge step.

To demonstrate this visually, we needed to find a place where the eels are both bold and hungry: a place with no commercial fishing and no feeding by people. Having selected a likely locality in the southwestern Fiordland, we were helicoptered in to a remote river, where the only stipulation was no eel fishing with hooks. For once, we were blessed with fine weather, and as we flew up the valley with our kit slung underneath us in a net, I alternated between gawping at the stunning mountainsides and the river below. From this vantage point I could see through the water to a clean, sandy bottom that appeared devoid of life. Despite our five hundred–foot altitude, the water clarity was so exceptional that if there had been any dark squiggles, I felt sure I would have seen them. Although the scenery was breathtaking, I suspected we might have come to the wrong place.

Nevertheless, we proceeded as planned. The idea was to duplicate, as closely as possible, the situation in which a deer hunter, carrying a bloody carcass on his back, comes to the banks of the river. He's hot, tired, and dirty, and the sandflies are biting. What could be more natural than to dump his burden on the grassy banks and plunge fully clothed into the river?

On the grassy riverbank I set about turning myself into human bait. In the absence of a deer carcass, I soiled my shirt by smearing shellfish guts over it. Underneath I wore a thin wetsuit because we were past summertime and the water was cold. This also meant that any eels would not be at their most active. But even so, I was not keen to have any bare flesh exposed. For this reason, I also wore protective cut-proof gloves. Stitched to these were finger-sized bobs made from mackerel strips to give my hands some flavor.

I get in at a small scoop in the bank, with no other signs of life visible. Just a few steps out, the water is up to my waist and washing a cloud of scent into the eddy around me, with a thin trail peeling off downstream. Inside just five minutes, I feel something bump my leg, but I can't see it because the bottom sediment is now stirred up. Five minutes later I can see perhaps half a dozen eels, each three or four feet long. Other long shapes are arriving from downstream, but the original ones came seemingly from nowhere. They must have been hiding under the trailing grass of the bank. I feel a nip on the inside of my right ankle and then a sharp twisting for a few seconds—good thing I'm wearing neoprene dive boots.

Steve, the director, tells me he has just counted more than thirty eels around me. Keeping an eye on them all is becoming difficult. A few are closing in on my crotch, and from time to time I reach down and push them away, my hand on the bulbous muscle of their heads, to which some react by rearing their heads back with open mouths. I start to touch others. They don't mind a hand gently on their backs, pushing them down onto the bottom, but they're sensitive about any contact on their undersides. I beckon some with my fingers and they close in, coming close to the surface, even pushing their horned snouts into the air to catch the dribbles running off my shirtsleeves. They appear to sniff my hands, and a few allow me to lift their heads out of the water. Two fish are very different in color from the rest, being brownish instead of dark gray. Both are thick bodied. There's one other of similar size, and it's closing in on my hand. Now it has gripped the wrapped mackerel strip and is working it back into its mouth. I move my hand and it clamps down to stop its prey from getting away. Only when I heave its twisting body fully clear of the water does it finally let go and crash back down, but this added commotion does not perturb the other eels. The animal that hung from my hand was about four feet long and, I'm guessing, about fifteen pounds in weight. A quick calculation tells me there's about twice my body mass writhing around me now. If just a few decided to latch on at once, I couldn't do much about it. I reckon I've done enough to prove the capabilities of these animals and the best thing now is to get out.

Safely on land, I start to wonder whether I could catch one of these big fish on a bob. But the rain is now tipping down, and even with the rain cover, we can't risk the camera being out in this. The rain falls constantly during the night, something I'm aware of because, for the first time here, I'm unable to sleep, a delayed effect of my dislocation perhaps. In the morning the river has risen seven feet. The small scoop in the bank is now a long, narrow inlet. I chum the water with the pungent liquid squeezed from abalone guts, being careful not to let any bits into the water because doing so might start to satisfy the eels' hunger.

When the rain eases, and with half an hour to spare before we have to pack, I pick up a six-foot pole from the end of which hangs a bob tied to three feet of 150-pound cord, and I creep toward the inlet. I'm looking for one of the brown-bodied fish, but another big one is in a perfect position: just a couple of feet out, pointing straight toward the inlet's gently shelving apex. If I can get it to take without alarming it, I should be able to drag it up here before it realizes what's going on.

I lower the bob into the cloudy water just in front of where I judge the eel's head to be, and the line instantly twitches and starts to inch out as the now-flexing body reverses away. I give a little line and then take up the slack and pull back in a long sweeping motion. The resistance I encounter almost dislocates my shoulder as I remember what Vic said about the impossibility of getting a big one in. Then, with a great eruption, the gray body is on land, still heavy but with no water now to grip. Several seconds pass before it releases its meal, then it writhes on the damp grass, sliding back toward the river. Throwing the pole down, I put myself in the eel's way, and with bent arms I scoop it up the bank. Only now do I try to pick it up. The thing is the size of my leg and has the strength of a constrictor. Under its smooth, moist, oddly sweet-smelling skin, its muscles are hard and I can't hold it. I try rolling it onto its back to induce tonic immobility, a tactic that worked on some smaller eels (and works on sharks), but this one isn't having any of it. So I do the counter-intuitive thing and stop trying to fight it.

As if sensing that something has changed, she stills and allows me to lift her. After all I've heard and seen, I feel certain I'm holding the monster described in Cook's journal. Eight feet long? Maybe that is a slight exaggeration, but who knows? And a shoal of eels even this size would have no trouble overpowering a weak or injured human in the water and then devouring the corpse.

However, more than two centuries later this serpent in paradise is still a creature of mystery. Patrolling river and sea, daylight and darkness, reality and imagination, it slips through our hands and escapes to regions where we can't follow. I wonder what Cook would make of its underwater navigation. Where are its charts? What instruments does it use?

A vibration of the air, getting closer and louder, is the signal that my time has come to leave this land. The chopper pushes through rain and drops us by our vehicles, and we drive to Queenstown airport where, after one aborted take-off, the 737 takes us back to Auckland. Then two nights between clouds and stars, homing in on a distant destination while the clear mountain streams retreat into memory.

EPILOGUE

WHAT ELSE IS DOWN THERE?

The wonderful mystery that there are fish at all
is the angler's first meditation.

Ted Leeson, *The Habit of Rivers*, 1994

SEPTEMBER 2000, ANOTHER AMAZON LAKE, small and crowded in by weeds—I was lying in a hammock, back from the water, resting after an exhausting day. Getting here from the river had taken us an hour and forty minutes along an uncertain bearing, wading through two swamps. Zé Carlos was one of just two people who knew the way, and he said no one had been here for years. On arrival we'd found the remains of a small dugout, which we'd patched with rags and mud. But the baits I'd cast to swirls on the weed margins had been scoffed by two-foot arowhana rather than the giant arapaima I had hoped for.

Our camp was in a small clearing, next to a fallen tree with its head in the lake. Above us an irregular window opened onto clear, still sky. The only sound was the whine of mosquitoes, crowding the gauze of my net. Then Zé Carlos spoke: "Jeremy, do you think that after all that black up there, if you go right to the very end, it's light again?" From someone whose normal topics of conversation were turtles and village girls, this was a strange question, and I wasn't sure how to reply. I said I didn't know, that some things are beyond the capacity of the human mind to understand.

After a silence he spoke again: "Jeremy, is it possible that somebody where you come from, one of your family perhaps, is thinking about you now, right at this moment?" I looked at my watch and then tried to explain about time zones, the fact that it would be 1 a.m. in England and that everybody would be asleep.

In the morning we set off early. I estimated we would be back at the river by 8 a.m. "Impossible," said Zé Carlos. "More like nine." He looked at my watch and told me it was wrong. Back at the village I discovered that, at some point during the night, it had stopped for exactly one hour.

Five nights later I arrived back at the town to find two figures on the waterfront: my friend Louro, who had been with me in the plane crash, and his wife. Louro told me that someone had been trying to reach me, on the town's radio-phone. Only Martin had this number, so I stayed up until 2 a.m. in order to call him before he went to work. Out of the speaker came the echo of a familiar voice. While I had been with Zé Carlos at the lake, our father had died.

TICK TOCK. Ten years later all that squelching in Amazon mud has at last borne fruit. Some people say I have the best job in the world. But with this come new challenges. A few people have accused *River Monsters* of stirring up hatred and fear of wild animals, even though these critics are anxious to make clear that they of course don't respond in that way, and anyone looking through my mail would find little evidence of it there. Part of the problem, for a few people, appears to be the title, and they can't see beyond this. "Monster" is a powerful word, with multiple facets and layers of meaning, and a charge that depends very much on the angle from which it is viewed. Children are intrigued and want to see what's behind the word, and they understand instinctively that it is a hook to snag the attention, but a few adults are so convinced of everyone else's simplemindedness and suggestibility and scarcely contained blood lust that it rouses them to a protective fury, and I have found myself the target of this strange, mutated attack reflex. Unlike snakeheads circling a fry ball or a wels catfish grabbing a leg, the motivation behind some human behavior is not so straightforward to unravel. And although human psychology is not my area of expertise, perhaps it was inevitable that making these programs was going to make me a coat hanger for a few people's preconceptions and the butt of their self-righteousness.

Then there are some nice things. Recently I was offered an eye-popping sum, about equal to what I make for a whole year's filming, to go into a studio for a day. It was my invitation to join the army of grinning sports people, actors, and the like who brandish stuff at the public in the commercial breaks. I turned it down, honestly wondering what these people spend it on and even more agog (now knowing what it pays to be a mouth for hire) at the depths of human insecurity. So although some others might disagree, I think I've managed, at least partially, to hang on to my soul.

Meanwhile, the other thing that has been trying to pull me down is still there—which makes it thirty-five years now. But although it hasn't surrendered, its weight has diminished to a point at which I scarcely notice it. I owe this in large part to the flesh-and-blood monsters in these pages. I think we've worn the fucker out. It feels like a victory of sorts.

There's one thing that bothers me though. In one respect the *River Monsters* television programs give a false impression. Many viewers tell me they would now think twice before getting in a river or lake—and so they should. But this is only part of the reality.

In north India, on the River Saryu, a mountain tributary of the Kali, there's a deep, swirling pool that has been excavated over the ages by monsoon floods colliding with a cliff. In my mind's eye I could see the leathery, sluglike shapes of huge goonch, wedged in holes between tumbled boulders and in the trench at the base of the rock. But for hours my lines hung limp and my anticipation drained away. Something was wrong.

Because this is a spring-fed river, the water, when not in flood, is clear. So I put on my dive mask and, having floated over the remains of a funeral shroud in the shallows, drifted through with the current. The water was much deeper than I expected; even a little way out I couldn't dive to the bottom. Then I had an idea. This being a film trip, I had a waterproof camera with me: a metal cylinder on the end of a cable that is plugged into a tape deck with a screen. I paddled across to the cliff in our miniature rubber dinghy and dangled this down, watching the aerial view it revealed of the underwater landscape. As I now suspected, there were no fish down there. The pool was dead apart from some cavorting tiddlers, only six inches long. So much for the Hindu belief that rivers are sacred, the way to new life. Those cremated remains had not been consigned to a living river but rather to a degraded ecosystem where the predominant life forms are mats of algae.

Meanwhile, in the Congo, at the village of Bonga, fishermen each put out one hundred baited hooks every night and pull them up in the morning empty. And in much of the Amazon, you'd be lucky to bring up anything other than tiny scavenging catfish. In fact, if you go to most rivers in the world, however remote, you *won't* find big fish. But if we made a TV program about fish in which we didn't actually show any, we wouldn't have any viewers. So we search out the few places where monsters still exist.

The reason for this sorry state, for the most part, is overfishing. In parts of India they fish with dynamite that has been acquired from road-maintenance teams. Fish concentrate in pools where only a couple of sticks, in a small river, can kill everything. Then there's the electro-fishing, using wires hooked up to power lines and run down to the water—an insanely dangerous method and indicative of a level of desperation that I, for one, can scarcely comprehend. Four thousand miles away in the Congo, catfish have been removed beyond immediate needs to be kept alive on ropes through their jaws and shipped downriver to buyers in Brazzaville. And in the Amazon, fishing boats will ditch the fish in their holds to make space for a catch of a more valuable species.

Add to this the effects of pollution, water removal, and damming, which blocks migration routes and alters age-old flow patterns, and river fish populations worldwide are in a very bad way—far worse than in the sea, if such a thing is possible, where some estimate we'll have no wild seafood by 2048.

The trouble is, though, that a river can look much the same whether it's alive or dead. Only by looking below the surface can you tell the difference. Casting a line, therefore, is like taking a sample of the planet's bloodstream—and the prognosis is not good.

In the Yangtze River they say there's a fish the length of four men that weighs over a thousand pounds, with a mouth that could easily engulf a human. Spending no part of its life in the sea, it could be the world's largest freshwater fish. But although monstrous in size, the Chinese paddlefish (*Psephurus gladius*) is not dangerous to people because it's a filter-feeder. The other reason we have no need to fear it is because it appears to be extinct. No adults have been seen since 2003, and no young since 1995.

The trajectory for other monsters is going steeply in the same direction. Alligator gar—wiped out from most of their ancestral range; freshwater sawfish—listed by the IUCN as critically endangered, next stop extinct in the wild; Mekong giant catfish—also critically endangered; freshwater whipray—"vulnerable." Recent research even suggests that *Arapaima gigas* may be extinct—all arapaima caught today appear to belong to closely related species. And the goonch, which Major A. St. J. Macdonald described in 1948 as "the vermin of the water," has become an underwater yeti.

When I finally caught a giant goonch for the cameras, some viewers asked why I put a potential man-eater back alive. But the river people see things a different way. Man Singh, who saw a goonch drag his buffalo into the Kali, told me, "If it's your time it's your time, and if it's not your time it's not your time." Killing what you fear will achieve nothing. In fact, this can even rebound on us—as it undoubtedly will if they ever try to wipe out the Breede River bull sharks. And the same goes for the casual killing of our fellow creatures that we are doing all the time through our now-untenable belief that our security is assured through ever-increasing consumption. Now, more than at any time in the past, the challenge facing every one of us is to learn to coexist with other life. Because the day the last monster dies is the day the river dies too.

And when that happens, we're not far behind.

REFERENCES &
FURTHER READING

Boote, Paul, and Jeremy Wade. *Somewhere Down the Crazy River: Journeys in Search of Giant Fish*. Swindon, UK: Sangha Books, 1992.

Buffler, Rob, and Tom Dickson. *Fishing for Buffalo: A Guide to the Pursuit, Lore & Cuisine of Buffalo, Carp, Mooneye, Gar and Other "Rough" Fish*. Minneapolis, MN: Culpepper Press, 1990.

Butcher, Tim. *Blood River: A Journey to Africa's Broken Heart*. London: Vintage, 2008.

Conrad, Joseph. *Heart of Darkness*. 1902; reprint London: Penguin Books, 1973.

Corbett, Jim. *Man-Eaters of Kumaon*. Oxford: Oxford University Press, 1944.

Ellis, Richard. *Big Fish*. New York: Abrams, 2009.

Fort, Tom. *The Book of Eels*. London: HarperCollins, 2002.

Goulding, Michael. *Amazon: The Flooded Forest*. London: BBC Books, 1989.

Grescoe, Taras. *Dead Seas: How the Fish on Our Plates Is Killing Our Planet*. London: Macmillan, 2008.

Hochschild, Adam. *King Leopold's Ghost: A Story of Greed, Terror and Heroism in Colonial Africa*. Boston: Houghton Mifflin, 1998.

Jeal, Tim. *Stanley: The Impossible Life of Africa's Greatest Explorer*. London: Faber and Faber, 2007.

Maisey, John. *Discovering Fossil Fishes*. Boulder, CO: Westview Press, 1996.

Marriott, Edward. *Wild Shore: Life and Death with Nicaragua's Last Shark Hunters*. London: Picador, 2000.

O'Hanlon, Redmond. *Congo Journey*. London: Hamish Hamilton, 1996.

Santos, Eurico. *Peixes da Água Doce: Vida e Costumes dos Peixes do Brasil*. 4th ed. Belo Horizonte, Brazil: Editora Itatiaia, 1987.

Spitzer, Mark. *Season of the Gar: Adventures in Pursuit of America's Most Misunderstood Fish*. Fayetteville: University of Arkansas Press, 2010.

Spotte, Stephen. *Candiru: Life and Legend of the Bloodsucking Catfishes*. Berkeley, CA: Creative Arts Book Company, 2002.

Thorson, T., ed. *Investigations of the Ichthyofauna of Nicaraguan Lakes*. Lincoln: University of Nebraska Press, 1976.

Vesey-Fitzgerald, Brian, and Francesca Lamonte, eds. *Game Fish of the World*. London: Nicholson & Watson, 1949.

von Humboldt, Alexander. *Personal Narrative of a Journey to the Equinoctial Regions of the New Continent, 1814–25*. Translated by Jason Wilson. London: Penguin, 1995.

WEBSITES

avaaz.org Transnational grassroots campaigns on environmental and other concerns.

elasmo-research.org Biology of elasmobranchs (sharks and rays).

fishbase.org Comprehensive information on fish identification and names.

fishonline.org More information from the MSC (see below) on sustainable fish stocks.

igfa.org (International Game Fish Association) The IGFA's "all-tackle" records are now public on their website. However, this is not a definitive big-fish list because it includes only rod-caught specimens from the last eighty years or so, and not all "record"-sized captures are submitted.

iucnredlist.org (The International Union for Conservation of Nature "Red List" of Threatened Species) According to the IUCN, "The freshwater system represents the most threatened of all ecosystems."

jeremywade.co.uk Information on upcoming programs and so forth.

msc.org (Marine Stewardship Council) Guidelines on how to eat fish with a clear conscience from certified sustainable sources.

ACKNOWLEDGMENTS

My twenty-five years of mostly solo travel have been aided by too many people to mention individually, principally the fishermen of the rivers I have visited. My more recent involvement in filming has been very much a team effort. Kieron Humphrey was the producer at Carlton TV in London who first saw the possibilities of a documentary about an outlandish Amazonian fish and who touted the idea for over two years. Leonie Hutchinson was the commissioning editor at Discovery Europe who finally made *Jungle Hooks* a reality, and Gavin Searle was the director who put me through the mill in the making of it. Wildlife filmmaker Lucy d'Auvergne first recognized the potential interest of fish mystery stories to a wider audience, and Harry Marshall at Icon Films in Bristol made these a reality, together with Charlie Foley at Animal Planet. For the subsequent making of these programs, my thanks go to the following: *Directors/producers*: Lucy d'Auvergne, Duncan Chard, Steve Gooder, Doug Hope, Charlotte Jones, Alex Parkinson, Barny Revill, and Luke Wiles. *Camera*: James Bickersteth, Mark Chandler, Duncan Fairs, Brendan McGinty, Rory McGuinness, Rick Rosenthal, Robin Smith, and Simon Wagen. *Other crew/support*: Poppy Chandler, Holly Cue, Natalie Dunmore, Claire Efergan, Bryce Grunden, Joseph Hassell, Dan Huertas, Lorne Kramer, Andrea Lawther, Becky Lee, Sam Mansfield, Che McGuinness, Dean Miller, Belinda Partridge, Nia Roberts, Robin Shaw, Chris Stitchman, Racquel Toniolo, Solange Welch, Erica Wilson, and Abi Wrigley. *Editors*: Rama Bowley, Darren Flaxstone, Thomas Kelpie, Matt Meech, Glenn Rainton, Sam Rogers, and James Taggart. *Executives*: Andie Clare, Laura Marshall, and Lucy Middelboe (Icon Films); Brian Eley, Mick Kaczorowski, Marjorie Kaplan, Jamie Linn, Lisa Bosak Lucas, and Kevin Tao Mohs (Animal Planet); Jo Clinton Davis, Diane Howie, and Katy

Thorogood (ITV); and Bethan Corney (Five). For the safe delivery of this book I am indebted to my agent Julian Alexander, Scott Hoffman and Erin Niumata at Folio Literary Management, and my editors Renée Sedliar at Da Capo and Rowland White at Orion. My thanks, too, to the K. Blundell Trust, administered by the Society of Authors, which provided a grant toward one of my early Amazon research trips. Finally, special gratitude goes to Tim Marks, John Petchey, Martin Wade, and the late David Bird.

PHOTO CREDITS

Goliath tigerfish © *Icon Films, by Dan Huertas.*
Five-hundred-pound bull shark © *Icon Films, by Natalie Dunmore.*
Half-eaten kob © *Icon Films, by Duncan Chard.*
Electric eel © *Icon Films, by Alex Parkinson.*
Stingray © *Icon Films, by Dan Huertas.*
Longfin eel © *Icon Films, by Dan Huertas.*

© Icon Films

JEREMY WADE has a BSc in zoology from Bristol University and a Postgraduate Certificate in Education (PGCE) from the University of Kent. He has worked as a secondary science teacher, a newspaper reporter, and a senior advertising copywriter. He has written for publications including *The Times, Guardian, Sunday Telegraph,* and *BBC Wildlife* magazine. His previous book, *Somewhere down the Crazy River* (with Paul Boote), was published in 1992 to stellar reviews. Prior to *River Monsters,* Jeremy made two documentary series for Discovery Europe: *Jungle Hooks* (2002, set in the Amazon) and *Jungle Hooks India* (2005), both since shown worldwide. He lives in southern England.

See www.jeremywade.co.uk for details of upcoming series and other news.